The
Reference Shelf®

The American Presidency

Edited by Christopher Mari and Paul McCaffrey

The Reference Shelf
Volume 80 • Number 4
The H.W. Wilson Company
New York • Dublin
2008

The Reference Shelf

The books in this series contain reprints of articles, excerpts from books, addresses on current issues, and studies of social trends in the United States and other countries. There are six separately bound numbers in each volume, all of which are usually published in the same calendar year. Numbers one through five are each devoted to a single subject, providing background information and discussion from various points of view and concluding with a subject index and comprehensive bibliography that lists books, pamphlets, and abstracts of additional articles on the subject. The final number of each volume is a collection of recent speeches, and it contains a cumulative speaker index. Books in the series may be purchased individually or on subscription.

Library of Congress has cataloged this serial title as follows:

The American presidency / edited by Christopher Mari and Paul McCaffrey.
    p. cm.—(The reference shelf ; v. 80 no. 4)
  Includes bibliographical references.
  ISBN 978-0-8242-1081-6 (alk. paper)
  1. Presidents—United States. 2. United States—Politics and government. I. Mari, Christopher. II. McCaffrey, Paul, 1977–
  JK516.A68 2008
  352.230973—dc22

2008026303

Cover: *Air Force One* flying over Mount Rushmore. Courtesy of the U.S. Air Force.

Visit H.W. Wilson's Web site: www.hwwilson.com

Printed in the United States of America

Contents

Preface

As the 2008 presidential race takes shape and the administration of George W. Bush winds to a close, now would seem an appropriate time to reflect on the American presidency, its origins, its evolution, and its remarkable endurance. For over two centuries, every four years, Americans have gone to the polls to elect their president. During that time the United States has expanded across the continent, fought wars at home and abroad, dealt with numerous social conflicts, and been transformed by technology. Yet the presidency and the Constitution, which established the office, have remained constant. This, in and of itself, is an impressive achievement, especially when one considers how tumultuous these past 200-plus years have been. In the 20th century alone, two world wars were fought, fascism and communism spread and retreated across the globe, religious conflict, ethnic strife, economic depression, colonialism, and countless other destabilizing elements continued to afflict humanity. Yet, during this tumultuous century, in the United States, the constitutional process was never circumvented, not even in the face of two presidential assassinations, an impeachment, and a resignation.

The articles contained in this volume provide a comprehensive examination of the office of the presidency, its constitutional genesis, its development over the years, and its relationship with the other branches of the federal government. Among the questions this book seeks to answer is why this office and the constitutional order it represents have remained so stable. Also included are varied assessments of George W. Bush's White House tenure and pieces exploring the dynamics of the current race between senators John McCain and Barack Obama,

In the first chapter, "The Evolving American Presidency," articles describe how the framers of the Constitution initially envisioned the country's highest office and how some of history's more noteworthy presidents have shaped it.

The 2008 presidential race has offered an illuminating window into the American electoral process. The Iowa caucuses, the New Hampshire primary, and the larger primary system have all taken center stage at various moments. Pieces in the second chapter, "Electing a President: From the Campaign to the Electoral College," describe the various mechanisms through which presidents are selected, balancing the current perspective with an historical one.

Wary of imbuing the presidency with too much influence, the framers of the Constitution sought to place limits on the powers of the office. As the head of the executive branch, the president is dependent on both the legislative and judicial branches, headed by the Congress and the Supreme. To pass a bill, the president must first win the approval of Congress, and then the Supreme Court may decide on whether the initiative is constitutional. Pieces in the next two chapters, "The Separation of Powers: Congressional Influence on the 'Imperial Presidency,'" and "Checks and Balances: The Courts and the President's Executive Power," examine how Congress and the courts influence and restrain presidential authority.

George W. Bush's presidency will conclude in a few short months. Having come to office in a disputed election and served through September 11, the wars in Iraq and Afghanistan, Hurricane Katrina, and times of economic uncertainty, Bush has not surprisingly generated strong feelings among the American populace, inspiring deep loyalty in supporters and fierce enmity in his detractors. This divergent response is reflected in the entries in the fifth chapter, "Too Early to Tell? The Legacy of George W. Bush," which attempt to place the president in historical context.

Pieces in the final chapter, "Who Will It Be: The 2008 Campaign, the Candidates, the Issues," consider the 2008 presidential race, describing both major party candidates and anticipating which issues are likely to play a definitive role in the outcome, in particular the war in Iraq, the economy, and health care.

In conclusion, we would like to thank the many friends and colleagues at the H.W. Wilson Company who have assisted in this project, especially Richard Stein, Joseph Miller, and Carolyn Ellis. We would also like to extend our appreciation to the authors and publishers who have generously granted their permission to reprint their material in these pages.

Christopher Mari and Paul McCaffrey
August 2008

1

The Evolving American Presidency

Editor's Introduction

The Founding Fathers were fearful of granting the head of their new government too much power. Having fought a long and bitter war for independence from Great Britain, they were wary of replacing their former sovereign with the republican equivalent of royalty. Consequently, they checked the president's authority by balancing it against the powers of the United States Congress and Supreme Court. In doing so, they created three separate but equal branches of government—the executive, legislative, and judicial—and a system of checks and balances that have endured for over 200 years.

According to the United States Constitution, the president's authority is limited to enforcing national statutes, signing bills passed by Congress into law or vetoing them, creating a cabinet, and granting pardons. With the "advice and consent" of the U.S. Senate, the president can also negotiate treaties and appoint ambassadors, federal officers, judges, and justices of the Supreme Court. Though the president cannot directly introduce legislation, he or she can influence the legislative agenda through the State of the Union, the executive's constitutionally mandated report to Congress, or by asking individual legislators to sponsor bills. Perhaps the president's greatest power comes as commander in chief of the nation's armed forces, though the actual authority to declare war resides with Congress.

Despite these limitations, presidential power has proven to be remarkably elastic—expanding in times of crisis or war, shrinking in times of peace or in the wake of scandals. From the 18th century to the mid 20th, American presidents—with such notable exceptions as Theodore Roosevelt and Woodrow Wilson—were generally more influential at home than abroad. This was due in part to the country's traditional non-interventionist foreign policy, which had first been advocated by George Washington, who warned his fellow citizens against "foreign influence" in his Farewell Address. Since the end of World War II, however, when the United States emerged as the world's greatest military and economic power, the president has been perceived as the most influential figure on Earth. Presidential authority waned somewhat in the 1970s as Congress became more assertive in its efforts to end the Vietnam War and curtail Watergate-style abuses of power. Even with this executive retrenching, presidential power has never retreated to pre-World War II levels, mostly because of perceived threats from abroad, particularly from the

Soviet Union during the Cold War or, more recently, from Al Qaeda and other terrorist organizations.

In this first section an overview of the evolving American presidency is presented along with biographical pieces on some of the most influential individuals who have held that office: George Washington, Abraham Lincoln, Franklin D. Roosevelt, and Ronald Reagan. In "The American Monarchy," Frank Prochaska examines the revolutionary era and recalls how the Founding Fathers, despite their misgivings about royalty, instilled in the presidency many of the same ceremonial protocols and powers that had been held by King George III. Richard Brookhiser, in "The Character of George Washington," notes that our first president was trusted with power by his contemporaries because he was so willing to cede it, not once but twice: first by returning his commission as commanding officer of the American armed forces at the end of the Revolutionary War and then by limiting his time as president to just eight years, creating a two-term tradition not broken until Franklin D. Roosevelt was elected four times. In the next piece, "Lincoln and Leadership," Thomas E. Schneider examines the deliberations that preceded the Emancipation Proclamation, seeing in them a window into Lincoln's leadership style.

The country's longest-serving president, Roosevelt is the subject of William J. vanden Heuvel's "FDR's Place in History," in which he argues that while Roosevelt may have occasionally overstepped his presidential authority, few in hindsight would deny his extraordinary leadership during the trying years of the Great Depression and World War II. Though widely regarded as one of the nation's greatest presidents, FDR is nevertheless subject to extensive criticism, particularly from conservatives. His internment program of Japanese Americans during World War II and his effort to "pack" the Supreme Court with additional justices after some of his initiatives were declared unconstitutional are almost universally viewed as egregious mistakes and damaging to his legacy. However, some conservatives go further, holding that Roosevelt's New Deal policies were unnecessary, counterproductive, and constitutionally suspect expansions of federal power.

The leading light of the modern-day Republican Party, Ronald Reagan is the subject of this chapter's final piece, "The 1980s and the Age of Reagan," in which Glen Jeansonne contends that the 40th president's optimistic view of the United States combined with large tax cuts helped stir the country out of the economic and social malaise of the 1970s, while the increased military spending he initiated helped speed the end of the Cold War. Though Reagan has yet to be elevated to the ranks of Washington, Lincoln, and FDR, his impact on his party and American politics over the last 30 years is hard to overstate. At the same time, his policies, like FDR's among conservatives, evoked deep apprehensions especially among liberals. The main criticisms center around Reagan's response to the AIDS crisis, his record on race relations, his espousal of so-called "trickle-down" economics, his reliance on deficit spending, and the troubling constitutional issues raised by the Iran-Contra Affair.

The American Monarchy[*]

By Frank Prochaska
History Today, August 2007

*The pride, the glory of Britain, and the direct end of its constitution is political liberty . . . Thus have
we created the noblest constitution the human mind is capable of framing, where the executive power
is in the prince, the legislative in the nobility and the representatives of the people, and the judicial in
the people and in some cases the nobility, to whom there lies a final appeal from all other courts of
judicature, where every man's life, liberty and possessions are secure.*

—King George III

In September 1761, the colonial Englishman Benjamin Franklin, on tour in the
Low Countries, eagerly anticipated a return to his home in London to attend the
coronation of George III. With his invitation secured, he reached London in time
for the festivities, but a storm delayed his arrival at Westminster Abbey and he had
to content himself with watching the pageant from a distance. From his vantage
point, Franklin would not have known that the ceremony itself was a shambles.
Among other mishaps, the authorities had forgotten the canopy, the sword of
state and chairs for the King and Queen; and the Dean of Westminster, it was said
by an eye witness, 'would have drop'd the Crown, if it had not been pin'd to the
Cushion'.

Franklin, fascinated by royalty, would have forgiven the King had he sat on the
Crown. He wrote to a friend that George III's virtue and sincerity would dissipate
faction and predicted that His Majesty's reign would 'be happy and truly glorious'.

Franklin's admiration for his monarch had few limits. After a dinner at Versailles
hosted by Louis XV in 1767, he reported that 'no Frenchman shall go beyond me
in thinking my own king and queen the very best in the World and most amiable'.
As a frequent guest at court, he attended George III's birthday festivities in 1771,
and the following year wrote to his son of the King's 'great regard' for him.

As Franklin's devotion to royalty illustrates, it was no easy matter to break with

* Article by Frank Prochaska from *History Today*, August 2007. Copyright © *History Today*. Reprinted with permission.

so universal a system of government as monarchy, especially for colonial subjects who thought of themselves as patriotic Englishmen and their King as a guardian of the Protestant faith and the 'father of his people'. George III was no less revered in America for being so remote. Distance made him a more difficult target and enhanced the monarch as symbol. With an ocean between them, few colonists ever set eyes upon a member of the royal family, but they demonstrated their allegiance through ritual celebrations of royal birthdays, coronations, and marriages.

Royal authority was slow to weaken in a land of English-speaking emigrants on the fringes of the known world, whose leaders looked to the King for political legitimacy. As the colonists believed the monarchy to be the guarantor of their rights, even the disaffected were hesitant to blame the King for their discontents. Popular indignation centred on the ministry and not the King, who was typically described in resolutions as 'the best of sovereigns'. Oliver Wolcott, a signatory of the Declaration of Independence, wrote that the reservoir of respect for George III had been so deep on the eve of the Revolution that 'the abilities of a Child might have governed' the colonists.

The colonial tradition of looking to the Crown for redress was powerful. While Americans often acknowledged the authority of Parliament, they found reasons for refusing to accept it in specific cases, such as taxation. Dismissing the monarch was more difficult given the deep roots of royalism in the colonies. Parliament, subject to party politics, had little symbolic importance in American political rituals, whereas, in the words of Brendan McConville (2006), the King was 'the empire's living embodiment'. Franklin said he could understand the sovereignty of the Crown but not the authority of Parliament. As John Brooke observed in his biography of George III (1972), 'the fathers of the American republic were the heirs of the Tory tradition in British politics'. He added: 'perhaps the only true Tories in the world today are to be found in the United States'.

Although the colonists' regard for George III was slow to wane, events on the ground increasingly strained their patience. In the 1770s, the tightening of political authority and the behaviour of the British Army towards colonial civilians heightened fears that the American arcadia was being sacrificed to satisfy European dynastic interests. As the crisis deepened, it became more common for the colonists to depict the King as the head of a tyrannical government. Pamphleteers fuelled the growing anxieties as the crisis turned violent at Lexington and Bunker Hill. The King, intent on defending his authority, played into their hands by resolving to bring the colonists to heel. As Jeremy Black notes in his life of George III (2006), the result was a breakdown of the paternalism that marked relations between the King and the colonists, whom he had described as his 'rebellious children' at the beginning of the conflict.

While the 'rebellious children' denounced the King as a despot in turn, it is debatable whether George III was even the 'executive' in British government in view of the constraints on his prerogatives. A century later Walter Bagehot observed in *The English Constitution* (1867) that the framers of the American constitution assumed that the King was the executive when in reality he was but 'a cog in the mechanism'. Though George III publicly approved of a harsh policy towards the colonists, he did not declare war on America nor lead the nation into battle. He advised and reprimanded but deferred to his Cabinet on strategy and generally followed the lead of his ministers. Thomas Jefferson wrote in the Declaration of Independence in 1776 that King George had shown himself 'unfit to be the ruler of a free people', yet Parliament carried every measure against the colonies by large majorities.

The defiant colonists needed a scapegoat and the zealous denunciation of George III in the Declaration of Independence, though unwarranted, was an astute propaganda device. Jefferson understood the value of personalizing the enemy. Having discredited Parliament, the revolutionaries needed to discredit the monarchy in order to define their cause and rally the troops. Thus Jefferson took aim at the King, describing him as 'a Prince, whose character is thus marked by every act which may define a Tyrant'. Most of the Declaration of Independence is a litany of royal 'injuries and usurpations' heaped on the colonists, from the King's refusal to assent to laws for the public good, to destroying lives. Nothing did more to shape the unhappy reputation of George III in America than what Samuel Adams called this 'catalogue of crimes'.

George III loomed large in America's foundation myth, and thus became a fixture in US history, an antitype of the Founding Father. A belief in the despotism of the King was invaluable in shaping the vision of the United States as a nation founded in patriotic struggle. In turn, the rejection of European dynastic and political interests contributed to the conviction that America is a nation uniquely blessed, which has characterized American self-perception since the Revolution. But the belief in American 'exceptionalism', like the belief in the 'free-born Englishman' that nourished it, has always been better propaganda than history, for America was, and remains, less exceptional than it takes itself to be. The Puritan John Winthrop fashioned his 'City upon a Hill' in the hills of Suffolk, England, not the hills of Massachusetts.

The hostility to Britain and its King during the Revolution has tended to obscure the constitutional affinities between the two nations. Americans, as Franklin's grandson Benjamin Franklin Bache put it in 1797, created a constitution before they 'had sufficiently un-monarchized their ideas and habits' (his italics). Republics, such as Venice, and 'elective' monarchies, such as Poland, existed in the western world; but hereditary monarchy was the principal constitutional model on which Americans had to draw before the French Revolution. The forms of government on offer to the Founding Fathers were essentially variations of monarchy, 'the rule of one'. Moreover, most colonists had looked favourably on Britain's hereditary monarchy before the Revolution. So too had leading eighteenth-century European political philosophers.

Though few Americans said it openly after 1776, many of them believed that limited hereditary monarchy was a practical system of government. As John Adams wrote to Benjamin Rush in 1790:

> No nation under Heaven ever was, now is, nor ever will be qualified for a Republican
> Government, unless you mean . . . resulting from a Balance of three powers, the Mo-
> narchical, Aristocratical, and Democratical . . . Americans are particularly unfit for any
> Republic but the Aristo-Democratical Monarchy.

Such phrases as 'Aristo-Democratical Monarchy' suggest just how arbitrary definitions of republican—and monarchical—government were in the late eighteenth century. Even Thomas Paine recognized that kingship was not inconsistent with republican government. As he put it in the Rights of Man, 'what is called a republic, is not any particular form of government'. King George, though often described as a tyrant, was himself a classical republican, wholly supportive of a balanced constitution.

Not all the Founding Fathers were averse to kingship, at least of the undespotic, limited variety, a point made nearly a century ago by the American historian Louise Dunbar. Various American thinkers, most notably John Adams (d. 1826) and Alexander Hamilton (d. 1804), leaned towards incorporating monarchical elements in the American constitution, a tendency that fuelled the hostility of their critics. As an officer at Valley Forge in 1778, Hamilton had signed an oath in which he repudiated any allegiance to George III. But his mind had been shaped by the British constitution, which he believed, like many of his contemporaries, to be the finest in the world. His admiration for England led to a good deal of ridicule from his enemies, who retailed stories that he was in league with British paymasters. Jefferson had the New Yorker Hamilton in mind when he wrote to La Fayette that the champions for a king, lords, and commons were often from the east,

> . . . and are puffed up by a tribe of Agioteurs which have been hatched in a bed of
> corruption made up after the model of their beloved England.

Jefferson had a point when he accused Hamilton of monarchical sympathies. Hamilton wrote in his notes in 1787 that republics suffered from corruption and intrigue, while monarchical power provided vigorous execution of the laws and acted as a check on the other branches of government.

> The monarch must have proportional strength. He ought to be hereditary, and to have
> so much power, that it will not be his interest to risk much to acquire more.

In his subsequent remarks on constitutional questions, Hamilton dropped all references to the virtue of 'hereditary' monarchy. In the Federalist essays he mocked those who equated the authority of the President with that of a hereditary British King. In a purposeful sleight of mind, he inflated the monarchy's powers so as to make the powers of the presidency, which he wished to be extensive, seem relatively modest. Like other Americans with royalist leanings, Hamilton judiciously covered his tracks and retreated from any notion of replicating in the republic a hereditary institution that had been complicit in so much turmoil. For years, he sympathized with the idea of what he called an 'elective monarch', who could serve for life on 'good behavior'. Indeed, he put forward this proposition in a long speech to the Constitutional Convention in 1787. The delegates rejected the idea, yet in the end the Constitution did not preclude the emergence of an elective monarch for life, at least in theory, for it permitted a President to be re-elected for successive four-year terms. As the Founding Fathers were aware, monarchy did not necessitate the hereditary principle or life tenure. Elective monarchy had a long history, with examples from Anglo-Saxon England, the Holy Roman Empire, Poland and the Vatican. As Hamilton noted, 'monarch is an indefinite term. It marks not either the degree or duration of power'. As Johnson's English Dictionary defined it, monarchy was simply rule by a single person.

The distinction between absolute monarchy and limited monarchy was often lost on American politicians, particularly anti-federalists with a political axe to grind. But in looking for a viable constitutional model, the Founding Fathers turned naturally to British precedent. They scrupulously avoided any identification of the model with George III, for having savaged him as a tyrant they could hardly use him as a prototype. A 'pure democracy' had little charm, for it was widely seen as at best impractical and at worst anarchical.

The theory of mixed government of King, Lords and Commons had a compelling logic to many Americans who desired security, a just measure of liberty, and the avoidance of arbitrary rule.

Americans sought to widen the definition of republic to embrace more fully the affairs of the public at large; but while they strained to reconcile egalitarianism with mixed government, their colonial experience eased the translation of King, Lords and Commons into President, Senate and the House of Representatives. Adams wrote to Jefferson in December 1787 on the new Constitution, observing that 'you are apprehensive of Monarchy; I, of Aristocracy. I would therefore have given more Power to the President and less to the Senate'.

The constitutional system adopted in the United States, with its ideal of checks and balances, was a creative modification of classical republican ideas suited to American social realities. But when those checks and balances do not operate effectively—as happens from time to time in American history—the powers of the presidency are arguably more akin to those of an absolute monarch like Charles I than to those of a limited monarch like George III. The effective American propaganda campaign skewed American perceptions of George's power, but it should not be assumed that as a constitutional monarch he had powers comparable to those granted the President, which have been interpreted at different times to be virtually unlimited. It is one of the great ironies of the US constitution that the Founding Fathers invested more power in the presidency than George III exercised as King.

For all their revolutionary rhetoric Americans treated 'His Excellency' George Washington as a republican version of 'His Majesty' King George. Some Americans, sensitive to the symbolism of power, believed the President required a title and pored over the titles of the European princes to find one that had not been appropriated. Thomas McKean, Chief Justice of Pennsylvania, thought 'Most Serene Highness' desirable. Washington himself was said to have preferred the style of 'High Mightiness' used by the Stadtholder of the Netherlands. The reigning Stadtholder, William V, was among the Europeans who saw George Washington as an uncrowned monarch. As he said to Adams: 'Sir, you have given yourselves a king under the title of president'.

In the Senate a titles committee suggested 'His Highness the President of the United States of America and Protector of the Rights of the Same'. Adams, who believed that social distinctions and love of ceremonial were innate human characteristics, took the lead on the issue; but the Senate rejected his suggestions for titles, 'His Elective Majesty' or 'His Mightiness'. In the end, the Senate, like the House of Representatives, voted that Washington should be called simply 'The President of the United States'. But the question of how the President was to be addressed did not end there. Article 2 of the Constitution gave the President the more significant and problematic title, Commander in Chief, which had long-standing royal associations, having first been used by Charles I.

Whatever his title, the President was not short on authority and prestige. Given American uneasiness with unmerited privilege, the Founding Fathers rejected the hereditary principle. But as Bagehot observed, the President was 'an unhereditary substitute' for a king, an elective monarch serving for a fixed term. Though the source of Washington's authority was not biological, as President he was given 'semi-royal status' that suited his august demeanour and vital role in the revolutionary struggle. The African-born Phillis Wheatley paid poetic tribute, which suggested just how common it was at the time to think of the presidency as a variant of kingship:

> A crown, a mansion, and a throne that shine/With gold unfading, Washington! Be thine.

Every parent believes in the hereditary principle. The want of a hereditary monarchy, what Bagehot called 'a family on the throne', has only propelled the emergence of political dynasties in the United States, from the Adamses to the Bushes. John Adams took comfort from the admixture of kingship in the presidency:

> Limited monarchy is founded in Nature. No Nation can adore more than one Man at a time. It is a happy Circumstance that the object of our Devotion [Washington] is so well deserving of it.

During the framing of the Constitution, the office of President came under attack as an instrument of monarchy. Some like George Mason and James Monroe in the Virginia Convention worried lest an 'elective monarchy' prevail. Patrick Henry, another Virginian, famously denounced the Constitution's 'deformities' and saw the presidency 'squinting' towards monarchy:

> If your American chief be a man of ambition and abilities, how easy is it for him to render himself absolute. The army is in his hands, and if he be a man of address, it will be attached to him . . . Away with your president! We shall have a king: the army will salute him monarch.

Various commentators worried about insufficient checks on presidential pretension given the extraordinary powers invested in the Commander in Chief, which in practice gave the President a free hand in foreign affairs. With the power to make treaties, grant pardons, fill vacancies, appoint supreme court judges, ambassadors, consuls, and 'all other officers of the United States', it was not surprising that critics saw American kingship in the making, for these powers resembled—indeed exceeded—the prerogative powers residing in the British Crown. Rawlins Lowndes, in the South Carolina Convention, declared the proposed presidential office 'the best preparatory plan for a monarchical government he had read'. It 'came so near' to the British form that, 'as to our changing from a republic to a monarchy, it was what everybody must expect'.

American commentators, having demonized the King, had little inclination to understand the limits of constitutional monarchy in the reign of George III. So when they said that America would lapse into monarchy, they meant something more absolute than the limited monarchy in Britain. William Short, the American chargé d'affaires in Paris, feared that 'the President of the eighteenth century' would 'form a stock on which will be engrafted a King in the nineteenth'. Alarmed by the moral temper in the early republic, Benjamin Rush wrote that 'a hundred years hence, absolute monarchy will probably be rendered necessary in our country by the corruption of our people'. In 1787, Franklin, with philosophical detachment, observed in the Constitutional Convention:

> It will be said that we do not propose to establish kings. I know it. But there is a natural inclination in mankind to Kingly Government. It sometimes relieves them from Aristocratic domination. They had rather have one tyrant than five hundred. It gives more of the appearance of equality among Citizens, and that they like.

It was of no small significance that the Founding Fathers made the President both the executive and the ceremonial head of state. Doing so ensured that the nation's highest office would have monarchical overtones, with much of the attendant, uncritical awe associated with kingship. Later European republics, those of France and Germany for example, separated these roles as a safeguard against the abuse of power. In combining its executive and ceremonial roles, the United States lacks a non-political head of state who can provide consensus and a focus for national pride in times of crisis or political division. The constitution encourages Americans to revere the President as head of state even when they disapprove of him as the executive or Commander in Chief. The result is a disconnection between thoughts and feelings in the citizenry, which leads to perplexity while diluting criticism of presidential abuse.

The Founding Fathers turned naturally to British precedent to answer constitutional questions but also to answer questions of political etiquette. They cast off British rule, but retained a liking for British ceremonial practices and customs. As Gordon Wood points out in *Revolutionary Characters: What made the Founders Different?* (2006), Hamilton urged Washington to follow the forms of 'European courts', while Adams advised him to indulge in a show of 'Splendor and Majesty'. Washington's presidency illustrates that a 'Republican Court' emerged, complete with artillery salutes, parades, martial music, odes set to the music of 'God Save the King', bewigged footmen, levées, lavish dinners, a presidential barge manned by thirteen river pilots in formal dress, and travels through the states that were reminiscent of royal 'progresses'. The courtly formality enraged radicals and anti-federalists, who thought it recreated the divisive rituals of monarchy.

The first inaugural in 1789, which set the tone for future administrations, had many of the elements of a crowning. Dignity and grandeur, thought essential to the union and the nation's highest office, were the order of the day. In a pale imitation of George III's golden state coach pulled by eight cream Hanoverian stallions, David McCullough describes how:

> Washington rode to Federal Hall in a canary-yellow carriage pulled by six white horses and followed by a long column of New York militia in full dress.

Back at the Senate, the President called his address 'His Most gracious Speech', which raised a few eyebrows, for it was noted that those words were the same as those placed before the speech of the King at the annual opening of Parliament. When a critic protested that the usage represented 'the first Step of the Ladder in the Ascent to royalty', the President greeted the complaint with surprise, saying that it was 'taken from the Practice of that Government under which we had lived so long and so happily formerly'.

George III, always attentive to etiquette and ritual, approved of the royal overtones of the American court. He would have been amused to discover that the former colonists celebrated Washington's birthday rather as his British subjects celebrated his own, with the sound of cannon, bells, and drums. It was followed by a levée, a formal reception long associated with royalty. Though frowned upon by many democrats, the levée became a fixture of the nineteenth-century American court. Even Jefferson, who discontinued the practice on becoming President, held one in 1805, to the dismay of some of his admirers. In a striking union of republican content and monarchical form, James Madison celebrated July 4th with a levée. Such practices fed the popular criticism of the nation's monarchical tendencies and the penchant of presidents for pomposity and seclusion from the people.

At his levées, George Washington played the king to weekly audiences, while Mrs Washington, in imitation of Queen Charlotte, opened her drawing room on Friday evenings. After witnessing one of Washington's receptions a colonel from Virginia despaired for the safety of the nation. As he observed, the President's 'bows were more distant and stiff than any he had witnessed at St James's.' Attacks on these formalities, the 'mock pageantry of monarchy', were a recurring feature in the young republic. John Adams, dubbed 'His Rotundity' and the 'Duke of Braintree', was often criticised for his princely style. His love of decorum led his enemies to conclude 'that he sought a hereditary monarch, with himself as king and son John Quincy groomed as his dauphin' (Ron Chernow, *Alexander Hamilton*, 2004).

America's adaptation of 'elective monarchy' and the borrowing of British ceremonial suggests just how deeply indebted the new nation was to its colonial past. In Britain, as Bagehot and a host of constitutional writers agreed, a republic had 'insinuated itself beneath the folds of a Monarchy'. In America, a monarchy had insinuated itself beneath the folds of a republic. The phrase 'Monarcho-Republicanism' was sometimes used to describe the British Crown in the nineteenth century. It had a variant in the US presidency, which many a participant in the Revolution recognized. Even Jefferson, the scourge of American royalists, felt that the spirit, if not the letter of monarchy, had persisted. He feared an eventual tyranny of executive power in Washington, which he believed to be a feature of Federalist politics. As he wrote to James Madison in 1789: 'We were educated in royalism; no wonder, if some of us retain that idolatry still'.

Contrary to Jeremy Black's excellent new biography, George III was not 'America's last King'. The Founding Fathers rejected hereditary monarchy, but a penchant for 'the rule of one' had a recurring echo in the republic, which the constitution did little to silence. Throughout American history references to the President as a king have been a feature of the nation's conversation about its political leadership. Such references have increased of late, as a glance at many a newspaper will attest. Stephen Graubard's recent survey of presidents from Theodore Roosevelt to George W. Bush sees them as a breed of would-be monarchs surrounded by courtiers, with vastly expanded executive authority and 'unmistakable signs of having assumed the trappings traditionally bestowed on European heads of state'. Brought up on trappings of royalty many Americans continue to succumb to the idolatry and charm of kingship. If they only knew, some of their presidents would give monarchy a bad name.

The Character of George Washington[*]

By Richard Brookhiser
USA Today Magazine, July 2007

There is a line in the song "America the Beautiful" of some significance: "Thine alabaster cities gleam, undimmed by human tears." It means that the cities of the U.S., unlike those of Europe, have not been torn and destroyed by war. That is not quite right. The city I live in, New York, has been attacked twice in American history.

The first was in the summer of 1776, and George Washington, commander in chief of the Continental Army, was responsible for the city's defense. The Declaration of Independence had been read for the first time in New York on July 9. That very week, residents of Long Island saw a British fleet moving toward New York Harbor. The British, who made camp on Staten Island, had at their command 10 ships-of-the-line, dozens of other vessels, and 32,000 professional soldiers—including Hessians. To oppose this force, Washington had no navy nor ships and a mere 19,000 soldiers, most of them untrained militia. Over the next few months, he and his men fought two battles: the Battle of Long Island, in what now is Brooklyn, and the Battle of White Plains, north of the city. They lost both.

The second attack on New York was on Sept. 11, 2001. New York lost almost 3,000 men and women on 9/11, far more than the several hundred American soldiers who were killed in the battles of 1776. However, for the rest of the Revolutionary War, the British kept all their American prisoners on ships in the East River, where they were not well fed, had no good air, and were given barely any water. Every morning the British would say, "Rebels, throw out your dead," and corpses would be pitched overboard. Eleven thousand men died on those ships and, for years, people in Brooklyn found skeletons on the waterfront.

We lost the two World Trade Center towers on 9/11, along with several smaller buildings. George Washington lost the entire city, which the British occupied for the remainder of the war. The British also could be said to have used weapons of mass destruction, as they encouraged slaves to run away from their American masters with the promise of freedom, but any slave who had smallpox was sent back in the hope that he would infect his fellow slaves and rebel masters.

The American Revolution lasted eight-and-a-half years. It was this nation's longest conflict—longer than the Civil War and our part in World War II put together—before Vietnam. So, we have our problems—especially in Iraq—but Washington had his as well. In many ways, his were worse: America was much weaker then, and the enemy it faced was much stronger. Washington's persistence through the Revolutionary War was remarkable. It did not end there, though. When the war was over and Washington retired to private life, he was called upon to serve again. He presided over the Constitutional Convention in 1787, was inaugurated as the first president in 1789, and served as the nation's leader for two terms. So, the full time of his service—including the war, the Constitutional Convention and his eight years as president—was 17 years. Washington's mother is supposed to have said, when told of one of his Revolutionary War victories, "George generally completes what he undertakes." He certainly did, and he did so through a lifetime of public service.

After persistence, the second quality of Washington's character worth exploring is the ability to let go and knowing when to let go. This quality, in a way, contradicted Washington's persistence and, largely for that reason, it is even more remarkable since it was a new thing at the time. Nowadays, we know that, in a republic, the military power serves the civilian power; elected officials serve for set terms and, that, if they fail to win reelection, they have to go home. This is part of our life today. It is what we expect. Yet, in Washington's lifetime, these were new ideas. Most of the rulers in the world were kings or monarchs of some sort. Holland and the Swiss Cantons were exceptions, but all of the major countries and most of the small ones were ruled by people who ruled them for life.

Washington lived in a time when royal rule began to be shaken. During his lifetime, the king of France was deposed and executed, and other monarchs would follow that path, but the new rulers who took their places did not, generally speaking, believe in letting go. Napoleon Bonaparte was a Corsican artillery officer who became first consul of France, then first consul for life, then emperor. His career as emperor eventually was ended, but it took a world war to do so—and that pattern has been repeated over and over again around the world.

Thus, at the end of the Revolutionary War, when Washington returned his commission to Congress, it was something very new. It similarly was new when, at the end of his second presidential term, he announced that he would not run a third time. These actions touch on a paradox of republican leadership: If you are a leader, there are times when you simply must take charge and be superior to the people you lead. This is most common in military situations, but it happens in peacetime as well. A leader must use his charisma or some other transnational force to get his way and, if he does not, things will fall apart. Every leader understands this. Yet, leaders in a republic also must understand that those times are temporary, that the term of leadership will pass, and that they then must pass from the scene. The reason is that the people they are leading are, in fact, their equals.

Washington kept both of those thoughts in mind throughout his career, which explains a feature of his rhetoric that comes up repeatedly. This feature is so common in his letters and speeches that I think of it as the "turn" in his rhetoric; it occurs when Washington takes the attention and the adulation that comes to him and turns it back to his audience. He does this to remind himself, as well as them, that he is a temporary leader of equals. We can see this in his Farewell Address, where he starts off with, "My friends and fellow citizens," and goes on to say that he has succeeded as president only because of the help the people gave him during his Administration. We also see it in the last message he wrote as commander in chief, where he said that the future happiness of the U.S. would depend on the people themselves—that their government is a good government, but that its survival is up to them.

One of the most striking instances of Washington turning attention from himself to others is what I believe to be the only authentic utterance we have from him on a battlefield. Of course, after he died, old veterans remembered a lot of things he said in battle, but much of this was embroidered. There was a Gen. Charles Scott, for instance, who remembered Washington at the battle of Monmouth cursing at Gen. Charles Lee. "He swore like an angel from Heaven," Scott recalled. "He swore 'til the leaves shook on the trees. Never in my life have I heard such wonderful swearing." The problem is, Gen. Scott was two miles away at the time, so he did not actually hear anything. There is one phrase, however, that comes up numerous times in the accounts of many different people, which is why I suspect it is a real quote. It is a phrase Washington used to address his troops— "my brave fellows."

At the Battle of Princeton, Washington is reported to have said, "Parade with me, my brave fellows. We will have them soon." Before the Battle of Trenton, when he was trying to get the troops to reenlist, he urged: "My brave fellows, you have done more than could be expected of you, but I'm asking you to do this one more thing and reenlist." Time and again he uses this phrase. In doing so, of course, he is asserting what remains to be seen. The soldiers, at the moment he addresses them, are not necessarily showing bravery. They may be confused. They may not know what is expected of them. They may be on the point of panic or fear, but he addresses them as "my brave fellows," which actually was Washington's way of saying, "My fellows, be brave."

This leads me to a final point about Washington's character, which is that it is unfinished, and I think that is by design. Washington made a bet with his life that the American people could bear the burden and responsibility of living in freedom. That bet is on the table for every generation. The completion of Washington's character, then, always rests with us.

Lincoln and Leadership[*]

By Thomas E. Schneider

Perspectives on Political Science, Spring 2007

To question whether the man generally regarded as our greatest president was a great leader will strike many as paradoxical. The question considered here is not Abraham Lincoln's stature, however, but whether it is appropriate to call him a "leader." Lincoln used the word infrequently, and when he did so before 1860 it was usually in the context of party intrigues. After 1860, a new context appears—Lincoln was determined not to jeopardize the distinction between his administration and the "leaders of the existing insurrection" in the South.[1] He seldom, if ever, used the word "leader" to refer to lawfully elected officeholders in their capacity as such (there is some ambiguity in the case of officeholders who were leaders of their parties), and his published speeches and letters contain no instance of its use in reference to himself.[2] When Massachusetts Governor John A. Andrew described Lincoln in September 1864 as "essentially lacking in the quality of leadership,"[3] he was expressing a judgment that (however mistaken in the conclusions he may have drawn from it) showed a genuine insight into the president's self-understanding.

Andrew probably had Lincoln's role as the Republican standard-bearer in mind—he was responding to a letter from three prominent Republican editors to Republican state governors concerning the advisability of replacing Lincoln (who had already been nominated) on the November ticket. Insofar as Lincoln can be called a party leader, he was clear-eyed about the somewhat dubious nature of that status. Party members, he observed, can be made to concur in a measure they would have dissented from as individuals, provided that it is represented to them as a "party necessity."[4] Party allegiances can be exploited for the purpose of diverting public opinion from its natural course, in effect "debauching" it.[5] On the other hand, parties moderate and give discipline to the expression of sentiments that might otherwise manifest themselves in violent or irregular ways.[6] The Re-

[*] *Perspectives on Political Science*, Spring 2007. Reprinted with permission of the Helen Dwight Reed Educational Foundation. Published by Heldref Publications, 1319 Eighteenth St., NW, Washington, D.C. 20036-1802. Copyright © 2007.

publican victory in 1860 testifies to Lincoln's skill in framing the question between the parties. He had succeeded in preserving the moral clarity of the antislavery and proslavery alternatives, as against the delusive attractiveness of Stephen A. Douglas's "popular sovereignty."[7]

As president, however, Lincoln would not assume the position of a leader in the partisan sense in relation to the American people as a whole. J. G. Randall quotes Andrew's remark in his essay "The Unpopular Mr. Lincoln" as indicative of a more profound disaffection than could have arisen from Republicans' fears about their party's fate in the 1864 election. It is admittedly not easy to distinguish dissatisfaction with Lincoln's administration from general dissatisfaction with the course of events since Lincoln took office, especially the slow progress of Northern arms. Nevertheless, in the case of the radical wing of the Republican Party it is possible to be reasonably precise. Randall writes,

> One must remember, that in the first eighteen months of his administration Lincoln withheld antislavery measures, overruled those who took liberating steps without authorization, showed a willingness to save the Union with slavery if that were possible, and in any case did not intend to impose abolition upon loyal men.

It might have been expected that the Emancipation Proclamation would silence Lincoln's radical critics. "It is true that he adopted emancipation in September 1862 (to become effective in January 1863), but this measure was considered to go only halfway since it did not decree abolition in the Union slave states, nor even in those portions of the seceded South where Union armies stood, such portions being specifically exempted." The proclamation did little to redeem the administration in the eyes of the radicals, because they perceived that Lincoln's reasons for issuing it did not coincide in all respects with their own views. Indeed, their "fiercest attacks . . . came after his famous edict of liberation."[8]

The root of radical dissatisfaction with Lincoln was not exactly that he had failed as a leader, but rather that he had failed *to be* a leader. That is the implication of this passage, for example, from a public letter of December 1862, addressed to Treasury Secretary Salmon P. Chase—known to be sympathetic to the radicals—by the social reformer Robert Dale Owen:

> With all the advantages of a just cause over our enemies, we have suffered them to outdo us in earnestness. We lack the enthusiasm which made irresistible the charge of Cromwell's Ironsides. We need the invincible impulse of a sentiment. We want, above all, leaders who know and feel what they are fighting for.[9]

The radicals were inclined to ascribe Lincoln's slowness in adopting the measures they favored to personal weakness or to a lukewarm convictions on slavery. One of them compared the president to a good-natured horse "that must be led!"[10] Their disparagement of Lincoln would be of slight interest to students of politics if it concerned the merits of a single public figure, but the radicals tended to assume that the people too "must be led." Lincoln has been called a pragmatist whose opponents were doctrinaires.[11] It is more correct to say that although his abolition-minded critics found it difficult to look beyond the fact of slavery's odiousness, Lincoln viewed the matter from a broader perspective—the need to be led implies an incapacity for self-government.

An old-fashioned military commander is a leader in the most straightforward sense—he goes ahead, and his men follow after him. (During the war Lincoln called on loyal Americans to offer prayers for "our brave soldiers and their leaders in the field."[12]) By analogy, Lincoln was himself a leader of this sort as commander in chief of the army and navy. Although vested in the same person, the president's other powers belong to a distinct class: the power to make treaties and to appoint ambassadors, judges of the Supreme Court, and other federal officers can be exercised only with the concurrence of the Senate. Frederick Law Olmsted cites the example of military discipline—the use of force to secure obedience—to make a point about the difference between slaves and free workers; the same point can be made about the difference between soldiers as such and citizens. If citizens are displeased with a law, they can petition for its repeal; as a last resort they can vote the lawmakers responsible for it out of office. Short of insurrection, soldiers, like slaves, have no recourse except to "obey the letter, but defeat the intention of orders that do not please them."[13]

There is little difficulty distinguishing leaders who rely on force from their elected civilian counterparts. In suppressing a rebellion of which slavery was "the root . . . or at least its *sine qua non*,"[14] the difficulty lay in restraining such leaders from employing military means to political ends. One of those who took liberating steps without authorization was General John C. Frémont. When Frémont tried to apply a military axe directly to this "root" by proclaiming emancipation on his own authority, Lincoln promptly overruled him.[15] In doing so, he made it clear that he regarded himself as subject to the same restraints: "Can it be pretended that it is any longer the government of the U.S.—any government of Constitution and laws,—wherein a General, or a President, may make permanent rules of property by proclamation?" Neither he nor Frémont had the right to "seize and exercise the permanent legislative functions of the government."[16] By canceling Frémont's edict, Lincoln gave assurance to the border states of his intention not to permit an exception to be made for slavery, but he incurred a political cost. In the words of Lord Charnwood, Frémont became for many Republicans "the chivalrous and pure-hearted soldier of freedom," whereas Lincoln seemed a "soulless politician, dead to the cause of liberty."[17] By attracting disaffected radicals to his candidacy, Frémont was briefly in a position to threaten Lincoln's prospects for renomination in 1864.

In ordinary circumstances slavery was a matter for the legislature. Lincoln was reluctant to conclude that even the circumstances of civil war were extraordinary enough to justify an executive proclamation. Almost a year would pass before events brought him to that conclusion.

Lincoln first revealed his thoughts on the matter to two members of his cabinet, Gideon Welles and William H. Seward, on July 13, 1862. As Welles reports it, Lincoln told them "he had about come to the conclusion that, if the rebels persisted in their war upon the Government, it would be a necessity and a duty on our part to liberate their slaves."[18] On July 22 he read his draft proclamation to the whole cabinet.[19] Seward persuaded him that the measure was inexpedient at that time, and Lincoln decided to wait for a more favorable moment. He waited two months, until after Lee's army had been expelled from Maryland, when he was able to issue the proclamation from a position of strength. In the meantime, Lincoln had to endure visits by groups bearing memorials urging him to take the very step on which he had already resolved. Much of what he told them would become irrelevant after September 22. Some of Lincoln's remarks, however, were not superseded by events; they remained valid insofar as they bear on the interpretation of what he did.

The best known of these groups is the one Lincoln met with on September 13, the "Delegation of Chicago Christians of All Denominations." It is not evident that the delegates or those they represented leaned very markedly toward radical views. Nevertheless, they clearly shared the feeling that the president had shown insufficient leadership on the emancipation question. Lincoln thought they had failed to give adequate consideration to the nature of his position. In the delegates' presence he voiced objections to a proclamation of emancipation that he had already weighed in his mind and rejected—above all, that it would necessarily be inoperative because it would apply only in areas where the Constitution could not be enforced. Lincoln's secretary-biographers Nicolay and Hay explain his seemingly odd behavior in this way: the president "felt himself under compulsion, which he could not resist, to state somewhat precisely the difficulties and perplexities under which he was acting, or, rather, apparently refusing to act"; his reply to the Chicago delegation "is in the nature of a friendly protest and polite rebuke against their impolitic urgency."[20] Apart from this, however, Lincoln no doubt wanted his decision to be seen in the proper light when he should choose to reveal it.

The delegates told Lincoln that a proclamation of emancipation would give the people of the North "a glorious principle for which to suffer and to fight." He replied, "I think you should admit that we already have an important principle to rally and unite the people in the fact that constitutional government is at stake. This is a fundamental idea, going down about as deep as any thing." Lincoln did not disagree with the delegates' rejoinder that "*nothing else has put constitutional government in danger but slavery*"—as a despotic element among American institutions, slavery was inconsistent with the others and had "caused free government to appear a failure before the world." Moreover Lincoln believed he was on safe constitutional ground in proclaiming emancipation, "for, as commander-in-chief of the army and navy, in time of war, I suppose I have a right to take any measure which may best subdue the enemy." The delegates, however, were inclined to see more in such a proclamation than Lincoln's view of the matter as "a practical war measure." They told him, "If the leader will but utter a trumpet call the nation will respond with patriotic ardor." The preliminary proclamation, issued just nine days later, was not the trumpet call they had hoped for but something more prosaic.[21]

One objection Lincoln had raised during the conference—"though it meet only your scorn and contempt"—was the opposition of the border states. The delegates replied that they were quite willing to "let the line be drawn at the same time between freedom and slavery, and between loyalty and treason."[22] In contrast, Lincoln based his border state policy on the premise that Unionism and opposition to slavery were to be kept distinct. "Lincoln could not expect the border people to favor his party or be attached to his administration . . . He had therefore to assume that people in this region would make a distinction between the Republican party and the Union cause."[23] Even before 1860 Lincoln had been careful to distinguish between them. He expected a crisis to follow the election of an antislavery president, but he knew that Southerners would never accept a president whose views on the moral question of slavery differed from theirs unless he could assure them in a credible way that their constitutional rights would be fully respected. Lincoln could not demand agreement concerning the moral evil of slavery, but he could and did demand loyalty to the Constitution and the government of the United States.

By 1862 secession and war had altered relations between the government in Washington and all but four of the slave states; still Lincoln persisted in maintaining separation between the question of freedom or slavery on one hand and that of loyalty or treason on the other. He began the preliminary proclamation by affirming that "hereafter, as heretofore, the war will be prosecuted for the object of practically restoring the constitutional relation between the United States, and each of the states."[24] Emancipation itself was made conditional on the failure of the states then in rebellion to reassume their rightful places in the Union before the end of the year.

During the conference Lincoln had also expressed skepticism about whether a proclamation from him "would have any greater effect upon the slaves than the late law of Congress . . . which offers protection and freedom to the slaves of rebel masters who come within our lines."[25] The fact that this law had already provided for "almost wholesale emancipation"[26] in the seceded states made an executive proclamation more rather than less likely—it removed the objection of usurping legislative functions.[26] Its passage precedes the reading of Lincoln's draft proclamation by just five days. The actual proclamation incorporates excerpts from this and another recent act of Congress on the same subject.

The radicals' approving use of the term "leadership" marks a stage in its rehabilitation since the time of the founding. Harvey Mansfield has pointed out that "leader" as used in *The Federalist* is practically synonymous with "demagogue." The older usage reflects something questionable in the notion of leadership—people may *govern* themselves, but they can only be *led* by another.[27] Clearly the word retained some of its questionable associations seventy-five years later. When Lincoln, in his last message to Congress, referred to Jefferson Davis as "the insurgent leader,"[28] he underscored the difference between himself and the Confederate president—the irregular nature of Davis's authority, at the head of a government that owed its existence to the repudiation of a constitutionally valid election. Lincoln's constitutional scruples distinguished him in a similar way from Frémont. Although Lincoln strove to keep the moral question of slavery distinct from the constitutional question of loyalty to the general government, they were not, after all, unrelated. Human beings show their fitness for freedom by successfully governing themselves. Their failure, if they fail, is the best argument for despotism. Lincoln's handling of the emancipation question reveals his concern to uphold, in deed as well as in speech, the distinction between constitutional government and extraconstitutional leadership. At a time when books on leadership proliferate and leadership studies is gaining recognition as an academic discipline, the distinction is easily overlooked. Lincoln's concern in this regard suggests that too little attention has been paid to the assumptions underlying the current preoccupation with leaders and leadership.

NOTES

1. Abraham Lincoln, "Message to Congress, March 6, 1862," in *The Collected Works of Abraham Lincoln,* eds. Roy P. Basler, Marion Dolores Pratt, and Lloyd A. Dunlap (New Brunswick, NJ: Rutgers University Press, 1953), 5:145.

2. In making this claim I acknowledge my debt to the Abraham Lincoln Association for its sponsorship of the electronic edition of Lincoln's *Collected Works.*

3. Quoted in J. G. Randall, *Lincoln the Liberal Statesman* (New York: Dodd, Mead, 1947), 81.

4. Lincoln 1953, 2:322,553.

5. Ibid., 3:423–25.

6. Ibid., 3:541–42.

7. Harry V. Jaffa, *Crisis of the House Divided: An Interpretation of the Issues in the Lincoln-Douglas Debates* (Chicago: University of Chicago Press, 1982), 275–409.

8. Randall 1947, 72–73. What is said here of the Radical Republicans applies *a fortiori* to the abolitionists (with individual exceptions); Randall tends to conflate them. The two groups did move closer together as the war progressed, although formal party membership remained a stumbling block for most abolitionists.

9. Charles M. Segal, ed., *Conversations with Lincoln* (New Brunswick, NJ: Transaction, 2002), 183.

10. Quoted in Don E. Fehrenbacher, *Lincoln in Text and Context: Collected Essays* (Stanford, CA: Stanford University Press, 1987), 200.

11. T. Harry Williams, "Shall We Keep the Radicals?" In *The Leadership of Abraham Lincoln*, ed. Don E. Fehrenbacher, 103–4 (New York: Wiley, 1970).

12. Lincoln 1953, 7:533.

13. Frederick Law Olmsted, *The Cotton Kingdom: A Traveller's Observations on Cotton and Slavery in the American Slave States* (New York: Da Capo, [1861] 1996), 101-2.

14. Lincoln 1953, 5:423.

15. Ibid., 4:506-7,517–18.

16. Ibid., 4:532.

17. Lord Charnwood, *Abraham Lincoln* (New York: Henry Holt, 1917), 270.

18. Segal 2002, 175.

19. Lincoln 1953, 5:336–38.

20. John G. Nicolay and John Hay, *Abraham Lincoln: A History* (New York: Century, 1890), 6:154, 158.

21. Lincoln 1953, 5:422–24. Lincoln used the same martial metaphor in an 1859 speech, but he used it to warn his listeners against the designs of the Democrats: where the Douglasite doctrine prevails that "there is a perfect right according to interest to do just as you please . . . the miners and sappers will have formed public opinion for the slave trade. They will be ready for Jeff. Davis and Stephens and other leaders of that company, to sound the bugle for the revival of the slave trade, for the second Dred Scott decision, for the flood of slavery to be poured over the free States . . . " (Lincoln 1953, 3:423)

22. Ibid., 5:423–24.

23. J. G. Randall, *Lincoln and the South* (Baton Rouge: Louisiana State University Press, 1946). 62.

24. Lincoln 1953, 5:433–34.

25. Ibid., 5:420.

26. Nicolay and Hay 1890, 6:157.

27. Harvey C. Mansfield, *America's Constitutional Soul* (Baltimore: Johns Hopkins University Press, 1991), 181,210. Elihu Root's 1920 address "Lincoln as a Leader of Men" concludes with the statement "Everyone ought to be, as Lincoln was"—everyone ought to be a politician, because "politics is the practical exercise of the art of self-government." This conclusion, unobjectionable in itself, reads strangely in the light of Root's theme: not everyone can be a leader. What Root calls Lincoln's "wise solicitude to keep the people upon whose support he relied close behind his leadership" was in the service of a wiser solicitude to keep them self-governing (Robert Bacon and James Brown Scott, eds., *Men and Policies: Addresses by Elihu Root* [Cambridge, MA: Harvard University Press, 1925], 69–75). (I thank the journal's anonymous reviewer for this reference.)

28. Lincoln 1953, 8:151.

FDR's Place in History[*]

By William J. vanden Heuvel
Prologue (Washington, D.C.), Winter 2006

The 20th century—that tumultuous, insane, brilliant, brutal, creative, awe-inspiring moment in the history of the world—is over. If democracy's victory over the Great Depression at home and the defeat of totalitarianism abroad in World War II is the defining challenge of the 20th century, then surely the historians are correct in judging Franklin Delano Roosevelt to be its greatest President. FDR's influence was profound—on the world, on his country, and on countless individuals who shaped the postwar world.

Franklin Delano Roosevelt was a New York patrician, a sophisticated and brilliant political representative of the Empire State; he was also a disciplined and intensely private person. He knew triumph and defeat as he transformed the nation by a social revolution that made hope, opportunity, and justice for all Americans our national commitment. In war, he defined the presidency as our commander-in-chief and led America to its pinnacle of strength. He brought a united people to understand its responsibilities of international leadership.

James Rowe, one of six anonymous administrative assistants to the President who constituted the White House staff during the years of the New Deal, has written about FDR that "all the staff adored him, and that's not true of any other President I know of. That complete charm was always there." He was as tough and demanding as any leader we have ever had, but his personal dominance was leavened by good humor, wit, and a respect for others built on self-respect and his sense of office. He knew who he was, comfortable in his own skin as the expression goes, confident and self-assured so that the paranoia of power never was his problem.

Isaiah Berlin, the incomparable British intellectual and philosopher, in an essay cataloging President Roosevelt's qualities of mind and spirit, wrote: "Above all, he was absolutely fearless. He was one of the few statesmen in the 20th or any other century who seemed to have no fear at all of the future." Confident of his own strength and ability to manage, FDR looked upon the future with a calm eye, his confidence inspiring confidence, his personal and public courage creating a moral authority that carried through the unprecedented years of his presidency.

There was probably no one FDR admired more than his cousin, Theodore Roosevelt. The extraordinary parallel of their careers was undoubtedly influenced greatly by that admiration. Those parallels include the following: both TR and FDR, separated by a generation in time, were elected to the New York State legislature (TR at 23, FDR at 28); both were appointed assistant secretary of the Navy (TR at 38, FDR at 31); both were vice presidential candidates (TR at 41, FDR at 38); both knew political defeat, TR as a candidate for mayor of New York (1886) and in his Bull Moose campaign for President (1912), FDR in the Democratic primary campaign for the United States Senate (1914) and as the running mate of James Cox in the 1920 presidential election; both married at a young age (TR at 22, FDR at 23); and both had four sons as brave participants in the two world wars. Both were Harvard graduates and recognized ornithologists. And, of course, both were Presidents of the United States—TR at age 42, serving 7½ years, FDR at 50, serving 12 years and 1 month. When Franklin and Eleanor were married in 1905, the President of the United States, Theodore Roosevelt, gave the bride away, remarking, "Well, Franklin, there's nothing like keeping the name in the family." The orphaned Eleanor Roosevelt was his godchild and favorite niece, and she became the conscience of Franklin Roosevelt's presidency. At the time of her death in 1962, Adlai Stevenson spoke at the United Nations and mourned "the First Lady of the World."

FDR's first battle in a lifelong struggle with the political bosses came shortly after his astonishing victory in 1910 for the state senate seat in Dutchess County, an election that had been won by the Democrats only once since the Civil War. The party elders thought the nomination was worthless. FDR seized the opportunity, campaigned night and day, listened to the voters, improved his speaking ability— and riding a national Democratic tide with a name—Roosevelt—more popular than any other in the nation, won by 1,140 votes. Within months, the fledgling state senator challenged Tammany Hall in a confrontation to nominate the next U.S. senator from New York. Tammany ended up with its own candidate, but to FDR's constituents, to journalists, and to politicians throughout the country, another Roosevelt had emerged who was tough, independent, willing to fight for democratic principles—and who enjoyed the battle.

With Woodrow Wilson elected President in 1912, FDR accepted appointment as assistant secretary of the Navy, a post he held for eight years. It allowed him to learn the ways of Washington, to witness the brilliance and destruction of Woodrow Wilson's presidency, and to gain a sharp sense of America's security interests as World War I became our battlefield. By 1920, he was a national figure of sufficient stature to be the Democratic candidate for Vice President. Even in defeat, FDR had added luster to his name. There was no doubt he would be heard from again.

In August 1921, at the age of 39, Franklin Roosevelt was stricken with infantile paralysis. It was an ordeal that many believe gave him the courage and character to become a great President, but the path to recovery was a tortured one with many crises of despair and anguish. The next several years were dominated by his determination to learn to walk again. It became the focus of his life. His forays into public places were carefully planned. Two-thirds of his personal fortune went into establishing the Warm Springs Foundation in Georgia. He transformed it into a major treatment center for polio victims. He created an enterprise that is today one of the most successful rehabilitation centers in the country. But he would never walk or stand again without help. With infinite patience, he learned to move again, to rely on the physical support of others, never giving in to despair, to self pity, or to discouragement.

In 1924, Governor Alfred E. Smith asked FDR to nominate him for President at the Democratic national convention in New York City. On the arm of his son, FDR, with his legs firm in locked braces, holding a cane in his other hand, advanced slowly without crutches to the podium in Madison Square Garden. It was a moment that no one who saw it would ever forget. His palpable courage, his eloquence, his magnificent voice, brought the delegates to their feet—and at that moment Franklin Roosevelt resumed a national political career. Seven years after his polio attack, Roosevelt was elected governor of New York. Roosevelt had perfected so effective an illusion of his strength and well-being that most Americans never realized until after his death that he was, in fact, a paraplegic. He founded the March of Dimes, which financed the research of Dr. Jonas Salk and Dr. Albert Sabin, resulting in the vaccine that conquered polio. FDR would have regarded that as one of his greatest accomplishments. The disabled the world over revere FDR, remembering his courage and steadfast support for the possibilities of their lives.

Franklin Roosevelt was elected to the first of his four terms as President in 1932. It was an election that changed Washington and America forever. Faced with a revolution in its streets, the country chose a revolution in its leadership. For only the third time since the Civil War, the Democrats gained power, with a leader who claimed the nomination of his party by pledging a New Deal for the American people. "The only thing we have to fear is fear itself," spoke Franklin Delano Roosevelt to his fellow citizens on the day of his inaugural in the midst of unparalleled national despair. The banking system had collapsed, 25 percent of the workforce was unemployed, and hunger, deprivation, and loss devastated the country as never before. Thus began the most innovative reform period of our history. With a commanding majority in the Congress and with the New Deal a magnet for thousands of the most talented, idealistic young Americans, FDR began his fabled 100 days of legislative accomplishment.

Having become President in the midst of the greatest economic crisis in the nation's history, FDR responded with a program that resulted in the Tennessee Valley Authority, the Works Progress Administration, the Social Security Act, the Rural Electrification Administration, the Securities and Exchange Commission, the Agricultural Adjustment Administration, the Civilian Conservation Corps, unprecedented programs of conservation, a bank moratorium and regulation, public and subsidized housing, and new rights for labor, for farmers, for the poor and the working man, the middle class, for a new society of decency and equality of opportunity for all Americans.

Both FDR and Eleanor Roosevelt received the special venom of the demagogues and anti-Semites who found the despair of the Depression to be a fertile ground for their hatred. The historic struggle between federal power and states' rights was altered de facto by the social contract rewritten by the New Deal. Roosevelt knew that the states' rights banner had often been used in our history as a cover for forces of selfishness, racism, and civil injustice, but he did not back away from the struggle. No President since Lincoln did more to restore the balance between federal and state responsibility.

By the winter of 1935, the Supreme Court had become the last hope of those who were committed to blocking the New Deal. FDR's concept of the constitutional powers of the President and the Congress to cope with the Great Depression was very different from that of his Republican predecessors who had appointed the dominant majority of the Supreme Court. The anti-New Deal forces started literally thousands of legal actions to stop the fulfillment of programs which the President had initiated, that Congress had legislated, and the people in landslide elections had approved.

The Court invalidated the Railroad Retirement Act. It then overturned the National Recovery Act as well as the Mortgage Moratorium legislation. In 1936 it ruled the Agricultural Adjustment Act unconstitutional. Harlan Fiske Stone, appointed by Calvin Coolidge, wrote a dissent accusing his colleagues of deciding on the basis of their own economic theories rather than fair constitutional interpretation. The Court proceeded to overturn legislation designed to bring order and safety to the desperate coal mining industry; it overturned the Municipal Bankruptcy Act created to save local governments across the country in financial distress; and then it ruled unconstitutional the New York State law establishing a minimum wage, outlawing child labor, and regulating the hours and labor conditions affecting women. Even the opponents of the New Deal were embarrassed.

FDR was reelected in 1936 in a landslide. The Court was about to decide the constitutionality of the Social Security Act, the Wagner Act establishing collective bargaining and protecting the right of labor to organize, and the minimum wage and employment laws. It was a dramatic moment in our history. Roosevelt understood that the economic and social revolution enacted by the elected representatives of the people could be defeated—not at the polls but by a Court whose majority philosophy the people had decisively repudiated. The justices who dominated the Court, though aged and in declining health, were determined to stay in office as long as Roosevelt was President in order to frustrate his programs. President Roosevelt took comfort in reading these words from Abraham Lincoln's first inaugural:

> The candid citizen must confess that if the policy of the government upon vital questions affecting the whole people is to be irrevocably fixed by decisions of the Supreme Court, the people will have to that extent practically resigned their government into the hands of that eminent tribunal.

Roosevelt had enormous respect for the constitutional framework of the balance of power and for the integrity of the Supreme Court as an independent branch of our government. But he stood with Lincoln in rejecting the concept that the Constitution was a rigid, inflexible instrument that could prevent the government from responding to crises that threatened to destroy the nation. FDR proposed that when a federal judge, including those on the Supreme Court, reached the age of 70 and chose not to retire, that the President could appoint a new justice to the Court.

Within weeks, under pressure from Chief Justice Charles Evans Hughes, the Court reversed its course, upholding the Wagner Act and the Social Security legislation and even the state minimum wage laws it had ruled unconstitutional just months before. Writers refer to FDR's court reorganization proposal as his attempt to "pack the Court," and they generally describe his "defeat" as the greatest of his domestic agenda and the turning point of the Roosevelt reform era. For FDR, there was no alternative—his challenge to the Court saved the New Deal. The political costs to FDR were significant, but he was twice again elected President by the American people after the struggle had settled.

As with so much of the New Deal, the Roosevelt challenge to the Supreme Court has contemporary resonance, as the bitter debates in the Senate in the last several years have shown. But the New Deal itself is part of the fabric of our nation, not beyond revision but beyond reversal—Dwight Eisenhower said of those who wanted to roll back the New Deal, "their number is negligible and they are stupid." In his presidential diaries, Ronald Reagan, who voted four times for FDR as President, expressed his anger at those who wanted him to challenge the achievements of the New Deal.

No one can talk of the Roosevelt legacy without mentioning the extraordinary contribution of FDR in the fields of conservation and environmental concern. His commitment to the conservation movement literally changed the landscape of our country. He regarded the majestic beauty of America, its resources, its soil, its water, its forests, to be the common heritage of all of our people. He brought a new sense of responsibility to land management to strengthen the role of the federal government, as TR before him in protecting the remaining wilderness and wildlife as national treasures of the country. Millions of acres were added to the national parks and to the public lands. The enemies of the countryside—catastrophic floods and droughts, deforested lands eroding, turning valleys of fertile plains into dust bowls—these destructive forces were met by the New Deal and by presidential leadership with top-priority programs to prevent their devastation. FDR invited our unemployed youth to join the Civilian Conservation Corps (CCC). It helped give meaning to their lives and remade the natural infrastructure of our nation. Even today, a major part of the infrastructure of every state—its schools, public buildings, its bridges, its airports—is the legacy of the Roosevelt presidency.

The 1938 elections reduced the Democratic majorities in the Congress. FDR in his famous "purge" had tried to defeat several of the key Democratic lawmakers whose conservative viewpoints had threatened the reforms of the New Deal. He was not successful, and the nation's press, as have later historians, regarded the election as a turning point for the reform era that FDR had so successfully led for the country. FDR, better than anyone, understood that no electorate can sustain on a continuing basis the energy, focus, and high resolve needed to advance a reform movement. As FDR approached the completion of his second term, the growing international crisis focused the question on who would lead America.

Events in Europe and the Far East threatened devastating war and destruction for much of the world. Japan, dominated by an inflexible militarism, had invaded China and sought to establish its domination of Asia. The dictators were on the march in Europe. Germany, re-armed under Hitler, began its march across Europe, occupying Austria and Czechoslovakia and on September 1, 1939, invading Poland, beginning the Second World War. As the American political parties were preparing their conventions in 1940, France surrendered to the Nazis. The world was stunned. Was this the "tremendous crisis" that Theodore Roosevelt had written of that would justify a sitting President to seek a third consecutive term? FDR was silent, like a sphinx, as reporters and politicians asked constantly whether he would run. He probably did not make a final decision until the world-shattering events played out around him. As Arthur Schlesinger has described in his brilliant memoir, the nation was more bitterly divided over the issue of the war in Europe and America's role and responsibility than by any other crisis of the 20th century. FDR's handling of the third term decision was a test of his consummate political artistry. He kept all of his options open. He accepted the nomination in the only way that the anti-third term tradition could have been broken—that is by a Democratic convention that truly drafted him. For those who thought that FDR had lost control in the purge of 1938, his nomination for a third term showed that he still dominated the Democratic Party. His victory over Wendell Willkie, a man of charm, culture, and conviction, showed FDR's command of the nation.

The achievements of the New Deal and the international role and responsibility that Franklin Roosevelt bequeathed to us, representing as they do a fundamental restructuring of our nation and the world, are under constant attack in contemporary politics. Of course, Roosevelt himself insisted that change was the order of the day—that programs and experiments had to be tried; if they worked then let them go forward, but if they needed to be reorganized, reformed, or abolished, then be not afraid to do so. He was a pragmatic idealist, and both of those words have bold meaning as biographers and historians search the archives continually seeking new evidence to reconstruct the complicated and extraordinary years of the Roosevelt legacy.

In this 125th anniversary year of his birth, we reflect on the major accomplishments of his life that time will not diminish:

Clearly the Grand Alliance, based primarily on the partnership of Winston Churchill and Franklin Roosevelt, was the most successful political, economic, and military partnership of modern history. It saved western civilization. Churchill has written that Roosevelt's life "must be regarded as one of the commanding events in human destiny." He described Franklin Roosevelt as "the greatest man I have ever known." They were characters worthy of a drama by Shakespeare. They were men of a different time—as Isaiah Berlin has written, Churchill was a man of the 19th century and Roosevelt a man of the 20th. Churchill was dedicated to the preservation of the British Empire. Roosevelt understood that the world that emerged from World War II would be profoundly different from what had been known before: that colonialism was nearing its end, that the threat of war in the nuclear age made it imperative for nations to find a means to work together to prevent violence and preserve the possibility of peace. At the helm of a profoundly isolated nation, with 84 percent of the American people registering their conviction against any involvement in European conflict, Roosevelt slowly, deliberately, and successfully educated his countrymen to the threat of Nazism and the calamity awaiting democracy if Great Britain should collapse.

Five weeks before Franklin Roosevelt took his first oath of office as President, Adolf Hitler became chancellor of Germany. Their epic confrontation would determine whether mankind's fate would be freedom or totalitarianism. Roosevelt's loathing of the whole Nazi regime was known the moment he took office. Alone among the leaders of the world, he stood in opposition to Hitler from the very beginning. He never wavered in his belief that the evil of Hitler and his followers had to be destroyed. Roosevelt confronted the profound isolationist attitude in the country and undid the public image that the isolationists had projected of themselves as peace-loving patriots. He turned the tide of public opinion against them.

At great political risk in the midst of a presidential campaign, Roosevelt engineered a deal that sent 50 desperately needed destroyers to Britain, a deed which helped save its lifeline from the unremitting attacks of German submarines. Hitler called it a belligerent act—it was. Roosevelt proposed lend-lease and built a bipartisan coalition to gain its congressional approval. He announced the Four Freedoms that would justify the terrible sacrifices that lay ahead, a speech that Margaret Thatcher has called one of the greatest of the 20th century. He met with Winston Churchill and announced the Atlantic Charter. All this—and America was not yet at war. Finally, the treacherous attack on Pearl Harbor by Japan brought us directly into the war that FDR had long regarded as inevitable. He now led a united country and mobilized it for victory, unleashing the colossal strength of America's military and economic potential.

Roosevelt as commander-in-chief was remarkably successful. He worked with his military commanders effectively and constructively, not harassing them with his own personal judgments, but always a welcome participant in the strategic decisions. His command appointments were the finest—Gen. George Marshall, Adm. Chester Nimitz, Gen. Douglas MacArthur, Adm. Ernest King. Together with General Marshall he chose Dwight Eisenhower to lead the D-day invasion, knowing certainly that the fame of his success would establish Eisenhower for a generation as a dominant leader of the nation. He would not allow Americans to be fearful, even when faced with a disaster like Pearl Harbor. He set about the supreme task of prevailing over our enemies in a mood of quiet, grim resolution, setting production goals for our factories that many thought unrealistic but all of which were surpassed. He called for sacrifice to be shared by the entire nation—16 million citizens entered the armed forces, business and labor cooperated to build an industrial capacity that remains a modern miracle, inflation was contained, rationing was accepted, heavy taxes were imposed, but our country was never more unified, never doubting the outcome of the greatest military conflict in history.

More than anyone else, Franklin Delano Roosevelt was the founder of the United Nations, a singular act of political creativity. While war was being waged, peace was being structured with the President personally directing the architecture of plans for the postwar world. The Four Freedoms would be the inspirational core of the universal effort that America would lead—Freedom of Speech and Expression, Freedom of Worship, Freedom from Want, and Freedom from Fear There were no illusions about the difficulties ahead. FDR understood very well the oppressive totalitarianism of communism under the Soviet Union, but he also understood that the United Nations' victory in World War II was due in substantial measure to the extraordinary sacrifice of the Russian people, who had lost 27 million dead with much of their country plundered and destroyed. He understood that we were about to enter the nuclear age and that conflicts among nations now required a forum for these conflicts to be resolved by means other than war. He saw the possibilities and potential for both China and India, insisting on China as a member of the Security Coucil and supporting the cause of India's freedom. Foreseeing the end of the colonial era, he tried to devise ways that would allow colonized nations to be led peacefully to independence and participation in the world order. If his successors had followed his views on Indochina, the Vietnam debacle almost certainly would have been avoided.

No single American did more to save the free enterprise system than Franklin Roosevelt. The capitalistic excesses of the 1920s that brought about the cataclysm of the Great Depression caused America to reconsider the balance of forces that made up its democracy. The trumpet had been sounded by Theodore Roosevelt when he said "of all forms of tyranny, the least attractive and the most vulgar is the tyranny of mere wealth, the tyranny of plutocracy." The progressive leadership of Woodrow Wilson introduced income and estate taxation, the central banking system, and rudimentary monitoring elements regarding the banking structure of the nation. Franklin Roosevelt was not against business or corporations. He understood the indispensable creative role that business had in creating wealth and jobs and economic opportunity, but he was determined that this immense power be regulated and restrained in the context of the national interest, a national interest that the President was elected to define and that the Congress was elected to advance. He saw the immense disparity of wealth that defined pre-Depression

America as a threat to Democracy. Many great capitalists were his allies. They shared his belief that wealth should be used to encourage purpose, achievement, and building a nation that no enemy could harm and whose example and democracy would inspire the world.

He was a master of the American political system, an intuitive genius regarding public opinion, a communicator who used the media of his time—radio—to amplify his magnificent voice into millions of households, becoming the neighbor and friend of most who heard him. Four times he was elected President of the United States; he led his party to seven consecutive congressional election victories. By temperament and talent, by energy and instinct, Franklin Roosevelt came to the presidency ready for its challenges—and he loved every aspect of the job.

We live in a world still guided and dominated by his strategic vision. Franklin Roosevelt's place in American history is with the Father of our Country and the Great Emancipator. In remaking America, Franklin Roosevelt made it possible to remake the world. It is that challenge that has left FDR's shadow as a dominating force in all of the administrations that have succeeded his presidency.

The 1980s and the Age of Reagan[*]

By Glen Jeansonne
History Today, August 2004

The 1980s were a time of paradox and change yet Reagan's friends believe he changed the world more than the world changed him. Reagan came to the White House underestimated, deemed a dullard who doled out tall tales and mixed Hollywood fantasy with political reality. He made peace with the Soviets, and bonded with their premier, before what he termed their 'Evil Empire' collapsed. He slashed taxes, mushroomed the military and created a national debt that was, as he quipped, 'big enough to take care of itself'.

His showman's experience enabled him to to deliver speeches glittering with inspiring generalities and tough talk. He felt for the poor as individuals, yet he believed more strongly in individual responsibility.

Ever since the New Deal Americans had looked to the Federal government to solve their problems. Once a New Dealer himself, Reagan warned that the Federal government could not expand infinitely. Franklin Roosevelt had intended massive federal intervention in the economy a temporary expedient; Reagan believed FDR would have been disturbed to learn that his minnow of a safety net had expanded into a whale.

'The Gipper', as Reagan was known for a movie role in which he played halfback George Gipp, believed, as Barry Goldwater, his John the Baptist, had warned, that 'a government big enough to give you everything you want is big enough to take away everything you have.'

It was said of FDR that he had 'a second-rate mind but a first-rate temperament'. This was equally true of Reagan. The New York aristocrat and the former California governor had other things in common, though they were poles apart on some things. First, was their ability to deal with people. Both were cheerful, born optimists, and benefited from a disarming sense of humor. Neither was a workaholic and they delegated many of their less important tasks.

1980s America was not particularly virtuous nor unselfish. Many Americans, especially those who became rich, went on a binge; 'restraint' was not a term that would be used to describe the decade. But the decade featured a President who clung to the wholesome image of the popular culture of the 1950s while the popular culture of his own presidential tenure went on a rampage. Americans had experienced a similar split personality in the 1920s; flappers danced the Charleston and guzzled bootlegged booze, then strolled into the voting booth and cast their ballots for Calvin Coolidge.

The election of 1980 was largely a revolt against the pessimism that had shrouded Jimmy Carter's America rather than the promise of an unknown future. Reagan understood that Americans were disillusioned after decades of national trauma, of Vietnam and Watergate, followed by stagflation, unemployment, international competition for jobs and the humiliating hostage crisis in Iran. Reagan denied that 'there are no simple answers': 'There are simple answers,' he said, 'but there are not always easy ones.' Eisenhower had seemed calm on the surface; Reagan was calm through and through. Nevertheless, there was the competitive streak of a college athlete in Reagan. Although not assertive in the realm of ideas, Reagan did not like to lose once proposals were on the table.

Americans accepted his laid-back style. He disliked detail and avoided it by delegating. The American people saw in Reagan someone who defied Lord Acton's epigram that no great men are good men. Reagan was a good man not in the sense that he was puritanical, but in the sense that he did not hold grudges, was not mean-spirited, and lacked a vindictive nature. He was not hard-hearted yet could be hard-headed. His friends called him principled; his enemies termed him stubborn.

Reagan was gifted in public speaking; in memorizing lines; in getting along with people; in making friends; in having a strong body that in youth possessed vigour and stamina; and in his relentlessly upbeat personality. He used his experience as an actor to guarantee a polished performance when working from a script. Yet when questions required him to respond extemporaneously, he faltered. Reagan did not think well on his feet. Unstructured situations fatigued the old warrior and when he became tired he sometimes grew flustered and made mistakes. Once he nodded off at an audience with the Pope. His spokesman conceded that the President often forgot the names of those he worked with.

He accepted his limitations with grace. An asset that caused his opponents to sneer was his gift as a born storyteller. He told stories with a twinkle in his eye, and people found his tales down-to-earth and humanizing. The American people did not want a rocket scientist for president, they wanted someone like them.

The 1980 election was more an anti-Carter referendum than a pro-Reagan vote. Yet by 1984 Reagan had a record to run on. At the time of his second election, America was proud, prosperous, and peaceful. Reagan evoked recollections of a time when the presidency was not only at the center of action but a rock of stability.

In his first term, Reagan's staff tried to shelter the President by selectively leaking to the press and making Reagan available under controlled situations. The press, even when it disagreed with Reagan's policies, found it almost impossible to dislike him personally.

In the second term, the new Chief-of-Staff Donald Regan decided the President should focus more on substance. Regan believed the President had been elected because of his personality and ideology, not in spite of them. He dismissed the idea that the President must be a figurehead.

This was not exploiting the President's strengths. After Reagan had spent weeks working on a policy agenda for the second term, the President simply said, 'OK' and did not bother to read it. The new Chief-of-Staff did not understand Ronald Reagan, and tried to push him faster than he wanted to go. Regan's colossal ego also irritated Nancy Reagan, a powerful First Lady. Most of the President's advisers had the good sense not to cross Nancy but when Don Regan, after a series of disagreements with the First Lady, hung up the telephone on Nancy, she shouted the equivalent of 'Off with his head,' and the guillotine fell.

Beneath the President's friendly exterior was a cold indifference, or perhaps simply a distracted personality, able to concentrate on only one thing at a time. He showed little interest in the families of federal officials outside his inner circle. He did not offer help to individuals who had served him loyally when they encountered legal problems. An unusual number of Reagan's advisers wrote harshly critical memoirs after leaving the White House.

The Republican party championed family values, yet the Chief Executive's own family was dysfunctional. Reagan espoused religion, yet rarely attended church and did not instill spiritual values in his children. Nearly all of Reagan's children, at one time or another, were estranged from their parents. Some felt the bond between the President and Nancy so great it shut them out.

People used to go the motion picture theatre to see the 'A' movie yet enjoyed Reagan's 'B' movies more. At every endeavor Reagan undertook he was expected to fail. Critics said he had gone as far in his radio career, in his acting career, in his political career as personality could take him. He was a romantic lost in the interstellar space of big-power diplomacy. When he told Margaret Thatcher that Communism's destiny was the dust-bin of history many of his own countrymen sneered. But he believed when he labeled Communism's clutch 'The Evil Empire' he was speaking literal truth. He pointed out that Communist leaders came to power by military coups or civil wars and remained there by force. They claimed public support yet dared not test it in a free election.

Reagan pushed the Soviet Union beyond its economic and military limits. The threat to build a defensive protection system against missiles, whether or not it would work, and regardless of how expensive it might be, cowed the Soviets more than any operable weapon in America's arsenal. The very expense of the system was what the Soviets most feared. A war of dollars was one they could not win.

When people pushed the laid-back President, he pushed back. Yet he was not all push and no give. As Soviet leaders toppled to diseases of old age, Reagan saw his entire first term elapse without a Soviet-American summit. Reagan complained: 'How am I going to meet them when they keep dying on me?'

He was the first Cold War president who did not fear his Communist adversaries, yet he was able, in his second term, to humanize them, to strike an arms deal with Mikhail Gorbachev and to forge a closer relationship with Gorbachev that any president in history had established with a foreign foe. Gorbachev respected Reagan because he knew he would not back down, however foolish he might have considered the American President's position. But he also knew that if he consummated a deal or a friendship with Reagan, it would stick. Fate brought them together in the same decade, just as it had brought FDR and Winston Churchill together, and they changed history. Historians will argue the extent to which to credit or blame Reagan for the events that occurred on his watch. Liberals will find it difficult to credit him with the collapse of Communism and the prosperity of most of the 1980s. Some believe that Reagan's role as a shaper of history was no more intentional than that of Mrs O'Leary's cow, who kicked over a lantern and started the Chicago fire.

Reagan accepted he would be judged partly on ideological terms because he was an ideological leader. He did not invent the idea that the federal government was too powerful and intrusive, nor did he demonise government in general; he had little negative to say about state and local governments. But he propelled the ideology of decentralization along a route it was already traveling. He presented a set of ideas for which there was a demand and exerted charm and subtle pressure to enact them into law. Some of his most important changes did not involve laws at all, but moods. A relentless cheerleader, he urged Americans to conquer defeatism. Slow to anger, he was a gentle warrior—yet a warrior nonetheless.

If Reagan was not a great president, neither was he a mediocre one. He came to office with a short agenda of big things and accomplished most of them. He demonstrated that common sense, sound judgment, and an uncanny intuition were more important than book learning.

Reagan hoped to spend his retirement at his ranch, riding horses, watching old movies and being with Nancy. Alzheimer's disease cut short this idyllic interlude, and 'the Gipper' slipped from life on June 5th, 2004, at 93 the oldest ex-president in history. If someone had tried to comfort Reagan by telling him that by dying he would be going to a better place, the fading warrior might have blinked, and asked, 'Is there a better place than America?'

2

Electing a President:
From the Campaign to the Electoral College

Editor's Introduction

For over two centuries, every four years Americans have gathered at the polls to elect a president. Through wars, both civil and foreign, during periods of intense economic and social unrest, this process has endured. Despite this seeming stability, the structure of our elections has changed drastically over the years. How major-party candidates are chosen has evolved, with the decisive factor shifting away from the political convention to the primary. Now two states, Iowa and New Hampshire, through their caucus and primary systems, have emerged as essential contests in any candidate's quest for the presidency. Still, amid these developments, the fundamental elements remain: The winning candidate has consistently hailed from one of the two major American political organizations, today the Republican and Democratic Parties; and the Electoral College continues to be the ultimate arbiter of who claims the office. The articles in this chapter provide an analysis of the American electoral process, balancing an historical perspective with an emphasis on the system as it exists today.

In recent years the Iowa Caucuses has been the first major hurdle in the race for the White House, with presidential hopefuls traversing the state in the hopes of gaining early momentum. The results of the 2008 Iowa Caucuses vividly illuminated just how important this unique contest has become, with the outcome fundamentally changing the nature of the race and foreshadowing the shape of the campaign to come. On the Democratic side, Illinois Senator Barack Obama achieved his historic victory over New York Senator Hillary Clinton, and former North Carolina Senator John Edwards; while in the Republican contest, former Arkansas Governor Mike Huckabee, scored the upset, defeating his more-established and better-financed opponents, with his grassroots support among evangelical voters tipping the balance. However, the Iowa Caucuses have not always played so influential a role in presidential elections. In fact, as Todd S. Purdum reports in "The Caucuses; Carter Put It on the Political Map and Iowa Hasn't Budged Since," the Iowa Caucuses have only recently become such a central fixture of American politics.

Following Senator Obama and Governor Huckabee's Iowa upsets, the campaign shifted to New Hampshire for the state's "first-in-the-nation" primary. With her campaign written off as all but dead, a revived Senator Clinton claimed the win, thus insuring that the race for the Democratic nomination would go on.

Meanwhile, Governor Huckabee failed to build on his Iowa momentum, and, as they did in 2000, New Hampshire primary voters backed Arizona Senator John McCain. This marked a stunning turnaround for McCain, whose bid for the White House pundits had declared doomed only months before, and reemphasized New Hampshire's prominent role in the campaign for the presidency. In "An Abridged History of the NH Presidential Primary," Michael McCord explores the origins and evolution of the first-in-the-nation primary.

With New Hampshire behind them, the candidates, Republican and Democrat alike, embarked on the larger primary campaign, competing in various states depending on the dates of their primary or caucus. While Senator McCain soon overcame his closest rivals, Governor Huckabee and former Massachusetts Governor Mitt Romney, to seal the nomination, Senators Obama and Clinton engaged in a protracted and combative battle before the race concluded with a narrow victory for Senator Obama. In "My Vote Means Nothing: How Presidential Primaries Backfired," David Greenberg critiques the primary system, maintaining that the way it is currently structured favors early momentum over long-term viability and gives early states a disproportionate influence. Though the 2008 Democratic race, in which momentum swung back and forth over many months and all but every state mattered, would seem to contradict much of Greenberg's analysis, the Clinton-Obama race was, given recent history, altogether unprecedented, suggesting that it is the exception rather than the rule.

After the primaries are complete, the political parties hold nominating conventions. In 2008 the Democrats hold theirs in Denver, Colorado, the Republicans in St. Paul, Minnesota. Today these gatherings are largely ceremonial and highly coordinated, geared toward convincing the voters watching on television to cast their ballots for the party's chosen candidate. This has not always been the case. In days past nominees were determined at the convention itself; if a consensus did not develop, boisterous and even violent confrontations could erupt. At other times the results would be determined in the so-called smoky back room, where party bosses would meet to settle on a candidate. In "Do Political Conventions Matter?" Peter Grier examines the history of these gatherings and how they've changed.

The final two pieces in this chapter offer dueling analyses of the Electoral College. According to the Constitution, rather than casting their ballot for a particular candidate on election day, voters are really choosing electors, delegates pledged to support a specific presidential aspirant. Electors are awarded on a state-by-state basis according to congressional delegation. Each state is awarded one elector for each senator and congressional representative. This results in a system that has weathered its share of criticism over the years, especially after the disputed 2000 presidential election. David I. Wells, in "Degrees of Democracy," argues that the Electoral College ought to be scrapped in favor of a more purely democratic system, while Michael M. Uhlmann maintains, in "The Old (Electoral) College Cheer: Why We Have It; Why We Need It," that the institution continues to serve a vital role in American life.

The Caucuses[*]

Carter Put It on the Political Map, And Iowa Hasn't Budged Since

By Todd S. Purdum
The New York Times, January 14, 2004

Exactly 28 years ago Monday, a little-known former governor of Georgia named Jimmy Carter polled just shy of 30 percent support in Iowa's precinct caucuses. He came in second, nine points behind "uncommitted," but the national news media proclaimed him the clear winner of the year's first presidential nominating contest, if only because he had finished so far ahead of everyone else.

Mr. Carter spent that caucus night not in Iowa, but in New York City, so he could be available for all three network news programs the next morning: none of them had sent anchors to Des Moines. Because he went on to win not only the Democratic nomination but also the White House, nothing about this state's politics has ever been quite the same.

Now the networks' mobile newsrooms roll through the frigid streets, and Tom Brokaw takes a table at 801 Steak and Chop House, Des Moines's meatery of choice. And depending on your viewpoint, the Iowa caucuses have become either an established ornament of American democracy or an unrepresentative abomination, in which candidates can win by losing if they run a good race, or lose by winning if they perform below expectations. The contest does not produce a single convention delegate but only begins the county and state selection process. It is far from a reliable predictor of the eventual nominee.

But together with New Hampshire, which votes next week, the Iowa caucuses lead the pack. So a once-obscure former governor of Vermont, aided by Mr. Carter's old organizer, Tim Kraft, and a batch of high-profile members of Congress are all hoping that Iowa will be their own breakthrough.

The contest looms all the larger this year because the primary schedule is now so compressed: of the delegates needed for nomination, more than one-tenth will be allotted by Feb. 3, and nearly 60 percent by March 2.

"It just keeps going," said Hugh Winebrenner, a retired Drake University professor and the author of "The Iowa Precinct Caucuses: The Making of a Media Event." "There have been attempts by the parties, the candidates, by other states to derail it or at least put it in some kind of perspective, and none of that has succeeded. But the original meaning has been transformed strikingly. There's been no little-known candidate come out of Iowa and win the nomination since Carter. Now it's a winnowing of the field, which is very different."

The race here is seen as so close that all the major candidates could conceivably survive to fight on. The front page of The Des Moines Register was plastered Sunday with big red up and down arrows detailing its latest poll, which showed some candidates rising and others falling, but all within reach of one another.

On Jan. 19, 1976, the notion of the caucuses as a big event was such a novelty that the Iowa Democratic Party had raised $4,000 to help defray the caucus costs: selling tickets, at $10 a head and $1 a drink, so the public could watch the national reporters at work on election night. Now, the party uses the caucuses as a vital fund-raising tool, and the candidates pay tribute, as Senator John Edwards of North Carolina did by donating computer equipment worth thousands of dollars for use during this election cycle.

"That's getting very close to, I don't know what the right word would be—not corruption, but something," said former Senator Gary Hart of Colorado, who first saw the Iowa caucuses as a way to build early support when he was George S. McGovern's campaign manager in 1972. Mr. Hart's own candidacy caught fire after his surprising second-place finish here behind Walter F. Mondale in 1984 helped propel him to victory in New Hampshire.

"In a perfect world, caucuses would be a very good way of figuring out which of the candidates has been persuasive," Mr. Hart added. "But what started out as a person-to-person, humanized event has gotten to be very organized and professionalized. The deliberative aspect of it—getting together in a rural Iowa farmhouse to debate the candidates' merits—is the ideal, and I think we've strayed very far from that."

"Caucus" is an Algonquin Indian word meaning elder, and Iowa's system dates to its statehood, in 1846. But for most of their history, the caucuses remained comparatively obscure. Only after the debacle of the 1968 Democratic Convention in Chicago and the subsequent revision of the party's rules to emphasize grass-roots power did Mr. Hart and others in the McGovern campaign seize on the caucuses as a way to make an early splash on a low budget.

It was all partly an accident: because the Iowa Democrats could not book a suitable meeting place for the state convention until May 20, 1972, and because new rules required 30 days between each party gathering (local, county, Congressional district and state convention) the latest possible date for the precinct-level caucuses was Jan. 24. For the first time, that put Iowa ahead of the New Hampshire primary, until then the initial test of candidates' strength.

Mr. McGovern, then a senator from neighboring South Dakota and a strong critic of the Vietnam War, headed a special Democratic commission that proposed changes in the national party rules. A young aide, Richard G. Stearns, sketched out a plan to win support in the 28 states where national delegates were chosen by caucuses or conventions, with easier potential for organizing, instead of primaries, with their higher turnouts and costs.

"Because caucus turnout was historically so low, on a fairly low budget you could organize the kind of attendance that could not only be competitive, but dominating," said Mr. Stearns, now a Federal District Court judge in Massachusetts.

In the summer of 1970, Mr. Stearns went to Iowa with Gene Pokorny, who had built a reputation as a wunderkind organizer. They carried the names of about 160 people who had written Mr. McGovern about the war, "went and saw everyone" and left with a skeletal organization in place, Mr. Stearns recalled.

Eighteen months later, the smart money favored Senator Edmund S. Muskie of Maine, but on caucus night—in a blizzard with a wind-chill factor of 56 degrees below zero—Mr. McGovern came in third with nearly 23 percent, and Mr. Muskie was virtually tied with "uncommitted" at almost 36 percent. R. W. Apple Jr. of The New York Times praised Mr. McGovern's "surprisingly strong showing," and ABC News declared, "The Muskie bandwagon slid off an icy road in Iowa last night."

So began a three-decade obsession with the Iowa results, whose meaning has varied wildly. Ronald Reagan lost here to George Bush, but went on to win New Hampshire and the nomination in 1980. Mr. Bush finished third here in 1988, after Bob Dole and the Rev. Pat Robertson.

On the Democratic side that year, Michael S. Dukakis finished third behind Representative Richard A. Gephardt of Missouri (whose political life now depends on winning outright) and Senator Paul Simon from Illinois.

Four years ago, Al Gore handily defeated Bill Bradley in Iowa, only to face a strong challenge from him in New Hampshire. And President Bush finished first here, where John McCain did not compete, only to lose to him in New Hampshire.

So why do candidates keep coming back?

Mr. Hart offers a clue. Asked if he has ever regretted begetting such a beast, he laughed long and hard, and replied: "I did many times in the cold, cold winter of '83–'84, until I came in a very distant second. And then I thought they were manna from heaven."

An Abridged History of the NH Presidential Primary[*]

By Michael McCord
Seacoast Online, February 7, 2007

The New Hampshire Presidential Primary began modestly as a little-noticed reform act of the state legislature in 1913 as a way to select delegates for the national party conventions.

Lying mostly dormant for some four decades, the primary grabbed its first national headlines in 1952 when it began direct voter balloting. The major names on the ballot included President Harry Truman who was upset in the Democratic primary by Sen. Estes Kefauver of Tennessee who endeared himself to the local population by riding around in a snowmobile in a coonskin cap.

On the Republican side, Gen. Dwight Eisenhower, the World War II hero, won the contest while not setting foot in the state. He was busy serving overseas as commander of NATO while the Korean War raged on in Asia. Ike used the primary victory as a stepping stone to winning the nomination and the presidency in the general election. He oversaw a cease fire agreement that ended the Korean War in 1953.

In 1968, the primary attracted wide attention when Sen. Eugene McCarthy, D-Minn, ran an anti-war platform against President Lyndon Johnson. McCarthy's young campaign volunteers cut their hair and dressed well to be "Clean for Gene." Johnson did not formally enter the primary but though he won the primary with 50 percent of the write-in votes, he had been politically wounded. Johnson became the first "winner" of the primary to lose the political and media expectations contest. It happened to Democratic primary winner Edmund Muskie of Maine in 1972, who was remembered for his emotional reaction to stories in the Manchester Union Leader, and later to President George H. W. Bush in 1992, who defeated insurgent candidate Patrick Buchanan but showed political vulnerability.

The breakthrough win in 1976 by Jimmy Carter, the former Georgia governor and peanut farmer who was virtually unknown on the national stage, cemented the primary's status as a major player in the nominating process—and a solid candidate predictor for the rest of the nation.

Carter's campaign showed how a lesser known but highly organized candidate could utilize the state's smaller geographic size and accessible, active citizenry to gain national recognition and overcome money and stature hurdles.

In 1977, the state legislature sanctioned the primary's first in the nation status by enacting a law that "eliminates any possible future encroachment on the state's being first" by being held "on the Tuesday at least seven days immediately preceding the date on which any other state shall hold a similar election, whichever is earlier." Over the years, [the] primary date has changed from early March to various dates in February and finally into January in the 2004 primary.

Due to dramatic changes with the primary process—when John. F. Kennedy and Richard Nixon won the 1960 primary, New Hampshire was one of 15 holding primaries—the state's first in the nation status has been targeted repeatedly during the past two decades by challengers and political parties determined to "frontload" the schedule to benefit establishment candidates.

In 1983, the state abolished signature filing requirements for the primary. Any American citizen willing to pay the filing fee [of] $1,000 can be listed on the ballot. This has led to an increase in the eclectic citizen candidates, some who campaign vigorously (at least until they run out of money) and some who never show up, who add to the primary's unique atmosphere.

It's a theatrical atmosphere which has [been] fed as well by an ever-increasing national and even international media presence. The reason for this is simple: the primary has been the scene of some of the memorable sound bites and events during the past half-century of American political history. Ronald Reagan barely lost to President Gerald Ford in the 1976 primary but he went on to win a tough primary skirmish against George H. W. Bush in 1980. During a campaign debate he took control of a dispute over who would take part in the forum by telling the moderator, "I paid for this microphone."

In 1988, Sen. Robert Dole of Kansas lost to Vice President George Bush but reacting to the tough campaign tactics, told Bush "to stop lying about my record." Dole, who lost in 1980, would lose again in 1996 to Pat Buchanan, though he eventually won the party nomination that year. Richard Nixon, on the other hand, won primaries in 1960, 1968, and 1972.

Buchanan, a television commentator and staff member for Presidents Nixon and Reagan but someone who never held elective office, has been the only outsider to actually break through to victory. Television evangelist Pat Robertson finished fifth in 1988 and millionaire publisher Steve Forbes spent an estimated $3 million of his own money to finish fourth in 1996.

The primary has had its share of upsets, candidates who make a splash in public opinion polls before diving to defeat, surprising results and match ups. In 1984, Sen. Gary Hart of Colorado upset the heavy favorite, former Vice President Walter Mondale. Hart also bested Sen. George McGovern, whose presidential campaign Hart ran in 1972. Hart's win was orchestrated by Jeanne Shaheen of Madbury, who would later become N.H. Governor in 1996.

Before his infamous Iowa defeat "scream" in early 2004, and eventual primary loss to establishment favorite Sen. John Kerry of Massachusetts, Vermont Gov. Howard Dean made an insurgent bid for the Democratic nomination with innovative uses of the Internet as a fund-raising and organizing tool.

Dogged by scandal allegations, Arkansas Gov. Bill Clinton fought on and finished second to former Massachusetts Sen. Paul Tsongas in the Democratic primary of 1992. He proclaimed himself the "comeback kid" and went on [to] win the nomination and the general election against President Bush the elder. Clinton became the first successful presidential candidate since 1952 not to have first won the N.H. primary.

The second primary "loser" to become president was Bush's son, George W., who was the prohibitive favorite in the 2000 Republican primary. But Bush ran a lackluster campaign and was easily bested by the "straight-talking" style of Sen. John McCain of Arizona. Bush later won the general election against former Vice President Al Gore.

It's impossible to predict what will happen until voters head to the polls in January 2008. New Hampshire has proven reliably subversive to the best laid plans of campaign experts.

My Vote Means Nothing[*]

How Presidential Primaries Backfired

By David Greenberg
Slate, June 11, 2007

Presidential primaries were created to put power in the hands of the people—to make the choice of party nominees, once the preserve of the bosses, more democratic. But instead of producing what you'd expect from democracy—greater disagreement, difference, and unpredictability—the ascent of binding primaries has turned the pre-convention months into a dreary slog. After a flurry of excitement surrounding Iowa and New Hampshire, front-runners typically amass springtime victories like a college football team running up the score in the last quarter. Even junkies get bored and turn off the TV.

Why have the primaries become a tedious march toward the inevitable, rather than an exhilarating saga of democracy in action? And why do New Hampshire and Iowa continue to exert so much influence that the balance of the primary season feels like an afterthought? The answer in two parts.

Primaries were the brainchild of early-20th-century reformers. Previously, delegates had chosen their nominees by bartering and scheming at conventions. But in the Progressive Era, good-government types mobilized to disinfect the squalid backrooms of the party bosses. Over the course of a generation, they introduced a slew of political reforms, from the use of secret ballots in the 1880s to the direct election of U.S. senators in 1913.

Primaries were supposed to further this movement. Wisconsin, which passed the first significant primary law, is a case in point. Gov. Robert La Follette had watched with fury at the 1904 Republican convention as party chieftains seated business-friendly "Old Guard" loyalists instead of progressive delegations like his own. At his urging, his state passed a primary bill that let voters choose their party's convention delegates directly.

The Wisconsin law, though a step toward popular empowerment, wasn't transformative, because it didn't actually commit these popularly chosen delegates to any particular candidate. That step was taken by Oregon voters in 1910. Soon, primary fever swept the states. In 1913, President Wilson even endorsed a national presidential primary law in his State of the Union address. By the time the 1916 presidential race rolled around, 25 of 48 states had established primaries in which voters chose their party's convention delegates, expressed a preference among the candidates (a competition known as the "beauty contest"), or combined both policies to bind delegates to the beauty-contest winner.

Just when primaries seemed like the wave of the future, they receded from view. One general reason was the shrinking appetite after World War I for reform of any sort. More concretely, primaries proved to be costly, and voters weren't turning out en masse. As a result, candidates didn't treat primaries as necessary stops on the road to the White House. In the 1910s and 1920s, most successful aspirants mapped out other routes to the nomination. In 1920, the Republicans, deadlocked at their convention, chose Warren Harding of Ohio, who hadn't entered any primaries at all. On the Democratic side, so few primaries had lured the top candidates that the number of uncommitted delegates dwarfed the number pledged to any individual. With primaries seeming irrelevant, only one state, Alabama, enacted a new primary law between 1917 and 1935. Eight states actually abandoned theirs.

After World War I, democratic hopes had been dashed; but after World War II, these hopes were reinvigorated. Primaries made a comeback in the late 1940s on the promise that they would help fulfill America's egalitarian potential.

Particular events helped. One was the surprisingly strong showing in the 1948 GOP primaries of Harold E. Stassen, the former governor of Minnesota. Though New York's Thomas Dewey, the presumed front-runner, ultimately prevailed, Stassen scored several primary upsets along the way and gave the primaries new respectability. More states established primaries, and between 1948 and 1952 turnout climbed from 4.8 million to 12.7 million. (Also influencing this trend was New Hampshire's decision in 1949 to revamp its primary law, on which I'll say more tomorrow.)

Most important, television arrived. Suddenly, a politician like Democratic Sen. Estes Kefauver of Tennessee—who once would have had to bide his time and accrue seniority before seeking the White House—could gain instant fame through the tube, as he did in 1950 by presiding over dramatic hearings into organized crime. Kefauver parlayed his celebrity into a presidential bid, campaigning across New Hampshire in 1952 in a Daniel Boone-style coonskin cap and upsetting President Truman in the primary. Kefauver then won 12 of 15 primaries, and although he wasn't nominated—Democrats went for Illinois Governor Adlai Stevenson—his populist, media-driven candidacy (along with Eisenhower's defeat of Robert Taft on the Republican side that year) confirmed primaries as a viable way to outflank party bosses. In later years, Stevenson, John F. Kennedy, and Barry Goldwater all nabbed their party's nominations with key primary victories.

Party reforms after 1968 solidified the primaries' importance. That year, Sen.

Eugene McCarthy came within 4,000 votes of upsetting President Johnson in the New Hampshire Democratic contest, prompting LBJ to end his re-election bid. Robert Kennedy then jumped in the race—his primary fights against McCarthy would determine the party's nominee. RFK's assassination on June 5 was all the more devastating to his supporters because it happened the night he won the crucial California showdown. In August, at a deeply divided convention, the Democrats chose the plodding Vice President Hubert Humphrey, who had won none of the preliminary contests, whose selection met with despair, and who went on to defeat in November.

The Democrats appointed a commission led by South Dakota Sen. George McGovern and Congressman Donald Fraser to reform the nomination process. The McGovern-Fraser reforms required greater transparency in how states chose their delegates. To meet these new strictures, many states found it simplest to hold binding primaries—making delegate selection a function of the popular vote. (The Republicans, responding to the same democratizing pressures, did similarly.) Before 1972, an average of 14 states held primaries each election; today almost every state holds one. Turnout also climbed.

In theory, the greater power of ordinary voters should have made for more open conventions. It's easier for party insiders to close ranks behind an anointed candidate—or to bargain their way to a consensus—than it is for tens of millions of atomized citizens to do so. But since primaries became the main method of choosing nominees, the opposite has happened: Despite occasional upsets in the early going, front-runners have mostly held on to win the nominations by racking up primary victories. Voters, sheeplike, dutifully follow the winner.

Several interrelated factors explain this phenomenon. One is what pollsters call a bandwagon effect. Because people like to hold opinions that the majority shares, they will unwittingly adopt the opinions of the majority. After Gary Hart's victory over Walter Mondale in the 1984 Democratic primary, he gained 27 points in the Gallup poll overnight.

The second is the news media. Even if people don't consciously cast their ballots for the most "electable" contender, candidates enjoy a surge of positive news coverage after winning New Hampshire or Iowa. This golden glow makes them more attractive to voters in later rounds. In 1976, Jimmy Carter trailed the pack of Democratic aspirants when a victory in the Iowa caucuses landed him on the morning news shows and in the newsmagazines. Evening news programs allotted him five times as much airtime as any of his rivals. New Hampshire media coverage is even more intense. According to a study of the 1996 Republican race by political scientist Emmett Buell, the New Hampshire primary generated more than six nightly news stories per delegate at stake, compared with an average of 0.18 stories per delegate overall. The disproportionate media coverage that New Hampshire enjoys means voters in subsequent weeks are much more likely to be influenced by the outcome in the Granite State than in states where many more delegates are up for grabs.

Third, campaign-finance reforms passed in 1974 capped individual donations at $1,000 apiece (raised to $2,000 as part of the 2002 McCain-Feingold Act). Candidates' fund-raising thus became less dependent on big donors, more reliant on mass appeal. Poor showings in New Hampshire, or at other points early in the campaign, now dry up not just a candidate's publicity but also the dollars that publicity brings.

Finally, in 1972, the Democratic National Committee banned winner-take-all primaries. (The ban was lifted but imposed again in 1992.) This made it harder for candidates (at least for Democrats) who are lagging in the race to become viable later on. With winner-take-all primaries, a trailing candidate could regain viability with a first-place finish in a big state; now, with delegates allotted in proportion to how candidates place, a front-runner can steadily grind out a victory merely by doing well enough to maintain his lead.

Not since 1968, then, have voters felt the excitement of a June primary where the nomination is at stake. On the contrary, the trend of the last 40 years has been to front-load—to move contests earlier and earlier in the campaign season. The 2008 campaign is already looking radically different from those of years past, with nearly 20 states, including California, Florida, and New York, having pushed up their primaries or caucuses to compete with Iowa and New Hampshire.

But front-loading created another irony. So far, at least, it has strengthened the hand of those first states, making the states that follow them little more than dominoes waiting to tumble into place.

Do Political Conventions Matter?*

By Peter Grier

The Christian Science Monitor, July 26, 2004

The first party convention in United States history was held in 1831 in Baltimore by the Anti-Masons, a tiny movement dedicated to the notion that the benign fraternity of Freemasonry was in fact an insidious political cabal.

Strangely, that convention tapped as its presidential candidate a man who was himself a Mason. Some would say it has been all downhill from there.

One hundred and seventy-three years later the tradition continues, with Monday's opening of the Democratic National Convention in Boston, to be followed by its Republican counterpart next month in New York. Raucous, vulgar, vital, political conventions are democracy at its finest, except for the bits when they are democracy at its worst.

It has been many years since a convention actually picked a candidate. Shocking, isn't it?

Worse yet, much of the proceedings are stage managed to appeal to viewers on TV! Yet they remain an important way for the parties to rally their fractious faithful. And they provide journalists a quadrennial opportunity to use the word "hoopla" in their leads.

"I would argue that their theater and stagecraft are part of the point, that they're fun, and that they're intrinsic to politics," says David Greenberg, a Yale political historian.

From 1831 until the middle of the last century, the phrase "political convention" meant much more than speeches and a roll call of people wearing hats indicative of their state. Conventions were a political reform, meant to replace the congressional caucuses that picked candidates in America's early era. By gathering large numbers of people from the entire nation, they assured voters of inclusiveness. And they served as forums for debate on the great questions facing the US.

The Democratic convention of 1860 was riven by the question of slavery, for instance. Southern Democrats eventually walked out, hastening the onset of the Civil War. In 1932 the Republican convention struggled to decide whether to repeal Prohibition. In 1948 the Democrats began what would be a series of searing debates over the party's position on the need for civil rights for blacks.

Then there were the ballots. In 1880, the GOP denied former president Ulysses S. Grant a third-term nomination after 36 ballots, opting for James A. Garfield instead. In 1924, a Democratic convention at Madison Square Garden needed 103 roll calls over 17 days to nominate John W. Davis of New York.

Yet as Mr. Greenberg notes, these deadlocked conventions produced some of the worst presidents and nominees in history. And there weren't that many of them—only 10 GOP and 14 Democratic conventions have had to cast more than one presidential ballot. "We always remember the past as more dramatic, partly because we forget what was forgettable and remember the memorable," says Greenberg, author of "Nixon's Shadow: The History of an Image."

Then came TV, which provided politicians an opportunity to showcase their party for a mass audience. Perhaps more important, the rise of primaries, themselves another generation of political reform, drained drama from the meetings. The result: today's heavily scripted conventions. . . .

Do they matter? Of course. Whether they matter less than they used to, or whether they will always matter, may be items for debate.

Sure, the networks have mostly abandoned conventions. But the rise of other forms of news media have perhaps made the question "Do the networks matter?" more apropos. And for two weeks out of every four years the conventions interest at least some voters. "Of course, the conventions are all about razzmatazz and sparkle. But a little bit of substance manages always to sneak in," says Rick Shenkman, editor of George Mason University's History News Network.

Ironically, in the postwar years the nascent television industry used political conventions as marketing tools, promoting them as the reality shows of the day. Prior to the 1952 conventions, newspapers were filled with ads for televisions, notes Mr. Shenkman, author of "Presidential Ambition: Gaining Power at Any Cost."

Buy a Stromberg-Carlson "and you can see and hear more of the presidential conventions than the delegates themselves," said one ad. A GE ad said, "See History Made When They Pick Their Man For The World's Biggest Job."

In the end, the conventions may be important for another reason: they return some power from the media to political parties. "It's unhealthy in a democracy for the media to have as much power over our elections as they have accumulated," says Shenkman.

Degrees of Democracy[*]

By David I. Wells
The New Leader, November/December 2004

Of the 51 Presidential elections since 1804, when the present system went into effect, in four contests—1824, 1876, 1888, and 2000—the winning candidate did not have the largest number of popular votes. This proportion is substantial, yet by 2000 most Americans were only dimly aware that such an outcome was possible, let alone that it had happened before.

Congress last seriously examined the Electoral College more than 25 years ago, but lately we have begun to hear from various quarters about how the Presidential election process might be made "more democratic." Had 2004 produced a second consecutive election with a popular winner who was also an electoral loser, the issue would undoubtedly have generated fierce public debate. Though that did not come to pass on November 2, the 8 per cent of elections that have produced a President who received fewer popular votes than his opponent—and several near misses—are indicative of a deeply flawed system that merits more attention than it has received. Unfortunately, the two most frequently advanced proposals to make the system "fairer" would actually make it less democratic.

As established in Article II of the Constitution and subsequently modified by the 12th and 23rd Amendments, every state now receives as many electoral votes as it has members in Congress. Since every state, regardless of population, has two Senators and at least one Representative, each begins with at least three electoral votes. The number of House seats for each state beyond the initial one is determined by a complex formula that also fixes a state's electoral vote beyond the automatic three.

Over the years, the total number of votes in the Electoral College increased in tandem with the size of the House of Representatives—until 1912 when the size of the House was fixed at 435. There are currently 538 electoral votes: 100 to match the Senate, 435 for the House, plus an additional three for the District of

* Reprinted with permission of *The New Leader*, November/December 2004. Copyright © The American Labor Conference on International Affairs, Inc.

Columbia as specified by the 23rd Amendment. During the 19th century, many states split their electoral votes in different ways, but for the last century states have almost uniformly operated under a "unit rule" that assigns all of their respective electoral votes to the candidate who wins the state plurality, regardless of how large or small that margin is.

The two most common criticisms of the Electoral College are by now familiar: Its winner-take-all method cedes major influence to heavily populated states; at the same time, the three-vote minimum provides disproportionate leverage to voters in sparsely populated states. Though apparently contradictory, both views have a solid grounding in fact.

The Electoral College incorporates a set of advantages and disadvantages—or "countervailing inequities"—for particular states. In the most basic sense, this is undemocratic because it can put the loser of the popular vote in the Oval Office. That is not true of any other system of election for any major office in the United States today. (Georgia did have a somewhat similar way of filling statewide offices until the 1960s, but its "county unit system" was declared unconstitutional by the Supreme Court.)

The winner-take-all feature benefits large states—California, New York, Texas, etc.—because candidates know that even the slimmest popular vote edge there will bring them a treasure trove of electoral votes. For instance, President George W. Bush's 537-vote edge in Florida four years ago got him all 25 crucial electoral votes. Thus candidates often take positions with those states in mind and spend heavily on them in time and money, especially if they are perceived to be winnable "swing states."

Meanwhile, the three-vote minimum provides a quantifiable boon to the states with the fewest people. In this year's contest Wyoming had one electoral vote for every 216,000 residents, while Texas had one for every 651,000, giving Wyoming voters a better than 3:1 advantage. Cumulatively, California's 35 million people are outvoted 59–55 in the Electoral College by the combined votes of the 16 least populous states, with a total population of only 17 million. Aware of the sway it grants their constituents, politicians from these smaller states are consistently resistant to proposals for change.

Yet a third less widely recognized aspect of the system gives a special advantage to a different group of states, depending on their voter turnout. The allocation of electoral votes to states beyond the first three "automatic" ones is set according to a state's total population, without consideration for the number of people who go to the polls. A state enjoys the same number of electoral votes whether 9 or 90 per cent of voters show up on Election Day.

This favors those in states with low participation who do cast their votes. The fewer the voters, the more political leverage they have. In the past, this constituted a huge advantage for Southern states where blacks were excluded from voting. It is less crucial today, but it can still tip the balance, if only slightly, to voters in states where many stay away on Election Day.

We cannot definitively say which of these advantages is most significant—it depends on how a particular election plays out. But it is noteworthy that in all four contests where the Electoral College chose a candidate with fewer popular votes than his opponent, the more conservative nominee (in the context of the times) was the beneficiary: John Quincy Adams over Andrew Jackson, Rutherford B. Hayes over Samuel J. Tilden, Benjamin Harrison over Grover Cleveland, and George W. Bush over Al Gore.

To eliminate all the special advantages that obtain in the case of the Presidency, we would have to abolish the Electoral College altogether and switch to the same direct popular system we use for other elective offices. But so far critics who recognize at least some of the undemocratic aspects of the present setup have weighed in with proposals that would merely tinker with the Electoral College. One approach would even add a new danger.

The plan most frequently put forward is the so-called "proportional system," which would uniformly apportion each state's electoral votes according to its popular vote. But the disposition of electoral votes is currently governed by state, not Federal, law. (A referendum to adopt a proportional system for Colorado was defeated on November 2. Had it been adopted, the change would only have applied to Colorado.)

The other oft-touted proposal is a "district system." It would assign one electoral vote to the winner of each Congressional district, and would award two "at-large" votes to the statewide winner. That would simply shift the winner-take-all feature of the Electoral College from the state level to the districts. (Maine and Nebraska already do this.)

Because the existing scheme encompasses advantages and disadvantages for different states, modifying just one undemocratic facet would result in a more unbalanced situation. A proportional system would do away with the edge enjoyed by the more populous states, leaving untouched the numerical upper hand of small states and those with low voter turnout. A district system would have a similar impact, and would add another undemocratic feature: the risk of gerrymandering.

As we have seen time and again of late, increasingly precise computer-assisted gerrymandering profoundly affects the political composition of the U.S. House of Representatives and state legislatures. The recent gerrymandering of Texas' Congressional districts brought big GOP gains in the House this year. Allowing easily manipulated Congressional district lines to play a role in the election of Presidents is an appalling prospect.

Furthermore, if district boundaries were not deliberately carved for political advantage, the uneven distribution of the candidates' voting strength within a state could still distort the results. A contender with small pluralities in many districts could defeat a rival with large pluralities in a few districts despite the latter's capturing a statewide plurality.

Why not head straight for direct election? After all, it is the most purely democratic option, and polls have consistently shown that, when asked, an overwhelming majority of Americans prefer it. Well, to begin with, that would require amending the Constitution, and advocates despair that with so many states favoring the status quo for their own self-serving reasons, such an amendment would never come to pass. Second, defenders of the Electoral College hold dear the boost it affords them without considering its countervailing consequences. Perhaps if they understood how the present system victimizes voters practically everywhere in one way or another, direct election, which would make every vote everywhere in the country count equally, would be achievable.

Until then, no fiddling with the Electoral College can ensure that the winner of the popular vote will occupy the White House. Direct popular election alone can accomplish this; indeed, most of its proponents stipulate a runoff between the two top candidates if no one wins 40 per cent of the total vote, absolutely guaranteeing that the President is the choice of the majority.

It should be noted, however, that besides the politicians, commentators on the Left and the Right have raised objections to the seemingly unobjectionable. The arguments one hears cited most often are that direct election would encourage "splinter parties" and "spoiler" candidacies in Presidential races and would increase the chances of vote fraud.

Over the years, of course, scores of contestants have emerged from outside the two major parties with various motivations. Their impact has been restricted to contests where they managed to deprive one or both of the leading competitors in a tight race of electoral votes. A few third-party nominees have been strong enough in one geographic area to win states; Strom Thurmond in 1948 and George C. Wallace in 1968 won several in the South. In 2000 Ralph Nader tilted enough states away from Gore to throw the election to Bush.

With direct election, the potential of third-party candidates would be no different than what it is now. We know this because precisely the same pattern has applied in statewide races for Governor and Senator where direct election has long been in use.

The danger of vote fraud, on the other hand, would likely be reduced under direct election. Such irregularities have constituted a threat because efforts to steal an election can focus on one or just a few closely contested states—hence the concern about Florida in 2000. There were widely reported charges of vote fraud in Illinois in 1960, with some historians believing that John F. Kennedy owed his victory over Richard M. Nixon to vote-padding by Mayor Richard J. Daley's machine in Chicago. In 1876 chicanery was so widespread in several close states that Tilden's popular vote plurality and Hayes' Electoral College majority were subject to doubt. A special commission eventually decided in Hayes' favor.

Over the past century six elections—1916, 1948, 1960, 1968, 1976, and 2000—have been tight enough that a tiny shift of votes in one or two close states would have yielded a different President. Elections pivoting on so narrow a base practically invite tampering. Direct popular election would discourage vote fraud because the results for the entire country—not merely a state or two—would have to be tipped to change the outcome. The tightest popular vote margin during the past century was JFK's 119,000 in 1960; the closest ever was James A. Garfield's

7,000 in 1880. With upward of 120 million voters turning out, though, stealing enough votes to win nationally is far more daunting a task than using foul play to shift a tiny number in a critical state.

The underlying purpose of democratic elections is to translate public opinion into public policy as accurately as possible. The Electoral College made sense to the founders, who worried whether 13 formerly separate colonies could stand together. But we are now a venerable nation. Our political apparatus should be structured so that our only nationally elected officeholder truly reflects the nation's collective will. The present system is an impediment that has too often prevented that from happening. The Electoral College should be abolished. Failing that, it should be kept as is. Tinkering with it would only make it worse.

The Old (Electoral) College Cheer[*]

Why We Have It; Why We Need It

By Michael M. Uhlmann
The National Review, November 8, 2004

As the late Rodney Dangerfield might say, the Electoral College just don't get no respect. Polls show that most Americans, given the opportunity, would cashier it tomorrow in favor of so-called direct election. That they'd live to regret their decision only reminds us of H. L. Mencken's definition of democracy: a form of government in which the people know what they want, and deserve to get it good and hard. What the people would get by choosing direct election is the disintegration of the state-based two-party system; the rise of numerous factional parties based on region, class, ideology, or cult of personality; radicalized public opinion, frequent runoff elections, widespread electoral fraud, and centralized control of the electoral process; and, ultimately, unstable national government that veers between incompetence and tyrannical caprice. And that's only a partial list.

Dissatisfaction with the electoral-vote system has been a staple of populist rhetoric ever since presidential elections became fully democratized in the 1820s. More than 700 constitutional amendments have been introduced to change the system—by far the greatest number on any subject—and although reform prescriptions have varied greatly in detail, their common assumption has always been that our electoral rules prevent the true voice of the people from being heard.

But what is the "true voice" of the people? Public sentiment can be expressed and measured in any number of ways, but not all are conducive to securing rights. If ascertaining the consent of the people were only a matter of counting heads until you got to 50 percent plus one, we could dispense with most of the distinctive features of the Constitution—not only electoral votes, but also federalism, the separation of powers, bicameralism, and staggered elections. All of these devices depart from simple majoritarianism, and for good reason: Men do not suddenly become angels when they acquire the right to vote; an electoral majority can be just as tyrannical as autocratic kings or corrupt oligarchs.

The Founders believed that while the selfish proclivities of human nature could not be eliminated, their baleful effects could be mitigated by a properly designed constitutional structure. Although the Constitution recognizes no other source of authority than the people, it takes pains to shape and channel popular consent in very particular ways. Thomas Jefferson perfectly captured the Framers' intent in his First Inaugural Address: "All, too, will bear in mind this sacred principle, that though the will of the majority is in all cases to prevail, that will to be rightful must be reasonable; that the minority possess their equal rights, which equal law must protect, and to violate which would be oppression." By reasonable majorities, Jefferson meant those that would reflect popular sentiment but, by the very manner of their composition, would be unable or unlikely to suppress the rights and interests of those in the minority. Accordingly, the Constitution understands elections not as ends in themselves, but as a means of securing limited government and equal rights for all.

The presidential election system helps to form reasonable majorities through the interaction of its three distinguishing attributes: the distribution and apportionment of electoral votes in accordance with the federal principle; the requirement that the winner garner a majority of electoral votes; and the custom (followed by 48 of 50 states) of awarding all of a state's electoral votes to the popular-vote victor within that state. Working together, these features link the presidency to the federal system, discourage third parties, and induce moderation on the part of candidates and interest groups alike. No candidate can win without a broad national coalition, assembled state by state yet compelled to transcend narrow geographic, economic, and social interests.

Reformers tend to assume that the mode of the presidential election can be changed without affecting anything else. Not so. As Sen. John F. Kennedy argued in the 1950s, by changing the method of the presidential election, you change not only the presidency but the entire political solar system of which it is an integral part. The presidency is at once the apex of our constitutional structure and the grand prize of the party system. Our method of selecting a president is the linchpin that holds both together. Capturing the presidency is the principal raison d'être of our political parties, whose structure, thanks to the electoral-vote system, mirrors the uniquely federal structure of the Constitution. This means that two-party competition is the norm; in a country of America's size and diversity, that is no small virtue.

With (for the most part) only two parties in contention, the major candidates are forced to appeal to most of the same voters. This drives them both toward the center, moderates their campaign rhetoric, and helps the winner to govern more effectively once in office. Many factional interests, for their part, are under a reciprocal inducement to buy insurance with both sides, meaning the compromises necessary for successful rule will be made prior to and not after the election. Moreover, by making the states the principal electoral battlegrounds, the current system tends to insulate the nation against the effects of local voting fraud. All in all, the current system forces the ambitions of presidential candidates into the same constitutional mold that defines and tempers American political life as a whole. It thereby prevents the presidency from becoming a potentially dangerous tutelary force separate and apart from the rest of the Constitution's structure.

These and other salutary consequences would disappear under direct election, whose deceptive simplicities mask its truly radical character. If President Bush wins the 2004 electoral vote without a popular-vote plurality, you can be certain that the enactment of direct election will become a principal mission of the Democrats. And it may well become their mantra even if John Kerry wins. We came perilously close to enacting direct election following the 1968 contest, when George Wallace's third-party candidacy shattered the New Deal coalition of big-city machines and the one-party South. Fearing the long-run effects of Republican competition in the New South, Democrats tried to change the rules to their advantage. They will do so again as soon as the opportunity seems propitious, which it will if this year's election resembles 2000's.

In 1969, as President Nixon dithered and eventually ducked, direct election passed the House by a sizeable constitutional majority—including many Republicans who ought to have known better. But for a small and determined group of conservative Democratic and Republican senators who filibustered it to death, direct election would have been presented to the states in an atmosphere that greatly favored ratification. Sensible heads may prevail in today's Republican-controlled House, but don't count on it: On matters of electoral reform especially, congressmen have little stomach for resisting populist enthusiasms. A House that rolled over for McCain-Feingold, which enjoyed only mild public support, will not likely oppose the clamor for direct election. As for today's Senate, one would be hard pressed to identify a band of constitutional stalwarts comparable to those who courageously resisted popular currents in 1970. The next few years, in short, may test whether our nation has the patience or wisdom to preserve the delicate balances of our constitutional solar system.

Proponents of direct election indict those delicate balances for being "undemocratic." That is true only in the most superficial sense. If the Electoral College is undemocratic, so are federalism, the United States Senate, and the procedure for constitutional amendment. So is bicameralism and, for that matter, the separation of powers, which among other things authorizes an unelected judiciary. These constitutional devices were once widely understood to be the very heart and soul of the effort to form reasonable majorities. If all you care about is the achievement of mathematical equality in presidential elections, and if to achieve that goal you're willing to eliminate the states' role in presidential elections, what other "undemocratic" features of the Constitution are you also willing to destroy? And when you're done hacking your way through the Constitution, what guarantee can you give that your mathematically equal majorities can be restrained? How will you constrain the ambitions of presidents who claim to be the only authentic voice of the people?

The current system teaches us that the character of a majority is more important than its size alone. Americans ought to care about whether the winner's support is spread across a broad geographic area and a wide spectrum of interests. That is what enables presidents to govern more effectively—and what encourages them to govern more justly than they would if their majority were gathered from, say, an aggregation of heavy population centers. By ensuring that the winner's majority reflects the diversity of our uniquely federated republic, the current system also assures his opposition that it will not have to fear for its life, liberty, or property. Direct election can provide no such assurance and may, in fact, guarantee just the opposite.

3

The Separation of Powers:
Congressional Influence on the "Imperial Presidency"

Editor's Introduction

Historically, presidents have wielded extraordinary powers in times of crisis, although not always without controversy. John Adams, during the undeclared naval war with France, selectively employed the Alien and Sedition Acts of 1798 to stifle newspaper writers and editors opposed to his policies. In the only such instance in American history, a sitting president, Andrew Jackson, openly defied the Supreme Court when it decided that the federal government, not individual states, had authority over American Indians. During the Civil War, Abraham Lincoln used his war powers to suppress the civil liberties of citizens who favored the Southern cause, most notably by stripping them of the right to due process. When a fear of communism gripped the nation after World War I, Woodrow Wilson also suppressed civil liberties, including free speech, and deported immigrants for their suspected political views.

Though controversial, these broad presidential powers did not extend much past the period of crisis that spawned them. Afterwards, the balance of power typically reverted back to the levels prescribed in the Constitution. The first *sustained* use of expansive executive authority came during the administration of Franklin D. Roosevelt, who had been given broad powers by Congress because of the severe difficulties facing the country during the Great Depression and World War II. Since that time, however, the executive branch has never ceded these far-ranging powers because each presidential administration since Roosevelt's has operated in a mode of "permanent crisis." While the impetus for this change was the postwar rivalry with the Soviet Union, the permanent-crisis mindset has persisted into each presidential administration that followed the 1991 collapse of the USSR. Throughout the Cold War, as nuclear brinkmanship with the Soviet Union became an everyday reality to generations of Americans, and U.S. troops found themselves posted to hot spots around the globe to contain communism, the executive branch argued that it needed the freedom to use the president's powers as commander in chief at a moment's notice—*without* congressional oversight. The administration of George W. Bush uses this same reasoning today to retain far-reaching powers in its efforts to combat terrorism. Despite occasional congressional efforts to curtail presidential authority, both major political parties see the benefit of having a strong executive as a bulwark against foreign and domestic threats to American citizens—and as a way to push their own political agendas. This attitude has helped to foster what some have dubbed the "imperial presidency"—an executive branch that has, since the time of Franklin Roosevelt, often exceeded its constitutional limits and outstripped the other two branches of government in terms of power. Regardless of how one views this change, the president is now the driving force of the American government.

The articles presented here examine how power has been divided between modern presidents and Congress. In "Commanding Heights," Charlie Savage writes that expanded presidential power is nothing novel—presidents from both parties have developed new powers since the mid-20th century—but also delineates the ways in which George W. Bush's administration has sought to protect and expand executive authority. Michael M. Uhlmann, in "Taming Big Government," traces the rise of a powerful executive to Woodrow Wilson, who used his political party to circumvent the Constitution's checks and balances and craft a proactive executive branch that would serve as the driving force of an expanded federal government. Writing through the lens of recent history, Andrew Rudalevige chronicles Congress's efforts through the years to restrain presidential power in his article, "The Contemporary Presidency: The Decline and Resurgence and Decline (and Resurgence?) of Congress: Charting a New Imperial Presidency." In the final article of this section, "When Congress Stops Wars," William G. Howell and John C. Pevelhouse focus on the occasionally partisan reasons why Congress has exerted its oversight powers to curtail presidential influence.

Commanding Heights[*]

By Charlie Savage
Atlantic Monthly, October 2007

In January 2001, the members of the Bush-Cheney administration's new legal team gathered in the wood-paneled office of their boss, White House Counsel Alberto Gonzales, whose freshly unpacked family pictures and Texas mementos lined the bookshelves. After a genial introduction, Gonzales got down to business. The new president, he said, had given them two mandates. First, they were to push conservative judicial nominees quickly into the confirmation pipeline. And second, they were to seize opportunities, wherever they lay, to protect and expand presidential power. The institution had been weakened by George W. Bush's predecessors, Gonzales said, and the new president wanted them "to make sure that he left the presidency in better shape than he found it."

To at least one of the assembled lawyers, this second priority seemed at the time to be an injunction to help repair the damage Bill Clinton's scandals had done to the White House. But it now seems clear that something far more sweeping was being set in motion: the realization of Vice President Dick Cheney's dream of restoring what the historian Arthur Schlesinger Jr. had called the "imperial presidency"—the era of unchecked executive power that peaked during the Nixon administration, when Cheney began his political career.

Taken one by one, the Bush administration's efforts to expand presidential power seem familiar. Piled together, they are startling. The administration has asserted a power to imprison Americans without charges, to bypass laws such as those governing wiretapping and torture, to set aside the Geneva Conventions and scrap other major treaties without consulting the Senate, and more. It has rebuffed oversight and has expanded secrecy. And it has tightened White House control over federal agencies through an explosion of "signing statements" appended to new legislation, instructing the executive branch that it can ignore vast swaths of laws that restrict the president's authority.

It may seem that this presidency's most aggressive expansions of executive power have been curbed. The new Democratic Congress has launched many oversight hearings. Five of nine Supreme Court justices have held that presidents must obey the Geneva Conventions and need congressional permission to set up military commissions.

But the aftermath of the Nixon presidency suggests that any ebbing of presidential power from its new high-water mark may be only temporary. Richard Nixon had sought unchecked power on many fronts—he expanded secrecy, spied on his political enemies, fired the special prosecutor who was investigating him, and kept the Vietnam War going for two years after Congress revoked its authorization. Vietnam and Watergate eventually prompted Congress to impose new controls on executive power. Among other things, the new rules required presidents to consult lawmakers before sending the armed forces into combat, and to bring troops home after 60 days if Congress did not explicitly authorize a longer fight. Congress also created an independent counsel who could investigate the White House without being fired by the president.

The erosion of these and other checks began even before the post-Watergate furor had fully subsided. As early as 1975, Gerald Ford, without consulting Congress, was sending marines on a bloody rescue mission to Cambodia; by 1999, Bill Clinton felt free to order the Air Force to bomb Kosovo and Serbia, which it did for 78 days—all without any explicit congressional authorization. After the Iran-Contra and Whitewater investigations, lawmakers let the independent-counsel law expire.

Administrations from both parties also continued to develop new powers. Jimmy Carter set the precedent for unilaterally scrapping a ratified treaty when he pulled the United States out of a mutual-defense pact with Taiwan. Ronald Reagan's legal team invented the "Unitary Executive Theory," which undercuts the authority of Congress to regulate the executive branch. The imperial presidency was largely restored before Bush took office. While Cheney claimed that he and Bush were filling in a valley of executive power, they were actually building atop a mountain. Indeed, presidential power has been mostly growing—in fits and starts—since World War II. An early-20th-century president, such as Calvin Coolidge, had no large standing army to command, nor a CIA to use for covert operations. He would not have dreamed of launching a major overseas war without permission from Congress—as Harry Truman did in Korea. He could not utter the magic words state secrets or executive privilege to nullify lawsuits and evade congressional oversight—both of these precedents were set during Dwight Eisenhower's administration. By exploiting the sense of permanent crisis that surrounded the early Cold War, presidents of both parties cowed both Congress and the Supreme Court. Today, the war on terrorism has provided a similar rationale.

Most legal scholars believe that these changes to the structure of American democracy deviate from the vision of the Founders, who hated monarchies and had a pessimistic view of human nature. To reduce the damage that a bad leader could inflict, the Founders divided control over the government among three coequal powers so that each could check the others. Focused in particular on keeping the president from becoming an elected king, they gave Congress the power to make the big decisions about going to war and broad authority to regulate how the executive branch carried out its work.

Of course, since then the government has grown in ways that necessarily increased the authority of presidents, because newly created bureaucracies fall under their day-to-day management. But it was not inevitable that checks and balances would simultaneously shrink. The erosion of controls on the presidency is the achievement of several generations of "presidentialists." Convinced that the modern world is too dangerous and complex for the president's hands to be tied, they have taken advantage of the fact that even the most vigilant Congress has only limited and politically difficult options for resisting executive overreach.

And, of course, lawmakers are not always vigilant. During Bush's first six years, a friendly Congress largely abandoned oversight while passing laws that broadened the president's power over detainees and strengthened his ability to impose martial law. Today, Congress has changed, but those laws remain on the books. And the administration's departures from traditional restraints and its novel assertions of power are now historical precedents.

In 1944, Supreme Court Justice Robert Jackson warned that each new assertion of executive power, once validated into precedent, lies about "like a loaded weapon ready for the hand of any authority that can bring forward a plausible claim of an urgent need. Every repetition imbeds that principle more deeply in our law and thinking and expands it to new purposes."

In the six decades since, presidents of both parties have seldom hesitated to use all the powers available to them. So what will future presidents do with the arsenal they will inherit from Bush and Cheney? So far, the 2008 candidates have volunteered little about what limits, if any, they would respect if entrusted with the presidency. It's time to start asking.

Taming Big Government[*]

By Michael M. Uhlmann
Claremont Review of Books, Summer 2007

Sir Lewis Namier, the noted British historian of an earlier generation, once wrote that "when discoursing or writing about history, [people] imagine it in terms of their own experience, and when trying to gauge the future they cite supposed analogies from the past: till, by double process of repetition, they imagine the past and remember the future." Great controversies, which often feature adversaries citing the same historical materials to opposite effect, confirm the truth of Namier's cautionary observation. In the United States, where great controversies tend to be constitutional controversies, disagreement about our charter's origins and meaning has been a defining feature of American political discourse from the republic's earliest days.

After nearly 220 years, one could say that Americans have more constitutional speculation than they know what to do with—a fact readily confirmed by almost any volume of any law review, not to mention the proliferating gaggle of legal experts who fill the airwaves on cable news shows. A cynic might infer from differing scholarly opinions that debate about constitutional meaning is so much rhetorical gamesmanship. But if that is so, if politics may indeed be reduced to sophistry, why bother to have a written constitution at all?

Most Americans would reply that a written constitution is the only kind worth having. They bear a decent respect for their nation's origins and founding documents, which they have no trouble believing were inspired by divine providence. They come by the millions every year from all over the country to the National Archives in Washington, or to the National Constitution Center in Philadelphia, to gaze upon the original parchments of the Declaration of Independence and the Constitution. They take pride in knowing that the Constitution, which was up and running before Napoleon came to power, has survived innumerable crises, including a dreadful civil war, yet emerged largely intact.

Liberals are wary of pious attachment to the past, considering it an expression of foolish sentimentality or a mask for some contemporary venal interest, but in either event as an impediment to progress. They are particularly suspicious about the framers' motives, which they tend to explain in terms of narrow self-interest, and are dogmatically skeptical about our founding documents' natural rights principles, dismissing them as so much wrong-headed and outmoded philosophical speculation. The resultant Constitution fares no better. It, too, is suspect for many reasons—failing to abolish slavery for one—but most of all because it sought to instantiate a regime of limited government. But, in the end, liberals care little about what the framers may have meant, for times have changed. They may object to the crudity of Henry Ford's assertion that "history is more or less bunk," but they do not essentially disagree with his sentiment. Liberals esteem not history, but History, which to them confirms the law of ceaseless change.

They are stuck, nevertheless, with a people reared under the aegis of a written Constitution whose authors affirmed the permanence of certain political truths. Most Americans remain stubbornly convinced that the framers got things mostly right on government's basic principles. From the Progressive movement's early days until the present hour, the liberals' medicine for this notable lack of popular enlightenment has consisted in one long effort to deconstruct the founding. The permanence of the Declaration's truths is denied; the framers' inability or refusal to resolve the issue of slavery is attributed to moral hypocrisy; the architecture of the Constitution is read as a series of mischievous devices to frustrate majority rule or to protect the ruling class's interests. These and similar critiques, which by gradual degrees have worked their way into standard textbooks and school curricula, have taken their toll on patriotic sentiment.

Old habits, however, die hard, which helps to explain the intellectual chaos of contemporary constitutional debate. Respect for the founding principles, though wounded, refuses to die; the new dispensation, though powerful, has yet to triumph. Whatever else may have accrued from the effort to deconstruct the founding, this much seems clear: the once common ground of constitutional discourse has fallen away. Witness the current debate between originalists and proponents of the "living" Constitution: they disagree about the meaning of constitutional wording, to be sure; but their deepest disagreement has to do with whether and why 18th-century words and concepts should now matter at all.

WHAT WILSON WROUGHT

The outcome of this debate has yet to be determined, but it has produced a number of notable anomalies, particularly with respect to the separation of powers. Ever since Woodrow Wilson set pen to paper, liberals have expressed frustration with, if not outright scorn for, the separation of powers. They read it almost exclusively in terms of its checking-and-balancing function, i.e., as a barrier that for many decades prevented the national government from enacting progressive social and economic policies. The other half of James Madison's elegant argument for separating powers—energizing government through the clash of rival and opposite ambitions—seems to have escaped their attention altogether, as has the framers' understanding that government powers differ not only in degree, but in kind. Transfixed by their own deconstruction of the founding as an effort to frustrate popular majorities, liberals find it hard to believe that the framers could have imagined the need for powerful government or a powerful chief executive. Indeed, a dominant theme of early Progressive thought—one still widely shared today—advanced the notion that the Constitution meant to enshrine legislative primacy. Accordingly, energetic presidents prior to the modern era are seen as exceptions that prove the rule, their boldness being variously attributed to the peculiarities of personality, short-term aberrational events, or national emergencies such as the Civil War—to everything, in short, except the intended purpose of Article II of the Constitution. It was only after decades of struggle, so the argument continues, that a new constitutional order, with the president as its driving force, came to ultimate fruition in the New Deal.

This reading of the founding and of American political history has a surface plausibility, fed in no small part by the republican Whig rhetoric that was so fashionable in much early American discourse. Upon closer examination, however, it turns out that congressional dominance is not the only story that emerges from 19th-century political history. As a large and growing body of thoughtful revisionist inquiry has demonstrated, that history is no less the story of effective presidential leadership that drew upon Article II's deliberately capacious language. Notwithstanding, contemporary liberal doctrine remains deeply indebted to the original Progressive indictment of the founding, and especially to Woodrow Wilson's thought, which remains the philosophical wellspring of almost every constitutional prescription in the liberal pharmacopoeia.

After flirting with the idea of grafting a parliamentary system onto the American constitutional structure, Wilson made a virtue of necessity by reconceiving the Office of the President. The nation's chief executive would defeat the original Constitution's structural obstacles by, so to speak, rising above them. Wilson's chosen instrument for this purpose was party government, which would breach the parchment barriers dividing president and Congress and unite both through a common policy agenda initiated by the president. The president would make the case for policy innovation directly to the people. Once armed with plebiscitary legitimacy, he might more easily prod an otherwise parochial Congress to address national needs. Madisonian fears about the mischiefs of faction would be overcome by separating politics and administration: Congress and the president would jointly settle upon the desired policy agenda, but its details, both in design and execution, would rely on non-partisan expert administrators' special insight and technical skill, operating under the president's general direction and control.

The presidency, thus reconceived, would by turns become a voice for and dominant instrument of a reconceived Constitution, which would at last detach itself from a foolish preoccupation with limited government. The old Constitution's formal structure would be retained, insofar as that might be politically necessary; but it would be essentially emptied of its prior substantive content. In Wilson's view, the growth of executive power would parallel the growth of government in general. The president would no longer be seen as, at best, Congress's co-equal or, at worst, the legislature's frustrated servant. Henceforth, he would be seen as proactive government's innovator-in-chief, one who was best positioned to understand historical tendencies and to unite them with popular yearnings. In an almost mystical sense, the president would embody the will of the people, becoming both a prophet and steward of a new kind of egalitarian Manifest Destiny at home and, in the fullness of time, perhaps throughout the world.

UNINTENDED CONSEQUENCES

The result of Wilson's vision is the administrative state we know today. Although it has retained the original Constitution's structural appearances, the new order has profoundly altered its substance—though not precisely in the way that Wilson intended, as we shall see. The arguments that once supported the ideas of federalism and limited government have fallen into desuetude: state power today is exercised largely at the national government's sufferance, and if there is a subject or activity now beyond federal reach, one would be hard-pressed to say what it might be. As for the separation of powers, while the branches remain institutionally separate, the lines between legislative, executive, and judicial power have become increasingly blurred. The idea that government power ought to be differentiated according to function has given way to the concept that power is more or less fungible. The dominant understanding of separated powers today—see the late Richard Neustadt's widely accepted argument in *Presidential Power* (1960)—is that the branches of government compete with one another for market share.

While most liberals continue to celebrate the old order's decline, the more thoughtful among them have expressed reservations of late about certain consequences of the Wilsonian revolution. It is widely remarked in the scholarly literature on the presidency, for example, that we have come to expect almost impossible things of modern presidents, and that presidents in turn come to office with almost impossible agendas to match heightened public expectations. After many decades of living with the modern presidency, it can be argued that the effort to rise above the separation of powers has only exposed presidents the more to the unmediated whimsies of public opinion. Far from being masters of all they survey, modern presidents are pulled this way and that by factional demands generated by an administrative state over which they exercise nominal but very little actual control.

The presidency's transformation has radically altered our system of government, but it poses a particular problem for liberals. The difficulty begins in their appetite for big government. Indeed, liberals can identify enough unmet needs, unfulfilled hopes, and frustrated dreams to satisfy the federal government's redistributionist and regulatory ambitions as far into the future as the eye can see. An already large and unwieldy federal establishment, expanding to meet the rising expectations of an ever more demanding and dependent public, threatens to become yet larger, more powerful, and harder to control. But, despite what bureaucrats might wish to believe about the beneficial effects of their expertise, the administrative state is not a machine that can run itself. It requires coherent policy direction; it needs to be managed with reasonable efficiency; and it has to be held politically accountable. As a practical matter, only a president can do these things, but with rare exceptions, presidents are prevented, mainly by Congress but also by the judiciary, from performing any of these tasks well.

It is here that a bastardized version of the separation of powers remains alive and well. The short history of the administrative state since at least the New Deal is a tale of protracted conflict between Congress and the president for control of its ever-expanding machinery. After initial resistance, which remained formidable until roughly 40 years ago, Congress has finally learned to love big government as much as, if not more than, presidents do. As political scientist Morris Fiorina has shown, Congress loves it because it pays handsome political returns. The returns come from greasing the wheels of the federal establishment to deliver an increasing array of goods and services to constituents and interest groups, who reward congressional intervention with campaign contributions and other forms of electoral support. Such political benefit as may accrue from enacting carefully crafted legislation is much less, which is why legislators devote far more time to pleasing constituents and lobbyists than they do to deliberating about the details of laws they enact. Congress is generally content to delegate these details, which often carry great policy significance, to departments and agencies, whose actions and policy judgments can forever after be second-guessed by means of legislative "oversight."

THE NEW SPOILS SYSTEM

Indeed, congressmen have become extraordinarily adept at badgering this agency or that program administrator for special favors—or for failing to carry out "the will of Congress." In most cases this means the will of a particular representative who sits on the agency's authorization or appropriations committee, and who has been importuned by a politically relevant interest group to complain about some bureaucratic excess or failure. Modern congressional oversight has become an elaborate and sophisticated version of the old spoils system adapted to the machinery of the administrative state. When it comes to currying favors, Congressmen know how to home in on programs under their committee's jurisdiction to extract what they want in terms of policy direction or special treatment, and there is enough boodle in a nearly $3 trillion federal budget to satisfy even the most rapacious pork-barreler. Likewise, when it comes to bashing bureaucrats, Congressmen have little trouble identifying vulnerable targets of opportunity. The federal government is so large, and its administrators so busy trying to execute often conflicting or ambiguous congressional instructions, that Congress can, like Little Jack Horner, stick in its thumb and pull out a plum almost at random. The modern oversight investigation, which has less to do with substance than with conducting a dog-and-pony show for the benefit of a scandal-hungry media, has become a staple of the contemporary administrative state. And it almost always redounds to Congress's political benefit, for the simple reason that the exercise carries little if any downside risk. But political theater of this sort, however profitable it may be to particular representatives, is a far cry from the deliberative function that the framers hoped would be the defining characteristic of the legislative process.

It is an open question, to be sure, whether anything so large as the current federal establishment can be reasonably managed, and it is something of a miracle that it works at all. Even so, Congress would do itself and the nation an enormous favor if it devoted more time to perfecting the legislative art, which includes paying serious attention to the policy coherence and consequences of its delegated legislative authority. In general, however, Congress has little political motive or (given its internal dispersal of power to committees and sub-committees) institutional capacity for substantive evaluation of the many programs it enacts and ostensibly oversees. It complains endlessly about the administrative state's inefficiency and arbitrariness, but compounds the problem by creating new agencies and programs in response to political urgencies. As it does so, it takes care to protect its own prerogatives even as it denies to the executive the requisite authority to control the administrative system.

This reluctance to vest the president with control has sometimes expressed itself in the form of independent agencies (independent, that is, of the president), which mock the idea of separated powers by vesting legislative, executive, and judicial functions in the same institution. Consider Boston University law professor Gary Lawson's provocatively compelling description of the Federal Trade Commission, which typifies the workings of the system as a whole:

> The Commission promulgates substantive rules of conduct. The Commission then considers whether to authorize investigations into whether the Commission's rules have been violated. If the Commission authorizes an investigation, the investigation is conducted by the Commission, which reports its findings to the Commission. If the Commission thinks that the Commission's findings warrant an enforcement action, the Commission issues a complaint. The Commission's complaint that a Commission rule has been violated is then prosecuted by the Commission and adjudicated by the Commission. This Commission adjudication can either take place before the full Commission or before a semi-autonomous Commission administrative law judge. If the Commission chooses to adjudicate before an administrative law judge rather than before the Commission and the decision is adverse to the Commission, the Commission can appeal to the Commission. If the Commission ultimately finds a violation, then, and only then, the affected private party can appeal to an Article III court. But the agency decision, even before the bona fide Article III tribunal, possesses a very strong presumption of correctness on matters both of fact and of law.

This pattern has become an accepted feature of the modern administrative state, so much so that, as Lawson notes, it scarcely raises eyebrows. Presidents and Congress long ago accommodated themselves to its political exigencies, as has the Supreme Court, which since the 1930s has never come close to questioning independent agencies' constitutional propriety.

RAIDING EXECUTIVE AUTHORITY

When dealing with the executive branch as such, Congress frequently delegates and retains legislative authority at the same time. It does so, inter alia, through burdensome or unconstitutional restrictions on the exercise of presidential discretion, which it inserts in authorizing legislation, appropriations bills, or, sometimes, even in committee report language. It has also contrived a host of other devices to hamper executive control. For many decades, for example, it indulged broad delegations (e.g., "The Secretary shall have authority to issue such regulations as may be necessary to carry out the purposes of this Act"), but as the number of agencies expanded and as delegated regulatory authority began to bite influential constituencies, Congress responded by imposing (variously) two-House, one-House, or in some cases even committee vetoes over agency action. Although the Supreme Court declared most legislative vetoes to be unconstitutional in INS v. Cbadba (1983), Congress has improvised additional measures to second-guess the operations of the executive branch.

Confirmation hearings in the Senate, for example, are increasingly used to extract important policy concessions from prospective executive appointees, who learn very quickly that while the president is their nominal boss, Congress expects to be placated and, failing that, knows how to make their lives miserable. To underscore this point, in addition to the omnipresent threat of oversight hearings, Congress has enacted extensive "whistle-blower" legislation and created inspector-general offices for every department and agency, which operate as semi-demi-hemi-quasi-independent congressional envoys within the executive branch. For a time (until Bill Clinton got caught in the web), Congress was also enamored of special counsels, empowering them by legislation to investigate and prosecute alleged executive malfeasance, and at the same time ensuring that their activities were not only beyond the president's authority to control, but beyond the Congress's and the courts' as well. (Demonstrating that the separation of powers in our time is more honored in the breach than the observance, the Supreme Court sustained the legislation with only one dissent.)

One may say by way of summary that Congress has, without fully realizing it, succumbed to Wilson's plan to eviscerate the separation of powers. It has failed to realize it in part because the administrative state's growth has occurred gradually; in part because it has learned how to profit politically by the change; and in part because it has convinced itself that conducting guerilla raids against executive authority is the most beneficial expression of the legislative function.

TAMING THE ADMINISTRATIVE STATE

Presidents have chafed under congressional controls, rightly complaining that they interfere both with their constitutional powers and their ability to make the administrative state reasonably efficient and politically accountable. They have responded with various bureaucratic and legal weapons of their own. These include a greatly expanded Executive Office of the President (in effect, a bureaucracy that seeks to impose policy direction and managerial control over other executive bureaucracies), a massive surge in the use of executive orders, and increasing reliance on signing statements reserving the president's right not to enforce legislation he considers to be unconstitutional. Ever since the New Deal, and growing proportionately with the size of the federal establishment, a good deal of White House energy has been devoted to trying to manage and direct the administrative state— and to reminding Congress in diverse ways that the Constitution provides for only one chief executive. But modern presidents, like the modern Congress, have also succumbed to the lure of Wilson's theory concerning the separation of powers. They dearly enjoy the prospect of becoming the principal focal point for national policy, but once in office soon discover that the mantle of plebiscitary leadership can be assumed only at great cost. Unlike Congress, presidents remain politically and legally accountable for the administrative state's behavior. In order to execute their office as their constitutional oath demands, they must pay serious attention to the separation of powers in ways that Congress does not.

Presidents sometimes win and sometimes lose in their struggles with Congress, but each new contest only serves to compound the constitutional muddle that now surrounds the separation of powers, a muddle made all the more confusing by the Supreme Court's Janus-faced rulings in major cases, which also bear the mark of the political revolution launched by Wilson's indictment of the structural Constitution. On a practical level, presidents have only modest gains to show for their continuing efforts to manage big government. Overall, when it comes to controlling the administrative state, the operative slogan might well be "Congress Won't and the President Can't." So much for Wilson's vision of the rational ordering of public policy through neutral expertise under the benign guidance of inspired presidents working in cooperation with Congress. Wilson dealt the separation of powers a mortal blow without understanding the full implications of what he had wrought. Without a vigorously enforced, reasonably bright-line distinction between the kinds of powers exercised by the different branches, the very presidency he hoped to create has been frustrated in its ability to execute coherent policy, or to manage those charged with fleshing out its details. For its part, Congress as a whole is even less interested today in deliberating about the coherence of national policy than it was when Wilson inveighed against its parochialism and committee structure in the late 19th century. And, it may be added, with each passing year the administrative state whose birth Wilson midwifed becomes increasingly harder for any of the branches, jointly or severally, to control.

HAVING IT BOTH WAYS

Liberals are not particularly happy with the present state of affairs, but their enthusiasm for big government leaves them little choice but to support expansive presidential authority; it is the only available instrument capable of seeing to it that their desired social reforms are carried out. They encourage Congress to create or expand progressive programs, and generally applaud congressional bashing of bureaucrats (especially when the targets come from the opposite end of the political spectrum); but they do not otherwise wish to see Congress heavily involved in the business of directing public administration, for they rightly suspect that when Congress does so, the likely beneficiary will be some private interest rather than the public good. As for presidential direction and control of policy, liberals tend to favor executive discretion when Democrats occupy the Oval Office, but are generally dubious about it when exercised by Republican incumbents. Like Al Gore, they're in favor of reinventing government so long as it doesn't disestablish or interfere with favored agencies or programs.

Liberals, in short, will complain about the administrative state's inefficiency and unwieldiness, and while they would no doubt like it to work better they haven't a clue about how to reform it—other than by tinkering with its machinery at the margins. In truth, liberals have no desire for systemic change. They do not wish to reduce government's scope; and they certainly do not wish to revive the old Constitution's structural distinctions that separate the branches of government by function, for that, too, might diminish or eliminate many of the cherished programs they spent so many decades creating. The era of big government may be over, but only in Bill Clinton's rhetoric; big government itself is here to stay, as is the constitutional confusion that surrounds the separation of powers and threatens to extinguish its purposes altogether.

Although liberals generally applaud the demise of 18th-century constitutional strictures when it comes to domestic policy, they are not above extolling the old Constitution's virtues in foreign and national security affairs. The late Arthur Schlesinger, Jr., surely the model of 20th-century high-toned liberal sentiment if ever there was one, raised the execution of this intellectual two-step to a fine art form. He began his scholarly career by discovering in Andrew Jackson's administration a pre-incarnation of Franklin Roosevelt's plebiscitary presidency. Later, in his multi-volume hagiography of the New Deal, he defended the expansion of unfettered executive discretion in domestic affairs as a necessary concomitant of the burgeoning administrative state. In foreign affairs as well, Schlesinger praised FDR's aggressive use of executive power, not only during World War II (which is understandable enough), but also in the pre-war years (which is more debatable). Schlesinger took a similar tack in his praise of John F. Kennedy, who in Schlesinger's eyes was a kind of reincarnation of FDR. Then came Vietnam, Watergate, and the assorted excesses of Lyndon Johnson and Richard Nixon, as a result of which the presidential powers Schlesinger had previously celebrated suddenly became harbingers of imperial pretension. The imperial presidency motif disappeared once Jimmy Carter came into office, only to resurface periodically and vociferously during the Reagan years. It disappeared yet again while Bill Clinton held the office, and reappeared like clockwork in criticism of George W. Bush's anti-terrorism policies.

Schlesinger's personal tergiversations to the side, his ambivalence about executive power is a perfect measure of the modern liberals' dilemma: they want a chief executive capaciously adorned with constitutional discretion when it comes to pushing government to carry out their social and economic agenda, but sound constitutional alarms when their own theory of presidential power gets applied to the execution of foreign and national security policies they do not like. That constitutional theory is sometimes bent to short-term policy preferences is hardly novel or shocking. But there is a deeper constitutional problem here as well, arising from liberals' embrace of Wilsonian theory. One simply can't have it both ways when it comes to the Constitution's grant of executive power—a small presidency for foreign affairs, but a large one for domestic affairs. If anything, a stronger case can be made the other way around: the vesting clause, the take-care clause, and the oath of office are common to both cases, but in war-related matters the president has an additional claim of authority stemming from his powers as commander in chief.

CONSERVATISM AND EXECUTIVE POWER

Not so long ago, conservatives might have been accused of harboring a similar inconsistency. For a long time, they were deeply suspicious of the executive branch, correctly seeing in its growth the dangers that flowed inexorably from the Wilsonian revolution in political thought—a notable increase in presidential caprice and demagogy, and a notable increase as well in the government's size, driven by the engine of the plebiscitary presidency. The memory of FDR's arguable abuses of executive power remained deeply etched in the conservative memory for the better part of three decades. Well into the 1960s conservatives remained congressional partisans, having bought into the academic consensus—ironically, a consensus Wilson also helped to create—that the Constitution meant to establish legislative dominance. There was a second, more immediate, ideological reason: Congress, precisely because it represented a federated nation in all its diversity and complexity, was less likely to embrace utopian liberal schemes or an expansive federal establishment. Willmoore Kendall, the resident political theorist at *National Review* in its early days, was justly famous for his 1960 essay on "The Two Majorities," the central argument of which was (a) that a regime of presidential supremacy was not the government America's framers fought for; and (b) that Congress, in its geographically and culturally distributed collectivity, was a better and more legitimate expression of democratic sentiment than could be found in the modern plebiscitary presidency. (Kendall was at least half-right. His essay is in any event a remarkable exercise in good old-fashioned political science, published before the behaviorists took hold of the profession. Warts and all, it remains an engrossing and rewarding read.)

In the year before Kendall's essay appeared, James Burnham, another important *National Review* editor with impressive academic credentials, published *Congress and the American Tradition*, an extended paean to the framers' wisdom in elevating congressional power to preeminence. Burnham's argument, like Kendall's, was designed in part to encourage Congress to become more aggressive in checking what Burnham saw as a dangerous trend toward executive self-aggrandizement and arbitrariness. The book, however, was as much a lament as a prescription for reform, for even as he wrote Burnham feared that Congress had already lost its edge as a countervailing force against the exponential growth of government in general and executive power in particular.

Nowadays, of course, *National Review* and most conservatives have become strong supporters of unitary executive powers, particularly in foreign and national security policy. The change appears to have begun during the late 1960s, when the execution of the Cold War took a bad turn in Vietnam. Conservatives certainly had no love for Lyndon Johnson or anything resembling his Great Society, but they realized that a vigorous executive, armed with as much discretion as could decently be allowed, was essential to keeping the Communists at bay. Congress, hitherto the collective repository of conservative wisdom (including quasi-isolationist tendencies), could no longer be counted on to defend the West. The Kendall-Burnham argument lost favor.

Such reservations as conservatives once had about presidential power on the domestic front became decidedly secondary to the overarching goal of deflating the Communist threat. For the most part, those reservations have not been reasserted, but not because conservatives came to embrace Wilson's general theory of history or of the state; rather, conservatives reluctantly resigned themselves to the fact that the administrative state is more or less here to stay. They would prefer, of course, smaller government, but as long as big government remains the order of the day, conservatives argue that the only way to make it reasonably efficient and politically accountable is to vest the president with sufficient authority to run it. On the conservative side, then, there is a rough symmetry between their position regarding presidential power at home and abroad.

WAR MEASURES

Not everyone on the right has this disposition, and President Bush's mismanagement of the Global War on Terror (if that's what the administration still calls it) has prompted some conservative thinkers to revisit the arguments advanced by Kendall and Burnham and to reassert the case for congressional authority over war-making. In this, they have plenty of company from liberals, who are dusting off their copies of Anti-Federalist tracts, Max Farrand's *Records of the Federal*

Convention of 1787, and other primary source material on the framers' and ratifiers' intent.

But letting go of Kendall and Burnham is a lot easier for most conservatives than letting go of Wilson is for liberals. Much of the activity of the political science profession, as well as of the history profession, rests on the philosophical and political premises that made Woodrow Wilson famous and to which he devoted so much of his academic life. One takes a certain perverse pleasure these days in watching liberals wrap themselves in the arguments of James Madison (or at least the Madison who, in 1793, argued for the executive's limited role in foreign policy). One suspects they will not go much further into Madison's political thought than is necessary to bash George W. Bush or anyone else who supports expanded executive power in the war on terrorism—especially the "surge" in Iraq, military trials for the enemy combatants housed in Guantánamo, and the use of NSA intercepts. The Madison of 1793, and others from the republic's early days who were suspicious of executive authority, have their uses to Bush's opponents at the present hour, but liberals will not wish to carry their arguments so far as to undercut Wilson's justification for the modern presidency or his general indictment of the old Constitution's principles and structure: the entire liberal enterprise depends on holding on to that sacred Wilsonian bastion.

The Contemporary Presidency: The Decline and Resurgence and Decline (and Resurgence?) of Congress[*]

Charting a New Imperial Presidency

By Andrew Rudalevige
Presidential Studies Quarterly, September 2006

The presidency was designed to have limited power, suspended in a series of checks and balances. But executive authority expanded dramatically over time. It took the presidential excesses of Vietnam and Watergate to prompt a legislative resurgence, a sequence bookended by Arthur M. Schlesinger, Jr.'s *The Imperial Presidency* and James Sundquist's *The Decline and Resurgence of Congress*. Yet even before September 11, assertive presidents and fragmented Congresses had allowed the presidency to regain much of the initiative lost in the 1970s; and in the global war on terror, a "new" imperial presidency has been cemented, grounded in broad claims to a "unitary" executive branch. Will there be another legislative resurgence in response? The question goes to the legitimacy of representative government's responses to the crises that already define the twenty-first century.

"How Much Power Should They Have?" demanded the cover of *Newsweek* as 2006 began, as President George W. Bush and Vice President Dick Cheney glared out from underneath the headline. The question was prompted by a flurry of holiday season revelations centered on aggressive claims to, and use of, unilateral presidential powers. These ranged from the detention and treatment of imprisoned terror suspects around the world to phone taps placed on Americans without a court warrant. "We've been able to restore the legitimate authority of the presidency," the vice president insisted; others worried that the Constitution's checks were being unbalanced and that the "imperial presidency" of the Vietnam/ Watergate era had risen from the grave (Cheney 2005; Rudalevige 2005; Schlesinger 1973).

FRAMING QUESTIONS

However timely, *Newsweek*'s query was of course hardly new. Indeed, little at the Constitutional Convention of 1787 provoked more debate than the shape and scope of the executive branch. Delegates had to determine how the president would be selected, how long he should serve, whether he should be able to run for office more than once, how much power he should have—even whether the president would be a "he" or a "they."[1] Some of the Framers were unconvinced of the need for an executive branch in the first place. Others thought that executive power must be strictly divided, to impede future tyranny: for them, in Virginia Governor Edmund Randolph's phrase, a single executive was "the foetus of monarchy" (Rakove 1996, 257). And monarchy, of course, was what the Framers wanted to avoid.

In the end, the framework of presidential power was left largely in outline form, to be worked out in practice. Consider the very first sentence of Article II: "The executive power shall be vested in a President of the United States of America." What is "the executive power"? What might it allow the president to do? Here the document is silent. In other places the president was given a limited array of specified powers, many of them further truncated by a sort of congressional asterisk— the president can finalize treaties, or appointments, only with Senate approval; the execution of the law assumes its legislative passage; no money can be spent that is not first appropriated by Congress. How these shared powers might work was itself not clarified; the expectation was, in Madison's famous phrase from the *Federalist*, that interbranch interaction would allow institutional "ambition . . . to counteract ambition."[2]

The conflict that implied began immediately, when Treasury Secretary Alexander Hamilton and Congressman James Madison argued over the scope of President Washington's unilateral authority. Reduced to its essence, the dispute was— and is—relatively straightforward: is a president limited to the specific powers affirmatively listed in the Constitution or granted in statute, or can he take whatever actions he deems in the public interest so long as those actions are not actually prohibited by the Constitution? Theodore Roosevelt's iteration of Hamilton's position put it clearly: "My belief was that it was not only [the president's] right but his duty to do anything that the needs of the Nation required unless such action was forbidden by the Constitution or by the laws." Roosevelt's successor, William Howard Taft, clarified the opposing view. "The President can exercise no power which cannot be fairly and reasonably traced to some specific grant of power or justly implied within such express grant as proper and necessary to its exercise," Taft wrote. "There is no undefined residuum of power which he can exercise because it seems to him to be in the public interest" (Pyle and Pious 1984, 70-71; Roosevelt 1985 [1913], 372).[3]

Whatever the Framers' true intent, the Hamiltonian position won out over time. The growth in the size and scope of government during and after the Great Depression, and the national security apparatus built during World War II and the Cold War, effectively settled the argument. H. L. Mencken (1926, 185) noted that "No man would want to be President of the United States in strict accordance with the Constitution." But people do want to be president, for by the time Franklin Roosevelt's "modern presidency" was institutionalized by his successors, presidents had acquired many tools to work around their constitutionally mandated weakness. They used their formal powers strategically and proactively; they built an executive branch in their own image, with an extensive presidential staff to oversee and control it; and they continually and creatively interpreted constitutional vagueness in their favor to reshape the policy landscape, relying on a direct connection with the public to legitimize their actions (Greenstein 1988, 3). Arguably, a new framework for American government had been created along the way.[4]

Given the demands facing the nation, few were concerned about this development. Into the 1960s, indeed, most scholars were far more worried about a Congress seemingly unwilling or unable to meet the challenges of the postwar era; the president was largely seen as a "savior" (Hargrove and Nelson 1984, 4). Legislators' failure to prepare for World War II; their reluctance to commit to an expanded American role in the wider world after 1945; their slow deliberations in a nuclear age that required dispatch; their fragmented, seniority-dominated committee system that brought dullards to power; their tacit (and often not so tacit) defense of institutionalized racism; their short-sighted, sectional demands for local pork at the expense of wider public goods—looking at all this, many felt that leadership must be vested instead in the executive branch. If, as legal scholar Edward Corwin (1984, 4) concluded long before Watergate, "the history of the presidency has been a history of aggrandizement," that aggrandizement was generally well received.

Yet presidents soon plunged precipitately through the circles of paradise—from "savior" to "Satan" (Hargrove and Nelson 1984, 4)—as Vietnam and Watergate showed the dark side of presidential unilateralism. Arthur M. Schlesinger, Jr.'s iconic 1973 book, *The Imperial Presidency*, argued that recent presidents, especially Richard Nixon, had sought not presidential strength but supremacy. Schlesinger focused mostly on the war powers and "the rise of presidential war" independent of congressional authorization. However, he also criticized the efforts of the Nixon administration to centralize budgeting powers and unilaterally shape policy outcomes via impoundment (the refusal to spend appropriated funds); to build up a large, politicized staff; to greatly expand the "secrecy system"; and, relatedly, to broaden the notion of executive privilege. The Watergate era's indictment against the presidency began with petty campaign sabotage and quickly ratcheted up to burglary, bribery, extortion, fraud, destruction of evidence, domestic espionage, obstruction of justice, and abuse of various aspects of executive power from efforts to inflict punitive tax audits on political opponents to widespread impoundments to covert action and even secret warfare (Schlesinger 1973, x, 252; Genovese 1999; Kutler 1990).[5]

The romantic glow of Kennedy's "Camelot" thus dispersed in the harsh glare of Vietnamese rice paddies and Judiciary hearing rooms. If presidents before Nixon showed imperial ambition, it was under his administration that overreach led to the empire's fall; and in August 1974, faced with certain impeachment and removal from office, he became the first and only president to resign from office. "When the President does it, that means that it is not illegal," Nixon famously remarked (Ambrose 1992, 508). But Congress, having battled Nixon the president, was now ready to turn its attention to the institution of the presidency. It was ready, in short, to make it illegal.

THE RESURGENCE AND DECLINE OF CONGRESS

It did so in extensive fashion. In *The Decline and Resurgence of Congress*, James L. Sundquist (1981, 7) documents that, after a "Congress at nadir," post-Watergate legislators achieved "a collective resolve . . . to restore the balance between the executive and legislative branches. . . . A period of resurgence had begun." Throughout the 1970s, legislators erected a latticework of new laws aimed at reshaping executive-legislative relationships in the substantive areas where congressional prerogative had been slighted. Not surprisingly, the framers of this resurgence regime foresaw a much greater role for congressional input—for both advice and consent—than recent presidents had desired or allowed. "The President has overstepped the authority of his office in the actions he has taken," warned Representative Gillis Long (D-LA). "Our message to the President is that he is risking retaliation for his power grabs, that support for the counter-offensive is found in the whole range of congressional membership—old members and new, liberal and conservative, Democratic and Republican" (Sundquist 1981, 6). Congress intended to reclaim control over the nation's bottom line and forbid presidential impoundments, to have a key role in authorizing and overseeing America's military deployments and covert adventures, and to keep a close eye on executive corruption.

A partial list of enactments gives a sense of the scope of that ambition. For example, the Congressional Budget and Impoundment Control Act of 1974 prohibited unilateral presidential spending decisions and created important centralizing structures (the Budget Committees, the Congressional Budget Office [CBO]) to guide the legislative budget process. In foreign policy, the War Powers Resolution (WPR) was to ensure that Congress had a say in the use of American force and the Hughes-Ryan Amendment and Intelligence Oversight Act to keep it informed of covert operations. The Non-Detention Act and National Emergencies Act, as well as the Foreign Intelligence Surveillance Act (FISA) and the 1972 *Keith* decision, limited presidents' internal security powers at home. The executive branch's workings were to be made more transparent through an expanded Freedom of Information Act, various "government in the sunshine" laws, and the timely release of presidential documents; at the same time, the Supreme Court ruled in *U.S. v. Nixon* that the president's power to assert "executive privilege" was not absolute, and reviewable by the courts. The role of money in politics was to be diminished by a new Federal Election Commission; and should all this fail, investigations of executive malfeasance would be conducted under a new independent counsel operation.

Already by 1976, journalists were keeping track of "the score since Watergate" in a running battle of "the President versus Congress," and Congress was ahead. Indeed, President Gerald Ford would soon complain that "We have not an imperial presidency but an imperiled presidency. Under today's rules . . . the presidency does not operate effectively. . . . That is harmful to our overall national interests" (Bonafede, Rapoport, and Havemann 1976, 738; Ford 1980, 30).

It soon became clear, however, that the resurgence regime was itself built on fragile foundations. Even in the decade following Nixon's resignation, the office of the presidency retained a solid base of authority grounded in its ability to grab the public spotlight and set the agenda, the commander-in-chief power, its potential control over policy implementation, its role in appointments, and its veto leverage. Presidents starting with Ronald Reagan aggressively used executive tools—from regulatory review to signing statements—to enhance their influence over bureaucratic outputs and avoid legislative dictation. They resisted probes for information and asserted executive privilege, albeit by less inflammatory names, over a wide range of records while shielding even historical material from public release. Through appointing personal loyalists to executive positions across the bureaucracy, sometimes by recess appointment, they sought to "implant their DNA throughout the government" (Allen 2004).

The statutory side of the regime also crumbled. In some cases, efforts to specify the limits of presidential powers gave life in law to powers earlier exercised only informally; for example, the International Emergency Economic Powers Act, designed to limit presidents' powers to impose economic sanctions, led to the declaration of dozens of "national emergencies" since 1979. In other cases, Congress itself backed away from using the processes it had created to challenge the president, or failed to make them work. Most dramatically, the WPR did not rein in presidents' use of force, as deployments in Lebanon, Iran, Grenada, the Persian Gulf (in 1987-1988), Libya, Panama, Somalia, Iraq (in 1993 and throughout the "no-fly zone" period), Haiti, Bosnia, Sudan, Afghanistan (in 1998), and Kosovo suggest. Though the NATO War in Kosovo utilized some 800 U.S. aircraft flying more than 20,000 air sorties at nearly 2,000 targets throughout Yugoslavia, for example, President Clinton did not deem that troops had, in the language of the WPR, been "introduced into hostilities or into situation where imminent involvement in hostilities is clearly indicated by the circumstances." By the WPR's twenty-fifth anniversary even observers sympathetic to its intent argued it should be repealed (Fisher and Adler 1998).

The Congressional Budget Act, likewise, failed to bring discipline to federal spending; deficits veered upward in the 1980s, and after a brief blip into surplus in the late 1990s, by fiscal year 2006 the federal government was more than $400 billion in the red. As importantly, the deliberative process laid out in 1974 was often honored in the breach: though thirteen budget bills were required to be passed by October 1 each year, in the five fiscal years 2002 through 2006, a *total* of eight such bills were passed on time. Outgoing CBO Director Dan Crippen (2002) summed up the situation bluntly: "The Congressional budget process is dead." The beneficiary, he argued, was the president, for "without this kind of process . . . the Congress is going to be dominated by any President."

To be sure, not every element of the resurgence receded at once, or for all time. Most obviously, Clinton's impeachment and trial in 1998-1999 was the first since 1868 and the first ever of an elected president. Still, while it seems strange to talk about congressional deference in that context, even this period highlighted the potential powers of the president and renewed legislative acquiescence to their use. As Clinton himself suggested after the Democrats lost Congress in 1994, "I think now we have a better balance of both using the Presidency as a bully pulpit and the President's power of the Presidency to do things, actually accomplish things, and . . . not permitting the presidency to be defined only by relations with the Congress"—as witnessed by the 1998 headline "Clinton Perfects the Art of Go-Alone Governing." That summer, cruise missiles were fired at Sudan and Afghanistan at the president's order even as the House debated his fate. Clinton's success in achieving his preferred policy outcomes in this period by taking advantage of the congressional budget process and his veto power is also notable. Even the very process of impeachment—in the face of hostile public opinion—helped to discredit it and to encourage the expiration of the independent counsel statute in 1999 (Clinton 1995, 1475; Kiefer 1998; Adler 2002). If the 1970s seemed delayed affirmation of Bob Dylan's famous observation that "the times, they are a-changin'," the state of the presidency by 2001 seemed better described by the satirical observation of Dylan's fictional film alter-ego, Bob Roberts: "The times they are a-changin—back." The "imperial" infrastructure seemed largely rebuilt.

PREROGATIVE UNLEASHED: THE WORLD AFTER SEPTEMBER 11

Still, it is George W. Bush's presidency that provides the clearest—because most openly claimed and aggressively argued—case study of presidential unilateralism in the post-Watergate era. "I have an obligation to make sure that the Presidency remains robust. I'm not going to let Congress erode the power of the executive branch," Bush noted in 2002. His vice president—who got started in political life as a staffer in the Nixon White House—put the aim even more bluntly: "For the 35 years that I've been in this town, there's been a constant, steady erosion of the prerogatives and the powers of the president of the United States, and I don't want to be a part of that" (Bush 2002; Cheney 2002; Walsh 2006).

In some areas, that attitude was translated to action even before September 11. Operating under the "theology," as one close observer put it, "that we the people have made the White House too open and too accountable," the Bush administration cracked down on Freedom of Information Act releases and increased federal executives' ability to withhold information from public view, even reclassifying previously open documents (Milbank and Allen 2003, A15; Shane 2006). The Presidential Record Act was amended by executive order to expand past administrations' capacity to delay or bar the opening of historical records. The administration later went to court, successfully, to defend its ability to withhold—even without formally claiming executive privilege—documents from congressional auditors or others seeking information about the energy task force headed by Vice President Cheney (Rudalevige 2005, 189-91; Victor 2003).

The brutal attacks on New York and Washington did, however, bring a tidal wave of renewed visibility and leverage to the presidential office. President Bush's standing to lead soared, and he seized the reins. On a variety of fronts, legislators hastened to expand his authority. With just one dissenting vote in either chamber—most Senate discussion of the bill actually took place after the vote—Congress passed a resolution on September 14, 2001, stating that "the president has authority under the Constitution to take action to deter and prevent acts of international terrorism against the United States" and granting him the power to use "all necessary and appropriate force against those nations, organizations, or persons he determines planned, authorized, committed, or aided the terrorist attacks that occurred on September 11, 2001, or harbored such organizations or persons, in order to prevent any future acts of international terrorism against the United States by such nations, organizations, or persons." In the fall of 2002, Congress approved by wide margins another broad delegation of authority to use force against Iraq. On the domestic front, the USA Patriot Act, passed rapidly to administration specifications in October 2001, was designed to enhance the executive branch's prosecutorial tools and power to conduct criminal investigations by relaxing limits on surveillance and softening the barrier between domestic law enforcement and foreign intelligence gathering. Overall, Bush received historically high levels of legislative support throughout his first term. As 2006 began he had yet to veto a single bill, this five-year streak the longest since Thomas Jefferson's administration. When asked at a press conference about this, the president sounded bemused: "How could you veto . . . , if the Congress has done what you've asked them to do?" (Bush 2004; Rudalevige 2006).

Yet more often the president preferred to do, rather than ask. ("This administration," groused Representative David Obey [D-WI], "thinks that Article I of the Constitution was a fundamental mistake" [Caruso 2003, 2258].) Its interpretation of the commander-in-chief power was perhaps broadest and certainly most controversial. For example, in October 2001, President Bush issued a secret executive order authorizing the National Security Agency (NSA) to track communications between individuals abroad with suspected terrorist connections and Americans within the United States. On its face this action seemed to violate FISA, which had been passed in 1978 to regulate the process by which such intelligence was gathered after a series of surveillance abuses by the FBI, CIA, and NSA were revealed in the mid-1970s. Under the act, surveillance required a warrant from a special court. Where the targets were not Americans, obtaining a warrant required only that the Justice Department establish that they were working for a foreign power; for Americans, however, there had to be probable cause that the suspect was working on behalf of a foreign power in ways that might violate criminal statutes. FISA did allow for warrantless wiretapping for fifteen days after the declaration of war, and for emergency taps of up to seventy-two hours (increased from twenty-four hours after September 11) before a warrant needed to be obtained.

When the initiative was revealed in late 2005, the administration quickly dubbed it the "Terrorist Surveillance Program" and argued that the president had both inherent and statutory power to order such wiretaps. "My legal authority is derived from the Constitution, as well as the [September 2001] authorization of force by the United States Congress," President Bush told a news conference (Bush 2005a; Lane 2005). A forty-two-page white paper defending the NSA program, delivered to Congress by the Justice Department in January 2006, argued that "the NSA activities are supported by the President's well-recognized inherent constitutional authority as Commander in Chief and sole organ for the Nation in foreign affairs to conduct warrantless surveillance of enemy forces for intelligence purposes to detect and disrupt armed attacks on the United States." In any case, Justice claimed, far from violating the law (i.e., FISA), the president was following its letter, as the September 14, 2001, congressional resolution authorizing military force should be read as direct statutory approval for the program. In this reading, wiretapping was a "fundamental incident" of warfare similar to the detention of "enemy combatants" approved by the Supreme Court in the 2004 *Hamdi* case (see below). But in any case, neither FISA nor Congress generally could limit the president's "core exercise of Commander in Chief control"; any attempt to do so was simply unconstitutional (U.S. Department of Justice 2006, 1-2, 10-11, 17, 30-31).

The Department of Justice disquisition highlighted several important touchstones for presidential power. The notion that the president is "sole organ" of the nation for foreign policy dates to the 1936 Supreme Court case *U.S. v. Curtiss-Wright*, which argued for "plenary and exclusive" presidential power in international affairs. The idea that the executive power is indivisible (and that, for example, the commander-in-chief power is separable from Congress' overlapping powers to declare war and to provide for the regulation of armed forces and hostilities)[2] stems from a parallel theory of the "unitary executive." That interpretation of Article II's vesting clause implies that not only can Congress not infringe on presidential power but that only the president himself can set the boundaries of that power. In the Department of Justice white paper, for instance, the leading constitutional authority is often not the Supreme Court but the Justice Department's own Office of Legal Counsel. The brief stressed the "reasonable basis" underlying the surveillance decisions—and rather less plausibly, that this standard was equivalent to the modified "probable cause" required for a FISA warrant—but again, that determination was to be made entirely within the executive branch. Claiming the need for secrecy, the administration also declined to reveal to nonexecutive actors why it thought the FISA process was inadequate to defend national security (Bravin 2006; Bush 2006; U.S. Department of Justice 2006, 30, 34 n.18,

40).

Following a similar unilateral logic was the administration's treatment of prisoners captured during various antiterror operations and the Iraq War. Some were kept at so-called black sites run secretly by the CIA around the world. Hundreds more were imprisoned at the custom-built detention center at the U.S. naval base in Guantánamo Bay, Cuba. They were designated by the administration not as prisoners of war but rather as "unlawful enemy combatants," without the rights prisoner-of-war status confers. This decision was arrived at not by hearing (for which the Geneva Conventions provide) but by dictate: "Pursuant to my authority as Commander in Chief and Chief Executive of the United States," the president declared in February 2002, "I . . . determine that none of the provisions of Geneva apply to our conflict with al Qaeda in Afghanistan or elsewhere throughout the world." He added that "our values as a Nation . . . call for us to treat detainees humanely" and "consistent with the principles of Geneva." In practice, though, in Secretary of Defense Donald Rumsfeld's translation, those detained "would be treated in "a manner that is reasonably consistent" with the conventions— "for the most part" (Seelye 2002, A7). What the other parts might mandate was not then disclosed. However, with Rumsfeld's approval, previous Army regulations constraining interrogation methods were superseded. The secretary had already approved a highly secret program aimed at carrying out "instant interrogations— using force if necessary" around the world. As one intelligence official told reporter Seymour Hersh, the rules were to "grab whom you must, do what you want." That might include sexual humiliation, thought to be particularly effective in shaming Arab subjects to cooperate, and the use of attack dogs (Hendren 2004; Hersh 2004). These techniques were widely transferred to other military facilities in Afghanistan and Iraq, beyond the program's original intent and often in tragically embellished form. The most notorious example was at the Abu Ghraib prison outside Baghdad in 2004, where repellant photographs came to light. Charges that detainees' human rights had been violated continued to be an issue into late 2005 as the "black sites" and the practice of "rendition"—sending prisoners to countries less encumbered by due process than the United States—came to light. The president repeatedly insisted that "we do not torture," but a list of approved techniques for interrogation included such measures as hooding, sleep deprivation, the use of painful bound positions, and "water-boarding," meant to simulate drowning. By 2005 CIA personnel had been implicated in the deaths of at least four prisoners in agency custody (Fletcher 2005; Mayer 2005; Priest 2005; more generally, see Greenberg and Dratel 2005).

The president claimed that even American citizens, arrested within the United States, could be held indefinitely without charge or lawyer if they too were labeled enemy combatants. The determination of who qualified as an enemy combatant was, according to the president, entirely up to him, not the courts or legislature, and not even reviewable by those branches of government. The president also asserted the authority to create military tribunals outside the normal judicial system for terrorism suspects and issued an executive order doing just that. Indeed, as with the NSA program, the executive powers flowing from the September 11 attacks and September 14 resolution were deemed to be practically unlimited. "Congress can no more interfere with the President's conduct of the interrogation of enemy combatants than it can dictate strategic or tactical decisions on the battlefield," the Justice Department declared (U.S. Department of Justice 2002).

Further, the term "torture," Justice argued, was legally limited to acts sufficient to cause, for example, "organ failure . . . or even death," and then only if inflicting such pain (and not, say, gaining information) was the "precise objective" of the interrogator. In late 2004, the administration broadened this definition somewhat (though continuing to argue that any previously approved techniques were not torture). In any case, as a memo constructed by a working group of administration attorneys concluded, "In order to respect the President's inherent constitutional authority to manage a military campaign, 18 U.S.C. § 2340A [the prohibition against torture] as well as any other potentially applicable statute must be construed as inapplicable to interrogations undertaken pursuant to his Commander-in-Chief authority."[4] Congress could not encroach on the exercise of that authority. Thus, when legislators overwhelmingly approved a blanket ban on torture as an amendment to a defense measure in late 2005, the president said he would prohibit torture (as defined, presumably, by the administration). But he also quietly noted that he would implement the provision "in a manner consistent with the constitutional authority of the President to oversee the unitary executive branch and as Commander in Chief" (Bush 2005b). That is, he would decide how (and, arguably, when) to apply the ban. The vehicle was itself notable: this sort of "signing statement" was used more by George W. Bush than by all his predecessors combined, fencing off not only the commander-in-chief power but other requirements imposed by Congress—such as that the administration report to legislators on certain issues, or that appointees have certain qualifications (Bumiller 2006; Cooper 2005; Hutcheson and Kuhnhenn 2006). Again, the message was that the president would determine the limits of his power and of the law itself.

John Locke, in his *Second Treatise* of 1690, defines "prerogative" as the power of the executive "to act according to discretion, for the publick good, without the prescription of the Law, and sometimes even against it." For Locke, the executive needed discretion to implement the law or to set a policy course when law was lacking.

President Bush's efforts, building on those of his predecessors, amounted to the extensive broad practical application of this notion. The legalistic, even formulaic, nature of the language used in asserting these executive claims tended to conceal their extraordinarily broad affirmations of presidential power. But there should be no mistake: these claims effectively placed the president above the law, at least where national security is concerned. In so doing they recast the interbranch balance of power and did so without broad deliberation or debate.

Yet even Locke's version of prerogative had some crucial natural limits. It was only legitimate as it reflected the public commonweal and could only be temporary: executive control in the absence of legislative direction stood only until "the Legislature can be conveniently assembled to provide for it." Laws can be amended; but in a government under the law, they cannot be long ignored.

In that very American context, the constraints on prerogative are even stronger. While presidents' arguments have been distinctly unitarian, the Constitution is in turn devoutly trinitarian. Presidents, naturally, cherish the language of *Curtiss-Wright*; but it is far from clear that the Framers intended to give the executive—or any other branch—exclusive power over much of anything. In that context, "organ" is the right word only if by it is meant an instrument whose notes are defined by the full range of pressure on its keys.

However, despite its own clear claims to the constitutional ground presidents seek to barricade, Congress has not acted effectively to protect its own authority. As President Bush's claims regarding the September 14 resolution's relationship to the NSA program make clear, broad delegations of power can be used in ways legislators may not have anticipated.[6] Did legislators mean to allow for warrantless surveillance within the United States, bypassing FISA's requirements? Former Senate Majority Leader Tom Daschle (D-SD) said not: the topic, he wrote (2005, A21), "never came up. . . . [T]he 98 senators who voted in favor of authorization of force against al Qaeda did not believe that they were also voting for warrantless domestic surveillance." The resolution did "not authorize the President to do anything other than use force," Senator Dianne Feinstein (D-CA) added (Hutcheson 2006).

However, the president was right to note the breadth of the delegation of power at least implied by the resolution. And Congress did not act, at least immediately, to clarify its intent.

Such inaction was particularly notable because the September 14 resolution had already been interpreted once by the Supreme Court as encompassing a delegation of power not overtly specified. The case involved Yaser Hamdi, an American citizen captured on the Afghan battlefield and designated by the president as an enemy combatant. As a result, he was detained in a military brig for some two and a half years without charge. The courts did reject the administration's claim that Hamdi's detention could not even receive judicial consideration ("The court may not second-guess the military's enemy combatant determination," the Justice Department told the Fourth Circuit Court of Appeals). Further, the Supreme Court held that enemy combatants did require some sort of fair hearing. "A state of war is not a blank check for the President when it comes to the rights of the Nation's citizens," Justice Sandra Day O'Connor's lead opinion declared. "Whatever power the United States Constitution envisions for the Executive in its exchanges with other nations or with enemy organizations in times of conflict, it most assuredly envisions a role for all three branches when individual liberties are at stake."

This famous sound bite obscured important parts of the Court's overall finding. For instance, the Court did not specify what due process might entail, leaving that for the administration to determine—at least in the continuing absence of legislative action. And, crucially, it upheld the administration's basic claim: that the September 14 resolution (termed the "authorization to use military force" [AUMF]) constituted affirmative legislative delegation to the president sufficient to name enemy combatants. While the AUMF did not discuss such a procedure, the Court found that the 1971 Non-Detention Act did not apply to Hamdi's case: taking prisoners was deemed so central to armed conflict that "it is of no moment that the AUMF does not use specific language of detention." As a result, in the parallel case of another American citizen, José Padilla— arrested not on a foreign battlefield but at Chicago's O'Hare airport—a circuit court panel found that "the AUMF as interpreted by the Supreme Court in *Hamdi* authorizes the President's detention of Padilla as an enemy combatant" as well.[7] The *Hamdi* ruling was thus trumpeted in the administration's defense of the NSA program, which argued that wiretapping was similarly integral to warfare.[8]

Did Congress mean to authorize presidents to name and detain American citizens as enemy combatants? As with the NSA, the case was far from clear—even the Court was deeply divided, with O'Connor's opinion joined by only three other justices. But the courts are unlikely to rescue Congress from self-inflicted vagaries in statutory language. As Justice Lewis Powell once noted, "If the Congress chooses not to confront the President, it is not our task to do so" (Sievert 2001, 167). Indeed, one dissent in *Hamdi* emphasized "the need for a clearly expressed congressional resolution of the competing claims."[9]

Such clarity was slow to emerge, however. In late 2005 the antitorture language noted above was passed, along with requirements that Congress be given reports on military tribunal procedures, ensuring judicial review of the tribunals' decisions by the Washington, DC circuit court, and also limiting detainees' access to other American courts or for other claims. According to cosponsor Carl Levin (D-MI), this was not intended to affect ongoing cases (Levin 2006). But affirmative language to that effect was not included; and the administration quickly sought to take advantage of that imprecision. The Justice Department moved to dismiss all pending cases brought by detainees, including the *Hamdan* case on the constitutionality of military tribunals awaiting Supreme Court action. In oral arguments, Solicitor General Paul Clement told the Court that "if Congress wanted to put in a . . . clause" allowing review of those cases, "it would have been very easy." He argued they had not.

AMBITION RISING?

Still, that legislators had acted at all did suggest the stirrings of renewed legislative resurgence. In fits and starts, in fact, Congress had begun to grow restive as early as 2004, when that year's election seemed to heat up the frozen ambition of the other branches of government. Bush's Democratic opponent, Senator John

Kerry, fiercely criticized many of the administration's claims and policies, touting his own military service and challenging President Bush's leadership even on national security issues. The Supreme Court's 2004 decisions on the detention regime did at least serve notice of judicial concern regarding executive overreach. Further, as bad news from Iraq undercut the president's claim to a "mission accomplished," legislators began to question the administration's prewar claims and postinvasion occupation plan. Defense Department personnel testifying on behalf of additional appropriations for Iraq in 2004 were assailed for the request's lack of specificity, for the imprecision of prior spending estimates, and for the Abu Ghraib scandal. "This is a blank check," said Senator John McCain (R-AZ), and it seemed that blank checks were less fashionable than before (Schmitt 2004, A1).

After a pause following President Bush's narrow reelection victory in November and inspiring Iraqi elections in late January, such criticism escalated dramatically late in 2005 and into 2006. Abroad, continuing violence in Iraq, leading to casualties both military (U.S. troop deaths passed 2,500 in 2006, with another 15,000 wounded) and civilian (in December 2005 the president estimated the Iraqi death toll from the war at some 30,000), drove support for the war below 40 percent in many polls. Widespread negative assessments of the Iraq occupation's planning and administration did not help the public's outlook. At home, the anemic response to Hurricane Katrina shook public confidence in the government's ability to react to large-scale emergencies. The president was also criticized for having appointed underqualified political loyalists to crucial management posts (Michael Brown, the Federal Emergency Management Agency [FEMA] director, was forced to resign after Katrina); he had to withdraw a nominee to the Supreme Court, White House counsel Harriet Miers, when she faced similar attacks. And in October 2005, the vice president's chief of staff, Lewis Libby, was indicted on perjury charges related to the leak of a CIA operative's name to the press after the operative's husband questioned the administration's rationale for the Iraq War.

The controversy surrounding torture, rendition, domestic eavesdropping, and the like added fuel to the furor on Capitol Hill. Democrats used the hearings on the nomination of Judge Samuel Alito to the Supreme Court to score the Bush administration's claims concerning executive power; even some Republicans (especially those worried about midterm elections in 2006, or themselves considering presidential bids in 2008) began to express doubts. The Patriot Act, due to expire at the end of 2005, was originally given only a brief extension until February 2006 when several Republican senators worried about its potential for intrusiveness and abuse joined with Senate Democrats to prevent a vote on a conference committee report that made most of the act permanent. McCain pushed antitorture language into law; Judiciary Chair Arlen Specter (R-PA) convened hearings into the legality of the NSA program. On other fronts, too, legislators began to desert the presidential banner, most notably ignoring the president's support of a trade deal that would have placed administration of some major U.S. ports under the management of an Arab company, and demanding staff changes (which came when Chief of Staff Andrew Card resigned in March 2006). Even the reliable

Fourth Circuit Court of Appeals blasted the administration's decision to charge José Padilla in the civilian courts, on charges never mentioned during his detention as an enemy combatant, in order, the court suggested, to avoid possible reversal by the Supreme Court.[10]

In some ways the galvanizing effect of events, elections, court decisions, and legislative hearings came as no surprise. Political contexts had changed; the world had changed; but the Constitution, and the hold it gave each branch on each of the others, had not changed. It remained up to Congress to use its power and to do its job. Specter suggested that if Congress was not yet showing "muscle," at least it "is showing some tendons" (Kuhnhenn 2006, A3).[11]

Still, any obituary for presidential power was at best premature. The contemporary executive retained the tools to define the terms of debate and utilize the office's structural advantages. The fact that Congress is a divided body run by collective choices gives presidents inherent advantages of (in Alexander Hamilton's terms) "decision, activity, secrecy, and dispatch." Even if they do not get the last say, presidents often get to make the first move—which itself may shape the landscape over which subsequent decisions are taken. In late 2005, President Bush sought to do just this. Seeking to reframe opinion on Iraq, the president began an extensive schedule of speaking engagements defending his policy in Iraq, claiming steady progress, and suggesting that calls for a military withdrawal from that nation were at best premature, at worst unpatriotic (Wolffe and Bailey 2006). A series of nominees who had faced difficulty in obtaining Senate confirmation in the post-Katrina spotlight were installed in their posts by recess appointment (Edsall 2006). The White House refused to provide an investigatory committee materials documenting its internal response to Katrina, and even sought to prevent former FEMA Director Brown from testifying about his contacts with the White House during the crisis (Lipton 2006).

In early 2006 legislators renewed the Patriot Act, largely on the president's terms; and in a signing statement, he rejected the legislative requirement that Justice report regularly on how the bill's powers were used. Members of Congress, including 2004 Democratic nominee John Kerry, pressed to give the president some form of line item veto authority. And they dealt with the NSA issue by creating a process that allowed warrantless surveillance not for three days, but forty-five (Shane and Kirkpatrick 2006). In January 2006, the president actually rejected proffered legislative support for changing FISA itself. There was no need to "attempt to try to pass a law on something that's already legal" because the debate might reveal information that would "help the enemy." Emphasizing the war was clearly the president's battle plan for the year to come; for "conducting war," he argued, "is a responsibility in the executive branch, not the legislative branch." He added, "I don't view it as a contest with the legislative branch" (Bush 2006). And certainly, to that point, "no contest" was an apt description.

PRACTICAL ADVANTAGES AND GRAVE DANGERS

So is there a "new imperial presidency"? That is, has the interbranch balance of power shifted back to the president to an extent comparable to the Vietnam/Watergate era? And if so, what are the consequences?

The short answer to the first question is "yes": the 1970s resurgence regime has eroded, and presidential power has expanded to fill the vacuum. There are meaningful parallels between the justificatory language of the Nixon administration and that of our most recent presidents: each stressed the notion of "inherent" presidential power, the broad sweep of the constitutional "rights" of the office. This development would have endured even had a Kerry administration replaced the Bush administration in January 2005, albeit in different terms and context, for the argument is not individually but institutionally grounded.

As with most interesting questions, though, the short answer is rarely the full story. The narrative here depicts a set of linear trends: the rise of presidential power to the 1960s, the overstretch of the presidency past "savior" to "Satan," the resurgence of other political actors through the 1970s, the counter surge of presidential initiative starting in the 1980s and accelerating into overdrive after September 11, 2001. That is certainly accurate, as generalizations go. Precedents matter, and accrete, and future presidents will rely upon what is established now as the "normal" balance of presidential-congressional power.

Despite the consistent, and often successful, efforts of presidents to expand their institutional resources past the sparse grants of Article II, however, they ultimately remain subject to its constraints and part of a set of potential checks and counterbalances. The modern presidency has many potent tools, and a global reach, surely unforeseen by the architects of the Constitution. Yet the framework they designed remains. Presidential power, in a real sense, is the residual left over after subtracting out the power of other actors in the system.[11]

As such, the power of the president remains conditional. And our assessment of it must also be conditional, underlain by a fundamental tension: in the American system of government, strong executive leadership is at once unavoidable and unacceptable. Supreme Court Justice Robert Jackson perhaps put the dilemma best. "Comprehensive and undefined presidential powers," he wrote in 1952, "hold both practical advantages and grave dangers for the country."[12]

The advantages are clear. After all, how can one provide direction to an enormous nation, with an enormous national executive establishment, with enormous public expectations—and still hope to limit the authority necessary to meet those needs? More than four million civilian and military employees work in the federal executive branch, across fifteen cabinet-level departments and more than one hundred agencies. The annual federal budget verges on $2.5 trillion (as much as the 1960 through 1974 budgets, combined). A nation cannot meet crises, or even the day-to-day needs of governing, with five hundred thirty-five chief executives or commanders in chief driven by as many constituencies and spread across divided chambers. The problems of administration that arose during the Articles of Confederation period in a much smaller country, with a much smaller Congress, in what seemed a much larger world, were sufficient to drive the Framers to submerge their fear of monarchy and empower a single person as president. These days, the flutter of a butterfly's wing in Wellington shifts the climate of Washington; a globalized, polarized world seems to call out for endowing leadership sufficient to match its powers to the tasks at hand.[13]

On the other hand, presidential "leadership" is not by definition virtuous, if it does violence to constitutional tenets. To accede to presidential hagiography—and thus executive dominance—is extraordinarily problematic for a republican form of government. The words of the antifederalist patriot Patrick Henry echo over the years: "If your American chief be a man of ambition, and abilities, how easy is it for him to render himself absolute?" We want men and women of ambition and abilities to serve as our presidents. But to pledge that their preferences should without need of persuasion become policy, that they should as a matter of course substitute command for coalition building, is to cede something of the soul of self-governance. The dangers of unilateral authority are immense, because once those claims are asserted they logically admit no limits.

That is not meant to be alarmist; but nor is it hypothetical. Consider the logic of the NSA white paper traced above. Or, similarly, consider the administration's argument in the *Rumsfeld v. Padilla* enemy combatant case. The president claimed that he could, on the basis of "some evidence," remove someone from the court system and hold them without charge or trial. Paul Clement was subsequently asked during oral arguments before the Supreme Court to delineate the boundaries of this argument. If the September 14 resolution were insufficient authorization for such power, did the president still have the authority to deny trials to American citizens? Yes, Clement replied. Given the emergency created on September 11, "I think he would certainly today, which is to say September 12th [, 2001] or April 28th [, 2003]." And, in fact, "I would say the President had that authority on September 10th [, 2001]." In that case, could you shoot an enemy combatant, or torture him? asked a Justice. Well, no, said Clement, "that violates our own conception of what's a war crime." Still, he was pressed, what if it were an executive command, what if torture were deemed necessary to garner intelligence? "Some systems do that to get information."

"Well," replied Clement, "our executive doesn't."

"What's constraining? That's the point. Is it just up to the good will of the executive?"

"You have to recognize that in situations where there is a war—where the Government is on a war footing—that you have to trust the executive to make the kind of quintessential military judgments that are involved in things like that."

The result comes back to what Schlesinger decried in the 1970s as a "plebiscitary presidency," where presidents claim broad discretion to act, constrained only by quadrennial referendum on their decisions—a problematic model in the world of term-limited presidents and four elections in a row where the winner has received 51 percent of the popular vote or less. In the meantime, voters must trust that the president was acting in their interests. "Our executive doesn't," the administration claimed; but history suggests our executive could.

The point is too important to be a punch line. We must accept that executive discretion is, in fact, increasingly important. Still, within what framework ought that discretion to be exercised? Who gets to set the boundaries between the branches? Who, even in a war with parameters and enemies as fluid as in the "global war on terror," gets to decide when it starts and ends? Much as he might prefer it, the president is not alone in his responsibilities. Nor, even if he will not admit to mistakes, is the president always right. In our separated system, legitimating large-scale change requires bridging its divisions, building coalitions persuaded the president is right. There is a clear normative difference between a presidential assertion of power that stands because of congressional inertia and a power delegated to the president after full and free debate. Justice Antonin Scalia's dissent in *Hamdi* reminds us that "the Founders warned us about the risk, and equipped us with a Constitution designed to deal with it." Ambition must continue to counteract ambition.

The first branch's job is not to manage policy implementation on a day-to-day basis. Nor is it always to pass a new law; the resurgence regime bears witness to the inadequacy of creating a statutory framework in the absence of political will reinforcing its component parts. But Congress has a critical task nonetheless. Its job is to use debate and deliberation to distill priorities and set clear standards, to oversee and judge the decisions and actions of others by those standards, to expose both the bad and good efforts of government to public scrutiny, and to revisit its earlier debate in the light of later events. All this is Congress' job; and debate, judgment, and oversight are delegated to other actors in the system at our potential peril.

The goal of legislative deliberation is not to foster trust in government for its own sake; indeed, a healthy distrust of government is part of American history and a valuable tool of accountability. We should, in President Reagan's words, "trust—but verify." We should work to make difficult decisions and tradeoffs about the powers and goals of American government, about its very scope and direction. Indeed, given the crises that already define our new century, doing so is our highest national priority. But it will require the active involvement of *all* our ambitions. "We must recognize," said a young John F. Kennedy, campaigning in his first election in 1946, "that if we do not take an interest in our political life, we can easily lose at home what so many young men so bloodily won abroad" (Dallek 2003, 132).

REFERENCES

Adler, David Gray. 2002. Clinton in context. In *The presidency and the law: The Clinton legacy*, edited by David Gray Adler and Michael A. Genovese. Lawrence: University Press of Kansas.

Allen, Mike. 2004. Bush to change economic team. *Washington Post*, November 29, p. A1.

Ambrose, Stephen E. 1992. Nixon, vol. III, *Ruin and recovery, 1973–1990*. New York: Touchstone.

Bonafede, Dom, Daniel Rapoport, and Joel Havemann. 1976. The president versus congress: The score since watergate. *National Journal*, May 29.

Bravin, Jess. 2006. Judge Alito's view of the presidency: Expansive powers. *Wall Street Journal*, January 5, p. A1.

Bumiller, Elizabeth. 2006. For president, final say on a bill sometimes comes after the signing. *New York Times*, January 16, p. A11.

Bush, George W. 2002. *Weekly compilation of presidential documents*, March 13, 411.

———. President holds press conference. Office of the White House Press Secretary, December 20.

———. 2005a. Press conference of the president. Office of the White House Press Secretary, December 19.

———. 2005b. President's statement on signing of H.R. 2863. Office of the White House Press Secretary, December 30.

———. 2006. Press conference of the president. Office of the White House Press Secretary, January 26.

Caruso, Lisa. 2003. You've got to know when to hold 'em. *National Journal*, July 12.

Cheney, Richard. 2002. Interview of the Vice President by Campbell Brown, NBC News. Office of the White House Press Secretary, January 28.

Cheney, Richard. 2005. Vice president's remarks to the traveling press. Office of the White House Press Secretary, December 20.

Clinton, William J. 1995. *Public papers of the president*, September 25.

Cooper, Phillip J. 2005. George W. Bush, Edgar Allen Poe, and the use and abuse of presidential signing statements. *Presidential Studies Quarterly* 35(September): 512–32.

Corwin, Edward S., with Randall W. Bland, Theodore Hinson, and Jack W. Peltason. 1984. *The president: Office and powers*, 5th rev. ed. New York: New York University Press.

Crippen, Dan L. 2002. Observations on the current state of the federal budget process. Address at the Fall Symposium of the American Association for Budget and Program Analysis, November 22. Available from http://ftp.cbo.gov/ftpdocs/40xx/doc4001/BudgetProcess.pdf.

Dallek, Robert. 2003. *An unfinished life: John F. Kennedy, 1917–1963*. Boston: Little, Brown.

Daschle, Tom. 2005. Power we didn't grant. *Washington Post*, December 23, p. A21.

Edsall, Thomas B. 2006. Bush appointments avert Senate battles. *Washington Post*, January 5, p. A13.

Fallows, James. 2005. Why Iraq has no army. *Atlantic Monthly*, December.

Fisher, Louis, and David Gray Adler. 1998. The War Powers Resolution: Time to say goodbye. *Political Science Quarterly* 113(Spring): 1–20.

Fletcher, Michael. 2005. Bush defends CIA's clandestine prisons. *Washington Post*, November 8, p. A15.

Ford, Gerald R. 1980. Interview. *Time*, November 10.

Genovese, Michael A. 1999. *The Watergate crisis*. Westport, CT: Greenwood.

Glanz, James. 2006. Iraq rebuilding badly hobbled, U.S. report finds. *New York Times*, January 24, p. A1.

Greenberg, Karen J., and Joshua L. Dratel, eds. 2005. *The torture papers*. New York: Cambridge University Press.

Greenstein, Fred I. 1988. Toward a modern presidency. In *Leadership in the modern presidency*, edited by Fred I. Greenstein. Cambridge, MA: Harvard University Press.

Hargrove, Erwin C., and Michael Nelson. 1984. *Presidents, politics, and policy*. New York: Knopf.

Hendren, John. 2004. Officials say Rumsfeld OK'd harsh interrogation methods. *Los Angeles Times*, May 21, p. A1.

Hersh, Seymour. 2004. The gray zone. *New Yorker*, May 24.

Hutcheson, Ron. 2006. Presidential power a key issue in debate over eavesdropping. *Knight-Ridder*

Washington Bureau, January 23. Available from http://www.realcities.com/mld/krwashington/news/columnists/ron_hutcheson/13694124.htm.

Hutcheson, Ron, and James Kuhnhenn. 2006. Bush asserts power over laws. *Philadelphia Inquirer*, January 16, p. A1.

Kiefer, Francine. 1998. Clinton perfects the art of go-alone governing. *Christian Science Monitor*, July 24, p. 3.

Kuhnhenn, James. 2006. Senators taking reins of their watchdog role. *Philadelphia Inquirer*, January 29, p. A3.

Kutler, Stanley I. 1990. *The wars of Watergate*. New York: Knopf.

Lane, Charles. 2005. White House elaborates on authority for eavesdropping. *Washington Post*, December 20, p. A10.

Levin, Carl. 2006. Statement on the Department of Justice motion to dismiss the Hamdan case in the Supreme Court. Office of Senator Carl Levin, January 12.

Lipton, Eric. 2006. White House declines to provide storm papers. *New York Times*, January 25, p. A1.

Mayer, Jane. 2005. A deadly interrogation. *New Yorker*, November 14.

Mencken, H. L. 1926. *Notes on democracy*. New York: Knopf.

Milbank, Dana, and Mike Allen. 2003. Release of documents is Delayed. *Washington Post*, March 26, p. A15.

Priest, Dana. 2005. Covert CIA program withstands new furor. *Washington Post*, December 30, p. A1.

Pyle, Christopher H., and Richard M. Pious, eds. 1984. *The president, Congress, and the Constitution: Power and legitimacy in American politics*. New York: Free Press.

Rakove, Jack N. 1996. *Original meanings: Politics and ideas in the making of the Constitution*. New York: Knopf.

Roosevelt, Theodore. 1985 [1913]. *An autobiography*. New York: Da Capo.

Rudalevige, Andrew. 2005. *The new imperial presidency: Renewing presidential power after Watergate*. Ann Arbor: University of Michigan Press.

———. 2006. George W. Bush and Congress: New term, new problems—Same results? In *The second term of George W. Bush: Prospects and perils*, edited by Robert Maranto, Douglas M. Brattebo, and Tom Lansford. New York: Palgrave Macmillan.

Schlesinger, Arthur M., Jr. 1973. *The imperial presidency*. Boston: Houghton Mifflin.

Schmitt, Eric. 2004. Senators assail request for aid for Afghan and Iraq budgets. *New York Times*, May 14, p. A1.

Seelye, Katharine Q. 2002. First "unlawful combatants" seized in Afghanistan arrive at U.S. base in Cuba. *New York Times*, January 12, p. A7.

Shane, Scott. 2006. U.S. reclassifies many documents in secret review. *New York Times*, February 21, p. A1.

Shane, Scott, and David D. Kirkpatrick. 2006. G.O.P. plan would allow spying without warrants. *New York Times*, March 9, p. A20.

Sievert, Ronald J. 2001. *Campbell v. Clinton* and the continuing effort to reassert Congress's predominant constitutional authority to commence, or prevent, war. *Dickinson Law Review* 105(Winter): 157–79.

Sundquist, James L. 1981. *The decline and resurgence of Congress*. Washington, DC: Brookings Institution Press.

U.S. Department of Justice. 2002. Re: Standards of conduct for interrogation under 18 U.S.C. §§2340–2340A. Office of Legal Counsel, August 1

———. 2006. Legal authorities supporting the activities of the National Security Agency described by the president. January 19.

Victor, Kirk. 2003. Congress in eclipse. *National Journal*, April 5, pp. 1069–70.

Walsh, Kenneth T. 2006. The Cheney factor. *U.S. News and World Report*, January 23, pp. 40–48.

Wolffe, Richard, and Holly Bailey. 2006. The Bush battle plan: It's the war, stupid. *Newsweek*, January 30, p. 35.

FOOTNOTES

1. Whether the president should be a "she" was not, of course, discussed at the time; and in talking about the presidency I will defer to historical fact and use the masculine pronoun to describe the office's occupants. But "he" should be read as "he, someday she."

2. See, for example, Article I's designation of Congress' authority to regulate the "land and naval forces," "captures on land or water," the militia, and "letters of marque and reprisal" (i.e., to hire private contractors to carry out warfare).

3. President's Military Order of November 13, 2001; Government's Brief and Motion, August 27, 2002, *Jose Padilla v. George Bush, Donald Rumsfeld, et al.* (U.S. District Court, Southern District of New York, Case no. 02-4445).

4. See the Working Group Report on Detainee Interrogations in the Global War on Terrorism: Assessment of Legal, Historical, Policy, and Operational Considerations, U.S. Department of Defense, April 4, 2003, 21 and Section III generally; Mayer 2005.

5. While one can find isolated examples of the practice as early as the Jackson administration, it was Ronald Reagan who advanced it as a more systematic strategy aimed both to put the president's point of view in the "legislative history" (should the judiciary weigh in) and to better control executive branch behavior. Reagan's successors all used the tool, but none as aggressively as George W. Bush, who made more than 500 constitutional objections to legislation during his first term (by contrast, Bill Clinton made 105, over eight years). See Cooper 2005; Hutcheson and Kuhnhenn 2006; Bumiller 2006.

6. Further, presidents have become astute at adapting outdated or inexact statutes to current needs. President Roosevelt closed the banks in 1933 under the terms of a World War I law; President Clinton's 1996 designation of two million acres in Utah as conservation land, over the objections of state officials, was undertaken using a statute passed in 1906.

7. *Hamdi v. Rumsfeld*, 124 U.S. 2633 (2004); *Padilla v. Hanft*, 05-6396, Fourth Circuit Court of Appeals, September 9, 2005.

8. Oral argument in *Hamdan v. Rumsfeld*, 05-184 (March 28, 2006), 55. The Court rejected this question of jurisdiction in its 5–3 decision in *Hamdan*, handed down as this essay went to press; it affirmed both the need for due process in detainees' tribunal proceedings and for legislative involvement in defining that process.

9. For the civilian casualty estimate, see "President Discusses War on Terror and Upcoming Iraqi Elections," in Philadelphia, Pennsylvania, Office of the White House Press Secretary, December 12, 2005; for polling data, see the CNN/USA Today/Gallup Poll sequence provided at http://www.pollingreport.com/iraq.htm, accessed January 3, 2006. For a discussion of the Iraq occupation, see, inter alia, Fallows 2005; Glanz 2006.

10. The Supreme Court, however, allowed the shift and later dismissed the appeal (albeit with a warning to the administration not to remove Padilla again from the court system) on the grounds that Padilla's desired relief—to be charged with a crime in civilian court—had already been granted.

11. Thanks to William Howell and Jon Pevehouse for suggesting this formulation.

12. Concurring opinion to *Youngstown Sheet and Tube Co. v. Sawyer*, 343 U.S. 579 (1952).

13. From the transcript of the oral arguments before the U.S. Supreme Court in *Rumsfeld v. Padilla*, April 28, 2004, available from the Court's Web site, http://www.supremecourtus.gov.

When Congress Stops Wars[*]

Partisan Politics and Presidential Power

By William G. Howell and Jon C. Pevehouse
Foreign Affairs, September/October 2007

For most of George W. Bush's tenure, political observers have lambasted Congress for failing to fulfill its basic foreign policy obligations. Typical was the recent Foreign Affairs article by Norman Ornstein and Thomas Mann, "When Congress Checks Out," which offered a sweeping indictment of Congress' failure to monitor the president's execution of foreign wars and antiterrorist initiatives. Over the past six years, they concluded, congressional oversight of the White House's foreign and national security policy "has virtually collapsed." Ornstein and Mann's characterization is hardly unique. Numerous constitutional-law scholars, political scientists, bureaucrats, and even members of Congress have, over the years, lamented the lack of legislative constraints on presidential war powers. But the dearth of congressional oversight between 2000 and 2006 is nothing new. Contrary to what many critics believe, terrorist threats, an overly aggressive White House, and an impotent Democratic Party are not the sole explanations for congressional inactivity over the past six years. Good old-fashioned partisan politics has been, and continues to be, at play.

It is often assumed that everyday politics stops at the water's edge and that legislators abandon their partisan identities during times of war in order to become faithful stewards of their constitutional obligations. But this received wisdom is almost always wrong. The illusion of congressional wartime unity misconstrues the nature of legislative oversight and fails to capture the particular conditions under which members of Congress are likely to emerge as meaningful critics of any particular military venture.

The partisan composition of Congress has historically been the decisive factor in determining whether lawmakers will oppose or acquiesce in presidential calls for war. From Harry Truman to Bill Clinton, nearly every U.S. president has learned that members of Congress, and members of the opposition party in particular, are fully capable of interjecting their opinions about proposed and ongoing military ventures. When the opposition party holds a large number of seats or controls one or both chambers of Congress, members routinely challenge the president and step up oversight of foreign conflicts; when the legislative branch is dominated by the president's party, it generally goes along with the White House. Partisan unity, not institutional laziness, explains why the Bush administration's Iraq policy received such a favorable hearing in Congress from 2000 to 2006.

The dramatic increase in congressional oversight following the 2006 midterm elections is a case in point. Immediately after assuming control of Congress, House Democrats passed a resolution condemning a proposed "surge" of U.S. troops in Iraq and Senate Democrats debated a series of resolutions expressing varying degrees of outrage against the war in Iraq. The spring 2007 supplemental appropriations debate resulted in a House bill calling for a phased withdrawal (the president vetoed that bill, and the Senate then passed a bill accepting more war funding without withdrawal provisions). Democratic heads of committees in both chambers continue to launch hearings and investigations into the various mishaps, scandals, and tactical errors that have plagued the Iraq war. By all indications, if the government in Baghdad has not met certain benchmarks by September, the Democrats will push for binding legislation that further restricts the president's ability to sustain military operations in Iraq.

Neither Congress' prior languor nor its recent awakening should come as much of a surprise. When they choose to do so, members of Congress can exert a great deal of influence over the conduct of war. They can enact laws that dictate how long military campaigns may last, control the purse strings that determine how well they are funded, and dictate how appropriations may be spent. Moreover, they can call hearings and issue public pronouncements on foreign policy matters. These powers allow members to cut funding for ill-advised military ventures, set timetables for the withdrawal of troops, foreclose opportunities to expand a conflict into new regions, and establish reporting requirements. Through legislation, appropriations, hearings, and public appeals, members of Congress can substantially increase the political costs of military action—sometimes forcing presidents to withdraw sooner than they would like or even preventing any kind of military action whatsoever.

THE PARTISAN IMPERATIVE

Critics have made a habit of equating legislative inactivity with Congress' abdication of its foreign policy obligations. Too often, the infrequency with which Congress enacts restrictive statutes is seen as prima facie evidence of the institution's failings. Sometimes it is. But one cannot gauge the health of the U.S. system of governance strictly on the basis of what Congress does—or does not do—in the immediate aftermath of presidential initiatives.

After all, when presidents anticipate congressional resistance they will not be able to overcome, they often abandon the sword as their primary tool of diplomacy. More generally, when the White House knows that Congress will strike down key provisions of a policy initiative, it usually backs off. President Bush himself has relented, to varying degrees, during the struggle to create the Department of Homeland Security and during conflicts over the design of military tribunals and the prosecution of U.S. citizens as enemy combatants. Indeed, by most accounts, the administration recently forced the resignation of the chairman of the Joint Chiefs of Staff, General Peter Pace, so as to avoid a clash with Congress over his reappointment.

To assess the extent of congressional influence on presidential war powers, it is not sufficient to count how many war authorizations are enacted or how often members deem it necessary to start the "war powers clock"—based on the War Powers Act requirement that the president obtain legislative approval within 60 days after any military deployment. Rather, one must examine the underlying partisan alignments across the branches of government and presidential efforts to anticipate and preempt congressional recriminations.

During the past half century, partisan divisions have fundamentally defined the domestic politics of war. A variety of factors help explain why partisanship has so prominently defined the contours of interbranch struggles over foreign military deployments. To begin with, some members of Congress have electoral incentives to increase their oversight of wars when the opposing party controls the White House. If presidential approval ratings increase due to a "rally around the flag" effect in times of war, and if those high ratings only benefit the president's party in Congress, then the opposition party has an incentive to highlight any failures, missteps, or scandals that might arise in the course of a military venture.

After all, the making of U.S. foreign policy hinges on how U.S. national interests are defined and the means chosen to achieve them. This process is deeply, and unavoidably, political. Therefore, only in very particular circumstances—a direct attack on U.S. soil or on Americans abroad—have political parties temporarily united for the sake of protecting the national interest. Even then, partisan politics has flared as the toll of war has become evident. Issues of trust and access to information further fuel these partisan fires. In environments in which information is sparse, individuals with shared ideological or partisan affiliations find it easier to communicate with one another. The president possesses unparalleled intelligence about threats to national interests, and he is far more likely to share that information with members of his own political party than with political opponents. Whereas the commander in chief has an entire set of executive-branch agencies at his beck and call, Congress has relatively few sources of reliable classified information. Consequently, when a president claims that a foreign crisis warrants military intervention, members of his own party tend to trust him more often than not, whereas members of the opposition party are predisposed to doubt and

challenge such claims. In this regard, congressional Democrats' constant interrogations of Bush administration officials represent just the latest round in an
ongoing interparty struggle to control the machinery of war.

CONGRESSIONAL INFLUENCE AND ITS LIMITS

Historically, presidents emerging from midterm election defeats have been less
likely to respond to foreign policy crises aggressively, and when they have ordered
the use of force, they have taken much longer to do so. Our research shows that
the White House's propensity to exercise military force steadily declines as members of the opposition party pick up seats in Congress. In fact, it is not even necessary for the control of Congress to switch parties; the loss of even a handful of
seats can materially affect the probability that the nation will go to war.

The partisan composition of Congress also influences its willingness to launch
formal oversight hearings. While criticizing members for their inactivity during
the Bush administration, Ornstein and Mann make much of the well-established
long-term decline in the number of hearings held on Capitol Hill. This steady
decline, however, has not muted traditional partisan politics. According to Linda
Fowler, of Dartmouth College, the presence or absence of unified government
largely determines the frequency of congressional hearings. Contrary to Ornstein
and Mann's argument that "vigorous oversight was the norm until the end of the
twentieth century," Fowler demonstrates that during the post-World War II era,
when the same party controlled both Congress and the presidency, the number
of hearings about military policy decreased, but when the opposition party controlled at least one chamber of Congress, hearings occurred with greater frequency. Likewise, Boston University's Douglas Kriner has shown that congressional
authorizations of war as well as legislative initiatives that establish timetables for
the withdrawal of troops, cut funds, or otherwise curtail military operations criti-
cally depend on the partisan balance of power on Capitol Hill.

Still, it is important not to overstate the extent of congressional influence. Even
when Congress is most aggressive, the executive branch retains a tremendous
amount of power when it comes to military matters. Modern presidents enjoy
extraordinary advantages in times of war, not least of which the ability to act unilaterally on military matters and thereby place on Congress (and everyone else) the
onus of coordinating a response. Once troops enter a region, members of Congress face the difficult choice of either cutting funds and then facing the charge
of undermining the troops or keeping the public coffers open and thereby aiding
a potentially ill-advised military operation.

On this score, Ornstein and Mann effectively illustrate Bush's efforts to expand his influence over the war in Iraq and the war on terrorism by refusing to
disclose classified information, regularly circumventing the legislative process, and
resisting even modest efforts at oversight. Similarly, they note that Republican
congressional majorities failed to take full advantage of their institution's formal

powers to monitor and influence either the formulation or the implementation of foreign policy during the first six years of Bush's presidency. Ornstein and Mann, however, mistakenly attribute such lapses in congressional oversight to a loss of an "institutional identity" that was ostensibly forged during a bygone era when "tough oversight of the executive was common, whether or not different parties controlled the White House and Congress" and when members' willingness to challenge presidents had less to do with partisan allegiances and more to do with a shared sense of institutional responsibility. In the modern era, foreign-policy making has rarely worked this way. On the contrary, partisan competition has contributed to nearly every foreign policy clash between Capitol Hill and the White House for the past six decades.

DIVIDED WE STAND

Shortly after World War II—the beginning of a period often mischaracterized as one of "Cold War consensus"—partisan wrangling over the direction of U.S. foreign policy returned to Washington, ending a brief period of wartime unity. By defining U.S. military involvement in Korea as a police action rather than a war, President Truman effectively freed himself from the constitutional requirements regarding war and established a precedent for all subsequent presidents to circumvent Congress when sending the military abroad. Although Truman's party narrowly controlled both chambers, Congress hounded him throughout the Korean War, driving his approval ratings down into the 20s and paving the way for a Republican electoral victory in 1952. Railing off a litany of complaints about the president's firing of General Douglas MacArthur and his meager progress toward ending the war, Senator Robert Taft, then a Republican presidential candidate, declared that "the greatest failure of foreign policy is an unnecessary war, and we have been involved in such a war now for more than a year. . . . As a matter of fact, every purpose of the war has now failed. We are exactly where we were three years ago, and where we could have stayed."

On the heels of the Korean War came yet another opportunity to use force in Asia, but facing a divided Congress, President Dwight Eisenhower was hesitant to get involved. French requests for assistance in Indochina initially fell on sympathetic ears in the Eisenhower administration, which listed Indochina as an area of strategic importance in its "new look" defense policy. However, in January 1954, when the French asked for a commitment of U.S. troops, Eisenhower balked. The president stated that he "could conceive of no greater tragedy than for the United States to become involved in an all-out war in Indochina." His reluctance derived in part from the anticipated fight with Congress that he knew would arise over such a war. Even after his decision to provide modest technical assistance to France, in the form of B-26 bombers and air force technicians, congressional leaders demanded a personal meeting with the president to voice their disapproval. Soon afterward, Eisenhower promised to withdraw the air force personnel, replacing them with civilian contractors.

Eventually, the United States did become involved in a ground war in Asia, and it was that war that brought congressional opposition to the presidential use of force to a fever pitch. As the Vietnam War dragged on and casualties mounted, Congress and the public grew increasingly wary of the conflict and of the power delegated to the president in the 1964 Gulf of Tonkin resolution. In 1970, with upward of 350,000 U.S. troops in the field and the war spilling over into Cambodia, Congress formally repealed that resolution. And over the next several years, legislators enacted a series of appropriations bills intended to restrict the war's scope and duration. Then, in June 1973, after the Paris peace accords had been signed, Congress enacted a supplemental appropriations act that cut off all funding for additional military involvement in Southeast Asia, including in Cambodia, Laos, North Vietnam, and South Vietnam. Finally, when South Vietnam fell in 1975, Congress took the extraordinary step of formally forbidding U.S. troops from enforcing the Paris peace accords, despite the opposition of President Gerald Ford and Secretary of State Henry Kissinger.

Three years later, a Democratic Congress forbade the use of funds for a military action that was supported by the president—this time, the supply of covert aid to anticommunist forces in Angola. At the insistence of Senator Dick Clark (D-Iowa), the 1976 Defense Department appropriations act stipulated that no monies would be used "for any activities involving Angola other than intelligence gathering." Facing such staunch congressional opposition, President Ford suspended military assistance to Angola, unhappily noting that the Democratic-controlled Congress had "lost its guts" with regard to foreign policy.

In just one instance, the case of Lebanon in 1983, did Congress formally start the 60-day clock of the 1973 War Powers Act. Most scholars who call Congress to task for failing to fulfill its constitutional responsibilities make much of the fact that in this case it ended up authorizing the use of force for a full 18 months, far longer than the 60 days automatically allowed under the act. However, critics often overlook the fact that Congress simultaneously forbade the president from unilaterally altering the scope, target, or mission of the U.S. troops participating in the multinational peacekeeping force. Furthermore, Congress asserted its right to terminate the venture at any time with a one-chamber majority vote or a joint resolution and established firm reporting requirements as the U.S. presence in Lebanon continued.

During the 1980s, no foreign policy issue dominated congressional discussions more than aid to the contras in Nicaragua, rebel forces who sought to topple the leftist Sandinista regime. In 1984, a Democratic-controlled House enacted an appropriations bill that forbade President Ronald Reagan from supporting the contras. Reagan appeared undeterred. Rather than abandon the project, the administration instead diverted funds from Iranian arms sales to support the contras, establishing the basis for the most serious presidential scandal since Watergate. Absent congressional opposition on this issue, Reagan may well have intervened directly, or at least directed greater, more transparent aid to the rebels fighting the

Nicaraguan government.

Regardless of which party holds a majority of the seats in Congress, it is almost always the opposition party that creates the most trouble for a president intent on waging war. When, in the early 1990s, a UN humanitarian operation in Somalia devolved into urban warfare, filling nightly newscasts with scenes from Mogadishu, Congress swung into action. Despite previous declarations of public support for the president's actions, congressional Republicans and some Democrats passed a Department of Defense appropriations act in November 1993 that simultaneously authorized the use of force to protect UN units and required that U.S. forces be withdrawn by March 31, 1994.

A few years later, a Republican-controlled Congress took similar steps to restrict the use of funds for a humanitarian crisis occurring in Kosovo. One month after the March 1999 NATO air strikes against Serbia, the House passed a bill forbidding the use of Defense Department funds to introduce U.S. ground troops into the conflict without congressional authorization. When President Clinton requested funding for operations in the Balkans, Republicans in Congress (and some hawkish Democrats) seized on the opportunity to attach additional monies for unrelated defense programs, military personnel policies, aid to farmers, and hurricane relief and passed a supplemental appropriations bill that was considerably larger than the amount requested by the president. The mixed messages sent by the Republicans caught the attention of Clinton's Democratic allies. As House member Martin Frost (D-Tex.) noted, "I am at a loss to explain how the Republican Party can, on one hand, be so irresponsible as to abandon our troops in the midst of a military action to demonstrate its visceral hostility toward the commander in chief, and then, on the other, turn around and double his request for money for what they call 'Clinton's war.'" The 1999 debate is remarkably similar to the current wrangling over spending on Iraq.

LEGISLATING OPINION

The voice of Congress (or lack thereof) has had a profound impact on the media coverage of the current war in Iraq, just as it has colored public perceptions of U.S. foreign policy in the past. Indeed, Congress' ability to influence executive-branch decision-making extends far beyond its legislative and budgetary powers. Cutting funds, starting the war powers clock, or forcing troop withdrawals are the most extreme options available to them. More frequently, members of Congress make appeals designed to influence both media coverage and public opinion of a president's war. For example, Congress' vehement criticism of Reagan's decision to reflag Kuwaiti tankers during the Iran-Iraq War led to reporting requirements for the administration. Similarly, the Clinton administration's threats to invade Haiti in 1994 were met with resistance by Republicans and a handful of skeptical Democrats in Congress, who took to the airwaves to force Clinton to continually justify placing U.S. troops in harm's way.

Such appeals resonate widely. Many studies have shown that the media regularly follow official debates about war in Washington, adjusting their coverage to the scope of the discussion among the nation's political elite. And among the elite, members of Congress—through their own independent initiatives and through journalists' propensity to follow them—stand out as the single most potent source of dissent against the president. The sheer number of press releases and direct feeds that members of Congress produce is nothing short of breathtaking. And through carefully staged hearings, debates, and investigations, members deliberately shape the volume and content of the media's war coverage. The public posturing, turns of praise and condemnation, rapid-fire questioning, long-winded exhortations, pithy Shakespearean references, graphs, timelines, and pie charts that fill these highly scripted affairs are intended to focus media attention and thereby sway the national conversation surrounding questions of war and peace. Whether the media scrutinize every aspect of a proposed military venture or assume a more relaxed posture depends in part on Congress' willingness to take on the president.

Indeed, in the weeks preceding the October 2002 war authorization vote, the media paid a tremendous amount of attention to debates about Iraq inside the Beltway. Following the vote, however, coverage of Iraq dropped precipitously, despite continued domestic controversies, debates at the United Nations, continued efforts by the administration to rally public support, and grass-roots opposition to the war that featured large public protests. Congress helped set the agenda for public discussion, influencing both the volume and the tone of the coverage granted to an impending war, and Congress' silence after the authorization was paralleled by that of the press.

Crucially, congressional influence over the media extended to public opinion as well. An analysis of local television broadcast data and national public-opinion surveys from the period reveals a strong relationship between the type of media coverage and public opinion regarding the war. Even when accounting for factors such as the ideological tendencies of a media market (since liberal markets tend to have liberal voters and liberal media, while conservative districts have the opposite), we found that the airing of more critical viewpoints led to greater public disapproval of the proposed war, and more positive viewpoints buoyed support for the war. As Congress speaks, it would seem, the media report, and the public listens.

As these cases illustrate, the United States has a Congress with considerably more agenda-setting power than most analysts presume and a less independent press corps than many would like. As the National Journal columnist William Powers observed during the fall of 2006, "Journalists like to think they are reporting just the facts, straight and unaffected by circumstance." On the contrary, he recognized, news is a product of the contemporary political environment, and the way stories are framed and spun has little to do with the facts. In Washington, the party that controls Congress also determines the volume and the tone of the coverage given to a president's war. Anticipating a Democratic congressional sweep in

November 2006, Powers correctly predicted that "if Bush suffers a major political setback, the media will feel freed up to tear into this war as they have never done before."

CONGRESS CHECKS IN

With the nation standing at the precipice of new wars, it is vital that the American public understand the nature and extent of Congress' war powers and its members' partisan motivations for exercising or forsaking them. President Bush retains extraordinary institutional advantages over Congress, but with the Democrats now in control of both houses, the political costs of pursuing new wars (whether against Iran, North Korea, or any other country) and prosecuting ongoing ones have increased significantly.

Congress will continue to challenge the president's interpretation of the national interest. Justifications for future deployments will encounter more scrutiny and require more evidence. Questions of appropriate strategy and implementation will surface more quickly with threats of congressional hearings and investigations looming. Oversight hearings will proceed at a furious pace. Concerning Iraq, the Democrats will press the administration on a withdrawal timetable, hoping to use their agenda-setting power with the media to persuade enough Senate Republicans to defect and thereby secure the votes they need to close floor debate on the issue.

This fall, the Democrats will likely attempt to build even more momentum to end the war in Iraq, further limiting the president's menu of choices. This is not the first instance of heavy congressional involvement in foreign affairs and war, nor will it be the last. This fact has been lost on too many political commentators convinced that some combination of an eroding political identity, 9/11, failures of leadership, and dwindling political will have made Congress irrelevant to deliberations about foreign policy.

On the contrary, the new Democratic-controlled Congress is conforming to a tried-and-true pattern of partisan competition between the executive and legislative branches that has characterized Washington politics for the last half century and shows no signs of abating. Reports of Congress' death have been greatly exaggerated.

4

Checks and Balances:
The Supreme Court and the President's Executive Power

Editor's Introduction

In an article later collected in *The Federalist Papers*, James Madison, who would become the fourth president of the United States, argued that the three branches of government "should not be so far separated as to have no constitutional control over each other." This writing is widely credited with helping to establish the concept of judicial review, a power not explicitly granted to the Supreme Court by the Constitution. In its 1803 ruling in the case of *Marbury v. Madison*, the Supreme Court declared that it had the authority to overturn executive actions or laws it deemed unconstitutional. Today, this ruling establishing judicial review is viewed as consummating the system of checks and balances envisioned by the framers of the Constitution.

Designed to allow each branch of the federal government to serve as a restraining influence on the other two, this system of checks and balances has proven remarkably effective in the United States. Though the judicial arm of the federal government, headed by the Supreme Court, does not set the political agenda in the same way as the Congress or the president, its influence over the other two branches through judicial review often has far-reaching results. While all federal courts may judge the constitutionality of federal laws or executive actions, the Supreme Court has the final say, holding the authority to overrule or uphold lower-court rulings. For its decisions to be implemented, the Supreme Court usually relies on the other branches of the government. Occasionally individuals or localities defy Supreme Court rulings, as was the case following the court's 1954 decision in *Brown v. Board of Education* that desegregated public schools. In that case the Supreme Court's decision was enforced by the executive branch, most famously in 1957 when President Dwight D. Eisenhower deployed elements of the 101st Airborne and federalized the Arkansas National Guard to ensure that black students would be admitted to Little Rock High School.

Though dependent on the other two branches to carry out its decisions, the Supreme Court has on occasion checked the president and Congress when they were deemed to have exceeded their constitutional authority. In the 1930s Congress granted Franklin D. Roosevelt sweeping powers to help the country recover from the Great Depression, but a series of Supreme Court decisions struck down those laws, ruling that Congress had ceded its own constitutionally mandated authority to the president. During his presidency Richard Nixon frequently asserted executive privilege to avoid legislative oversight and invoked national security to expand his powers. When Nixon sought to suppress access to audio tapes made in the Oval Office pertaining to the Watergate criminal investigation, the Supreme Court unanimously declared that the president had exceeded his authority. Nixon subsequently handed over the tapes to investigators and resigned within weeks of the decision. Though other presidents since Nixon have asserted executive privilege, no president has ever again claimed it so broadly. A generation after the Watergate scandal, another American president, George W. Bush, is testing the limits of presidential authority in his administration's efforts to conduct the global war on terrorism.

The articles collected in this section provide an overview of how the Supreme Court limits executive power, both historically and as it pertains to the Bush Administration's handling of the war on terror. In "The Idea of America," Morghan Transue puts the issue of judicial review into historical context by describing the case of *Marbury v. Madison* in depth. Lincoln Caplan discusses the issue of expansive presidential power in "Who Cares About Executive Supremacy?" For *USA Today*, Joan Biskupic reports on the setbacks facing the Bush Administration after the Supreme Court limited the executive's wartime powers pertaining to the detention of two U.S. citizens who had been designated as "enemy combatants" and denied due process. In light of recent Supreme Court decisions, John O. McGinnis analyzes the administration's legal strategy in combatting international global terrorism in his article, "Executive Power in the War on Terror."

The Idea of America[*]

Marbury v. Madison and Checks and Balances

By Morghan Transue
Humanities, March/April 2003

In a nation established by peoples of differing languages, ethnicities, and religions, Americans find unity in the democratic principles of the founding fathers; principles that united the thirteen colonies after the American Revolution and continue to unite Americans during such crises as the attacks of September 11th. Fundamental doctrines associated with the Constitution are familiar to average Americans even today, two hundred years after its ratification. For example, Americans widely believe that governmental "checks and balances" safeguard American democracy by equalizing powers between the three branches of government: legislative, executive, and judicial. While most Americans probably remember how the first three articles of the Constitution address this point, many have no knowledge of the single most important event that elevated the federal judiciary to equal footing with Congress and the president: the case of *Marbury v. Madison*. Without this landmark Supreme Court case, the highest federal court would not have the power to render decisions substantial enough to change the face of American history.

During John Adams's presidency (1797–1801), his Federalist party began losing its strength to the ever-growing Republican party headed by Thomas Jefferson. As the election of 1800 came and went, the Federalists lost the presidency to Jefferson along with their congressional majority. Simultaneously, the Federalist lame-duck Congress passed the Judiciary Act of 1801 creating sixteen vacancies in federal judgeships and other judicial positions. Attempting to sustain the party, Adams appointed Federalists to these offices during his last day as president. These "midnight judges" never received their commissions because a new Republican Congress immediately repealed the Judiciary Act of 1801, destroying the

---

* Essay by Morghan Transue. Originally published as part of the National Endowment for the Humanities (NEH)'s "Idea of America" history essay contest.

positions. Jefferson therefore told Secretary of State James Madison not to deliver some commissions.

One "midnight judge," William Marbury, whom Adams had appointed as a justice of the peace for Washington, D.C., sued for his commission using the Judiciary Act of 1789.

Marbury requested that the Supreme Court give him a "writ of mandamus" (a court order requiring a specific action) that would force Madison to hand over the commission. Chief Justice John Marshall, a newly appointed Federalist justice, dismissed the case but went one step farther when writing the court's opinion. He argued that the portion of the Judiciary Act that allowed the Supreme Court to issue such writs was unconstitutional since the Constitution did not grant the judicial branch such authority. Therefore, any law including such writs was invalid. This decision, while avoiding a confrontation with the presidency over the writ's enforcement, set an important precedent for "judicial review," the Supreme Court's power as the final judge of a federal law's constitutionality. This authority raised the judiciary to a level equal to that of the legislative and executive branches, one able to check and balance the other two branches' power.

Americans need to remember the principle of checks and balances because without them, American democratic government would not survive. Checks and balances exist to ensure that one branch of government does not become too powerful. For example, if nothing restricts presidential power, the chief executive could become a dictator, commanding the military, vetoing laws not to his liking, and assigning overwhelming authority to executive agencies. An unchecked legislature could degenerate into "majority rule" with the potential to create laws that trample individual liberties or the welfare of less populated regions. An all-powerful judiciary could hand down cruel punishments that would be out of proportion to the crimes committed. To ensure that no government branch became too powerful, the founding fathers included explicit checks and balances in the Constitution so the legislative branch could restrain the executive branch and vice versa.

Article three governing the judicial branch however consists of only three small sections. The first describes the term of judicial appointments; the second, the cases it may accept; and the third, the terms of a treason case. Given these three sections, the judicial branch possessed little power over the other two branches. It therefore was considered the weakest branch of government. Before *Marbury v. Madison*, the Supreme Court had in fact never declared a law unconstitutional because the Constitution did not specifically provide this authority. Ironically, in denying the courts the additional writ authority and declaring the Judiciary Act of 1789 unconstitutional, Marshall gave the court the more important, implied constitutional authority of "judicial review," which was essential for effective checks and balances with the presidency and Congress.

Judicial review, a check, has had a large influence on American history. Foremost, it provided a nationally accepted process for individuals and states to oppose oppressive or unacceptable federal legislation without open rebellion or state nullification. In the Virginia and Kentucky Resolutions, nullification declared that a state could invalidate any federal law because the states comprised the national government. Nullification reached dangerous potential in 1833 when South Carolina nullified the tariff of 1828, almost provoking a civil war. If judicial review had not existed, such nullification controversies would have occurred much more often, leading to chaos, civil war, and the nation's ultimate collapse.

Many cases of judicial review involving individual civil rights have produced paramount effects on American society such as Southern desegregation in the 1950s. In 1896, the Supreme Court upheld Southern segregation in the *Plessy v. Ferguson* case, ruling that "separate but equal" facilities were constitutional under the fourteenth amendment. Fifty-eight years later in 1954, the Court reversed its earlier decision in the *Brown v. Board of Education of Topeka, Kansas* case. It decided that legislated segregation produced "inherently unequal" conditions in the schools, and therefore, segregation was unconstitutional. Without judicial review as a balance against state and federal legislatures and executives, African Americans might still face the oppressive Jim Crow voting laws and the humiliating segregation practices of previous decades.

Tragic events like the September 11th attacks may fragment Americans' lives and sense of security, but common principles pull us together into a unified nation. Checks and balances, a principle first established by the founding fathers, continues to support and safeguard our strong national government, which provides citizens security and aid in times of crisis. Without it, American liberties and ideals could be at the mercy of dictatorial presidents, majority rule, or cruel and irreversible judicial decisions. The possibility of continued segregation in the South, a military dictator, or an extensive list of capital offenses seems all too real. As a "check," judicial review exemplifies how the system has protected democracy and personal liberty against such terrors since its creation.

Without a strong system of constitutional checks and balances and the implied powers of judicial review from *Marbury v. Madison*, Americans today could not boast a truly free country.

Who Cares About Executive Supremacy?*

By Lincoln Caplan
The American Scholar, Winter 2008

The scope of presidential power is the most urgent—and fundamentally ignored—legal and political issue of our time

For more than a generation, the Watergate-tapes case stood for the principle that the Supreme Court has the last word in defining the reach of presidential power: Richard Nixon claimed that his power was unlimited, especially when it came to national security, and that his position gave him the privilege of refusing to turn over tape recordings made in the Oval Office. The Burger Court declared that, while the president of the United States is due "a high degree of respect," he isn't "above the law," and it unanimously ruled against him. Sixteen days later Nixon resigned in disgrace. The ruling illustrated a crucial purpose for the separation of powers, and for the checks and balances it was devised to provide.

The sweeping authority that Nixon claimed in theory, George W. Bush has acted on again and again. The preemptive attack on Iraq was the most visible of his presidency's actions resting on that claim—actions we can't fully count because so many have been undertaken in secret. This pattern has made the issues of presidential power and the separation of powers as important today as they have ever been. From 2003 through 2006, when the Republicans occupied the White House, controlled both houses of Congress, and held sway on the Supreme Court—and, really, since the administration came to power in 2001—there was little checking and balancing. Instead of ensuring that the executive branch was properly enforcing the law—holding meaningful hearings about Abu Ghraib, for example, or about the detention of enemy combatants—Congress often acted like an extension of the White House.

This year's resurgence of congressional oversight hearings after the Democrats gained control of both houses, especially those focusing on the Iraq war, the war on terrorism, and the upheaval at the Justice Department, has contributed to a loose consensus that our system is righting itself and operating as it's supposed

* Reprinted from *The American Scholar*, Volume 77, No. 1, Winter 2008. Copyright © 2007 by the author.

to. The 2006 Supreme Court ruling in *Hamdan v. Rumsfeld*, in which a five-to-three majority of justices rejected the plan of the Bush administration to try Guantána-mo detainees before military commissions, reinforced that consensus. The major-ity opinion of Justice John Paul Stevens in *Hamdan*—"The Executive is bound to comply with the Rule of Law that prevails in this jurisdiction," he asserted—was said to "demolish" the administration's arguments that the American crisis begin-ning on 9/11 requires the government to put aside ordinary legal rules.

The problem with that view is its emphasis on the design of government rather than on how the machinery actually works. By general agreement for the past half century at least, the Supreme Court has been granted the last word on what the Constitution means, including its meaning with reference to the president's power. But in reality, especially in "the domain of foreign affairs," as the legal scholar Cass Sunstein explained, "the central legal issues rarely come before the Court at all. The law is effectively settled within the executive branch, or by informal agree-ments between the president and Congress."

The so-called torture memo of August 2002, the best-known legal opinion of the Bush administration, was noteworthy because it justified the torture of pris-oners despite a statute outlawing the practice, but even more so because it made a far-reaching change to a little-known body of law that controls the president's obligations as well as his powers. Under the Judiciary Act of 1789, the attorney general is authorized to render legal opinions when asked for them by the presi-dent. Since 1950, this body of law has been made by the Justice Department's Of-fice of Legal Counsel (OLC). Beginning in 1977 its opinions have generally been published so that past findings can serve as precedents for future ones and so that the whole executive branch can have easy access to rulings by which it is bound.

For a generation, a fundamental debate carried on between Republican and Democratic OLCs concerns whether the separation of powers means that each branch has exclusive control of matters in its domain or whether the Constitution (as the legal scholars David Barron and Martin Lederman put it in a forthcom-ing article in the *Harvard Law Review*) generally gives Congress and the president "overlapping, or blended, powers, all of which are quite extensive, but none of which obviously serves as an absolute trump over the other." In 1996, during the Clinton administration, the OLC issued a legal opinion embracing the lat-ter judgment, which has been supported by the modern Supreme Court, most prominently in the opinion by Justice Robert Jackson in the landmark 1952 Steel Seizure case. "While the Constitution diffuses power the better to secure liberty," he wrote, "it also contemplates that practice will integrate the dispersed powers into a workable government. It enjoins upon its branches separateness but inter-dependence, autonomy but reciprocity."

On the other hand, in the Reagan administration and more notably in the George H. W. Bush administration, the OLC issued without fanfare opinions en-dorsing the view that each branch has exclusive control. They built on arguments about the president's inherent authority in foreign affairs that were articulated in an influential 1936 Supreme Court opinion by Justice George Sutherland in the case of *United States v. Curtiss-Wright Export Corp.* On grounds that Congress had left what it should have decided to the executive's "unfettered discretion," the company challenged an embargo proclaimed by the president against arms shipments to countries at war in South America. In rejecting the challenge, the Court held that the president had "plenary" powers in foreign affairs that didn't depend on congressional delegation. The Supreme Court hasn't recognized the scope of presidential power suggested by Sutherland. But his arguments were invoked to skirt restrictive laws passed by Congress in reaction to the Vietnam War; to justify undeclared wars, covert operations, and other divisive undertakings; and they laid the groundwork for the torture memo.

Even given the Reagan-Bush precedents, the view of presidential power asserted by the administration of George W. Bush stands out for the far-ness of its far-reaching scope: the Bush position is that the decisions of the president related to a war or national crisis are beyond the reach of statutory or court-made law, even if what he does is prohibited by Congress, the Supreme Court, or an international treaty signed and ratified by the United States. The presidential powers flowing from this position include going to war, detaining and interrogating prisoners, gathering information through electronic spying, and doing much more. When the administration, quailing from fiery criticism, replaced the torture memo with another saying it isn't lawful to torture prisoners, it didn't retract the first memo's stance on the scope of presidential power.

Thanks to articles this past October in *The New York Times*, we now know that in 2005, when the president said that he agreed with the bill that eventually outlawed "cruel, inhuman, and degrading" treatment of prisoners and a year after the Justice Department's revised legal opinion called such treatment "abhorrent," the department relied on its belief in the president's far-reaching authority to endorse the use of severe and relentless physical and psychological forms of interrogation: head slapping, simulated drowning, exposure to frigid temperatures. We know that, when the articles were published, the until-then-secret opinions laying out this view remained in effect. From the administration's viewpoint, according to the president himself, the opinions present sound law. Senator Arlen Specter, the Republican from Pennsylvania and ranking member of the Senate Judiciary Committee, called the opinions "shocking."

Since the Nixon era, one legal issue regularly debated in politics has been the scope of judicial power. Judicial review has been roundly attacked as undemocratic, based on the grounds that it undermines the freedom of the majority to govern. Recent legal thinking agrees that this concern has been overblown: scholars have shown that because judges are appointed by elected leaders who are subject to the pressures of politics and the scrutiny of public opinion, the leaders pick judges whose decisions generally track with the views of the majority. In addition, as recent legal history by William Michael Treanor documents, by the time of *Marbury v. Madison*, the 1803 super-precedent in which Chief Justice John Marshall first asserted for the Supreme Court the doctrine of judicial review, that power was exercised much more often than was previously recognized and courts "aggressively protected their power." This well-worn controversy about judicial power has led to extensive conversation on both sides about the role that the Supreme Court plays in our constitutional system. We know how to talk about rulings of the Court and its role in American governance. We come to pretty wide agreement about what is a respectable legal decision (*Hamdan v. Rumsfeld*) and what is a disgraceful political one (*Bush v. Gore*).

In contrast, the conversation about the law that the executive branch makes for itself takes place largely among a very small cadre of experts. In the wake of the uproar about the torture memo, a group of former OLC lawyers in Democratic administrations tried unsuccessfully to stir extensive talk by issuing a memo titled "Principles to Guide the Office of Legal Counsel." It summarized "longstanding practices" followed "across time and administrations," and made the case for the virtues of what they called "craftsmanship." The first principle was the most salient: "To fulfill this function appropriately, OLC must provide advice based on its best understanding of what the law requires. OLC should not simply provide an advocate's best defense of contemplated action that OLC actually believes is best viewed as unlawful." The unmistakable point was that the Bush OLC must have known its torture memo expressed a political, not a legal, judgment.

The principles memo didn't say that if the president and his administration don't subscribe to the interdependence/reciprocity view about the relationships among the branches, then the notion of the executive branch making law for itself is inconsistent with the tenets of checks and balances. But the thought is hard to dismiss, given how little executive-made law is reviewed by courts or appraised by Congress. If the president and his administration subscribe to the interdependence/reciprocity view, despite the lack of review and appraisal, then they are restrained by the view itself. It compels them to take account of the other branches' interests and to respect limits set in statutes and court rulings. If they don't subscribe to that view, though, they are effectively unchecked. The latest evidence is the Justice Department's secret opinions justifying the severe and relentless forms of interrogation that the president maintains are not torture—secret in the sense of hush-hush, because they are classified, and secret in the sense of deceitful, because they superseded an opinion expressly issued to give the opposite impression.

That thought about an unchecked executive branch relates to a more sweeping one developed in a provocative piece of recent scholarship about the separation of powers. Daryl Levinson and Richard Pildes in the June 2006 *Harvard Law Review* argue persuasively that the lack of competition between the branches during the Bush administration before this year was not a malfunction of the system; it was one piece of evidence among many that the system no longer works as it was intended. The Framers despised political parties, but it's the parties through which competition about ideas for governance now takes place. When the government is unified, with the same party controlling both elected branches as the Republicans did until last January, competition basically disappears.

If the scope of executive power were a burning topic of politics, the breakdown allowing the power to expand dramatically might not feel so momentous—whether you regard it as a breakdown in the American legal process or in the system of checks and balances. Among the current Democratic and Republican presidential candidates, however, none has attacked executive supremacy as forcefully as past candidates assailed judicial supremacy. None has made executive restraint a rallying cry. Torture, illegal surveillance, and other contentious practices of the Bush administration have drawn criticism from candidates of both parties, but not one of them has focused on the underlying problem.

The most urgent legal and political issue of our time might as well not exist. Since 9/11 our democracy has functioned like an autocracy. In making one significant choice after another, the Bush administration has repeatedly done what Nixon only threatened to. But this is a nonissue in the current presidential race. That is so even though what's at stake is a fundamental judgment about the nature of the presidency and, therefore, of the Republic.

High Court Limited Presidential Power[*]

By Joan Biskupic
USA Today, July 1, 2004

Since the Sept. 11 attacks, the United States' reputation as a guarantor of individual liberties has taken a series of hits.

The Bush administration's open-ended detentions of captives in the war on terrorism have been denounced worldwide, as have the president's moves to designate two U.S. citizens as "enemy combatants" and hold them incommunicado, without hearings.

In recent months, the abuse of Iraqis at Abu Ghraib prison near Baghdad has led critics to accuse the White House of flouting international laws that ban torture.

But during its annual term that ended this week, the U.S. Supreme Court offered several reminders that American democracy allows the court to protect civil liberties by limiting presidential power—even during wartime.

In the most closely watched cases of the term, the justices ruled that the president cannot indefinitely lock up foreign nationals and U.S. citizens without giving them a chance to show that they were wrongfully captured. The justices made clear that as the United States' leaders try to protect the nation from another terrorist attack, they should not abandon constitutional principles of freedom that have long made U.S. laws a model for other countries.

"It is during our most challenging and uncertain moments that our nation's commitment to due process is most severely tested," Justice Sandra Day O'Connor wrote as the court ruled that Yaser Hamdi—a U.S. citizen who was designated an enemy combatant after he was caught fighting with the Taliban in Afghanistan—has a right to be told why he is being held and should have a chance to make his case before a neutral judge.

The court also ruled that nearly 600 foreigners held incommunicado at the U.S. Naval Base at Guantánamo Bay, Cuba, may challenge their detentions in U.S. courts.

Overall, the justices tore apart President Bush's assertion that he had unfettered executive power to lock up the suspected al-Qaeda and Taliban operatives. Only one of the nine justices—Clarence Thomas, perhaps the court's most conservative member—fully agreed with the Bush administration's claim of unilateral power in the war on terrorism.

"The court was saying we need to maintain our status as a beacon to the world," says Washington lawyer Richard Klingler, a former law clerk to O'Connor.

"The court had two interests," he said. "It wanted to show that it was still independent and maintaining the ideals important to its prestige. But it also sought to enhance the country's standing overseas, which rests in part on how the judiciary protects the legal system and remains a bulwark of liberties."

In several other rulings during the term that began last fall, the justices clearly were focused on the basics of American democracy. In major cases concerning election law, the right to a jury trial, free speech and the meaning of the Pledge of Allegiance, their opinions were strewn with references to historic values, the democratic process and patriotism.

The justices in some cases indicated that they were concerned about how the United States might be perceived internationally.

In an opinion that criticized politicians' excessive manipulation of voting district boundaries, Justice Anthony Kennedy said that "the ordered working of our republic . . . depends on a sense of decorum and restraint in all branches of government."

He said the United States has an "interest in demonstrating to the world how democracy works."

CONCERNS ABOUT TORTURE

The court's rejection of unchecked presidential control comes at a difficult time for the Bush administration.

Polls indicate that public opposition to the war in Iraq is increasing, and declassified government memos have raised questions about how the administration's policies for aggressive interrogations might have set a tone that led to the mistreatment of Iraqis at Abu Ghraib and other facilities where the U.S. military is holding foreign prisoners.

Coincidentally, the first shocking pictures of abused Iraqis at Abu Ghraib were broadcast just a few hours after the justices had met on April 28 to hear arguments in cases involving Hamdi and Jose Padilla, a U.S. citizen who is suspected of plotting with al-Qaeda to blow up U.S. apartment buildings.

Both are designated as "enemy combatants," which under administration policy means they can be held indefinitely without being charged.

When a Justice Department lawyer said during oral arguments that the president should have broad authority to confine the men, several justices questioned why Hamdi and Padilla had not been granted a hearing so their cases could be reviewed. The justices also wondered what safeguards existed to prevent torture or other abuses.

In their opinions this week, the justices agreed that a post-9/11 congressional resolution had given Bush the power to detain enemy combatants indefinitely.

But they said that Hamdi should have a hearing, and their ruling could help guide the administration as it develops a process to review the Guantánamo detainees' cases. On a technicality, the justices declined to rule on Padilla's challenge to his detention; they said his attorney filed the claim in the wrong court jurisdiction.

The court's opinion in the Hamdi case did not mention Abu Ghraib, but "it is hard to believe that it did not affect the court and reinforce its view that unchecked power invites abuse," says Steven Shapiro, national legal director for the American Civil Liberties Union, which was among the groups that supported the challenges to the administration's terrorism policies.

David Rivkin, a Washington lawyer who worked in the Reagan and first Bush administrations, said the rulings should not be seen as a complete rebuke of the president.

"The court has fundamentally affirmed the legitimacy of the president's position that this is a real war," Rivkin said.

"The court has said, 'The president has formidable powers, but so do we.' This is constructive tension among the branches. This is an affirmation of the vigor of American democracy."

BASIC RIGHTS A COMMON THEME

Public attention has focused on the terrorism disputes, but the justices also used earlier rulings to stress the importance of individual rights and democracy.

By a 5–4 vote, the court upheld a federal overhaul of campaign-finance laws, endorsing Congress' goal of public confidence in elections. Justices referred to the "untoward consequences" of big-money contributors "for the democratic process." The McCain-Feingold law, named for its Senate sponsors, is aimed at limiting the influence of corporations and the wealthy on elections.

In a ruling hailed by defendants' rights advocates, the court said in a 5–4 decision that whenever a judge wants to increase a defendant's prison sentence beyond what is allowed under sentencing guidelines, a jury first must agree on the reasons for the increase beyond a reasonable doubt.

Dissenting justices warned that revising criminal sentencing rules to give jurors more responsibility will confound prosecutors, overburden juries, create chaos and squelch two decades of efforts by federal and state officials to have sentencing guidelines that make punishments more uniform.

On Tuesday, a federal judge in Utah ruled that the U.S. Sentencing Guidelines, which have been in effect for more than 15 years, are unconstitutional under the new court decision. In other cases nationwide, judges have begun to cut back defendants' sentences because of the ruling. Prosecutors, meanwhile, have sought to postpone indictments as they sort out how to meet the requirements of the Supreme Court decision.

Writing for the majority in the high court ruling, Justice Antonin Scalia reached back to the writings of John Adams and Thomas Jefferson to emphasize the importance of jurors—not a judge—deciding a defendant's fate.

In a case that reflected the emotions of tradition and patriotism during wartime, the justices examined whether the words "under God" in the Pledge of Allegiance were an unconstitutional government endorsement of religion. By reversing a lower court ruling, the justices kept the reference to God. But they did not resolve whether the practice of having students recite the Pledge amounts to religious indoctrination.

A five-justice majority said that Michael Newdow, the atheist father who brought the case against a California school district, lacked legal standing to sue because he did not have legal custody of his daughter, a student in the district. The court did not rule on the merits of his claim, but the majority's opinion was rife with patriotism.

Delivering the decision on June 14, Flag Day, Justice John Paul Stevens said the Pledge evolved from "public acknowledgement of the ideals that our flag symbolizes," and he referred to "our nation's indivisibility and commitment to the concept of liberty."

Executive Power in The War on Terror[*]

By John O. McGinnis
Policy Review, December 2007/January 2008

The Bush Administration's legal performance in the war on terror is much like its performance in the war in Iraq. In both cases it had plausible objectives but employed mistaken, often counterproductive and occasionally foolish strategy. The Bush administration itself has admitted mistakes in Iraq. But it is also important to describe the errors in its legal strategy to which it has not yet admitted so that future administrations will not suffer similar defeats in the courts of law and the courts of public opinion.

The errors in the Bush administration's legal strategy had common roots. One was an ideological focus on bolstering executive power and a consequent lack of pragmatic flexibility in choosing tactics that would maximize the chances of gaining public and judicial acceptance of its framework for detention, interrogation, and trial of terrorists as well as surveillance of individuals resident in America. The administration repeatedly failed to recognize that reliance on executive authority alone entailed a high risk of defeat at the hands of the Supreme Court.

Second, the administration radically underestimated the magnitude of the risk that the Court would curb the president's discretion, because it misunderstood the changed legal environment for litigation in the twenty-first century. Every aspect of American life has been increasingly subject to court-made rules. As a result of this trend, even discretion in the war on terror would likely be seen through the prism of legalism that applies to domestic criminal law. Moreover, foreign elites, particularly European elites, would seek to influence our judiciary so as to tie down what they regard as a dangerous hegemon.

The third systematic error was a failure to recognize that all administrations tend to lose power as they age, and wars run a high risk of exacerbating that loss as they become progressively less popular. Of course, the scandals at Abu Ghraib and the more general lack of success in Iraq could not have been predicted. But an administration's legal high command—and here I speak particularly of the White

House counsel and attorney general and not of mid-level attorneys on their staffs or those simply defending the policies in court—must choose strategies that take account of the worst possible outcomes.

As a result, the administration would have been well advised to take every step to bolster its legal position as early as practicable. It could have secured from Congress framework legislation for detention, military tribunals, surveillance, and perhaps even interrogation. Because citizens are generally most supportive of an administration at the beginning of a conflict (a phenomenon so well known among political scientists that is has been given the name "rally around the flag effect"), the terms of trade between the administration and Congress would likely have been favorable, even when the Senate was controlled briefly by the Democrats in late 2001 and 2002, not to mention in 2003 when Republicans took over both chambers and the United States was still savoring victory in Iraq. To be sure, nothing is certain in the legislative process, and deals would have had to be struck, but it seems almost certain the administration early on could have obtained legislation that would have met its strategic objectives. In this regard, the introduction of the Patriot Act is the paradigm the administration should have followed. It received overwhelming support in Congress for the new powers it sought. Its provisions have withstood judicial challenge, and the consensus support of the people's representatives has made its harsh critics seem politically isolated.

The consequences of eschewing Congress and relying on judicial vindication of executive power in court have been grave. Far from strengthening executive power, the administration's policies generated a series of Supreme Court defeats that have weakened it. These losses have contributed to a public perception that its policy for dealing with captured terrorists is in disarray and, still worse, that the United States is trenching on liberties as never before, when the reality is that the war in Iraq and the war on terror reduced domestic liberties less than earlier wars and even prisoners charged as war criminals had greater protections at trial than those charged previously.[1] The unnecessary reliance on executive power has also permitted foreign critics to claim that President Bush is a lone ranger, whereas legislative endorsement of specific policies would have underscored the reality that these policies reflect the consensus of the American people.

Of course, it may be argued that these recommendations suffer from hindsight bias. The administration was faced with a dangerous new kind of enemy after 9/11, one made all the more fearsome in an age of weapons of mass destruction, and the optimal tactics to use against such an enemy were unclear. But recommendations offered here do not depend on any argument that the administration misunderstood the enemy—rather, that it misunderstood both the historical patterns of executive branch strength and weaknesses and the modern realities of the judiciary.

Let me stress at the outset that the administration's errors were ones of prudence and judgment, not morality or ethics. The Bush administration's lawyers had to confront novel kinds of questions without a clear legal map. These errors do not make their service any less patriotic and admirable. Yet some critics have criticized the work of these lawyers as incompetent and unethical. Amnesty International has even called for investigation of administration lawyers as war criminals without any showing that these lawyers' arguments were made in bad faith or lacked a basis in law.[2] The translation of legitimate disputes about law into matters of ethics and criminal law threatens to cut off the legitimate debate by which law is made in a democratic and pluralist society.

GETTING SOME BIG THINGS RIGHT

Before analyzing the Bush administration's legal strategy on the war on terror, it is important to reject some lines of criticism made popular by its opponents. First, critics are wrong to suggest that terrorism requires only enhanced law enforcement rather than the use of war powers. Second, critics are also wrong to suggest that the United States is bound by international law even if that law is not incorporated into our domestic law.

First, the 9/11 attack on the United States was an act of war no less than Japan's attack on Pearl Harbor. Al Qaeda was a military organization that was attempting to harm and disrupt the United States as nation-state rather than simply harm individuals. As such, the action against it cannot be understood within a law enforcement paradigm, because that paradigm presupposes that the actors are within the bounds of civil society. Instead, al Qaeda and other Islamic terrorists act in a world that predates civil society, because between such strangers there is no common government responsible for law enforcement. Al Qaeda and its members are not part of our social compact and thus do not enjoy the rights that derive from it. Moreover, domestic criminal law is simply not adequate to deal with vast conspiracies that enjoy resources equivalent to those commanded by political entities rather than by a band of criminals.

Second, the administration should generally adhere to international law made binding domestically through the ratification of a treaty or incorporation into a statute. But when the critics of the Bush administration denounce it for violating international law, they do not confine themselves to complaints about international rules that have become domestic obligations. They complain, for instance, that Bush violated a norm of customary international law in invading Iraq or violated an interpretation of the United Nations Charter proclaimed by other nations or international bodies even if the United States has a different interpretation. They argue that the United States should follow interpretations of treaties made by international bodies and committees in treatment of enemy combatants.

The administration has no obligation to follow such norms. First, the Supremacy Clause of the United States Constitution makes only treaties and statutes the supreme law of the land. But it is more than a formal error for the United States to consider itself bound by international law unratified by the political branches. Such "raw" international law has a large democratic deficit.[3] It does not emerge from any democratic process but is instead shaped by unrepresentative elites in the form of international law professors or international jurists who sometimes hail from authoritarian nations.

Indeed, American law is not only likely better than unratified international law for Americans, but in many areas is also likely to aid foreigners. Because of the position of the United States as the dominant economic and military power in the international system, it has strong incentives to provide international public goods, such as appropriate detention of international terrorists, that benefit foreigners as well as Americans. Thus, the administration not only has been doing Americans a favor when it does not allow unratified international law to constrain the President's otherwise lawful discretion, but also has been doing a service for citizens around the world.

DETENTION

The United States faced three issues in adapting the war paradigm to hold prisoners of war captured in the war on terror. First, unlike conventional wars, prisoners taken in the war against al Qaeda and other organizations are generally not in uniform and sometimes do not in fact proclaim their allegiance to their organizations. Their uncertain and often opaque identity creates a greater risk that individuals will be captured in error. Second, the war against al Qaeda does not have as clear a stopping point as conventional wars, because conventional wars generally can be ended by capturing the enemy's territory or by peace negotiations. In particular, because these combatants are part of an irregular army and cannot be forced by their own domestic law to persist in or desist from fighting, their detention may extend long after their allegiance to the cause has dissipated.

The third difference affecting detention between conventional war and the war on terror is more general. The Bush administration should have realized that it would face a much more concerted legal effort to release these prisoners than would have been the case with respect to those captured in previous conventional wars. The precedents upon which the administration relied were generally from the World War II era. Yet since that time federal courts have constrained government discretion in running schools and prisons and ordered states to raise taxes. In 2000, they decided a presidential election. It is a short step to bringing more judicial regulation to war, particularly when that war is not conventional and may appear more closely related to law enforcement. Moreover, since that time the world has become smaller: Some of the justices of the Court have increasingly adopted a transnational perspective on constitutional jurisprudence—one that garners respect for the United States around the world and respect for themselves in their international networks of peer jurists.

In light of these potential problems, the Bush administration should have immediately acknowledged the differences that unconventional wars introduced into the legal framework for holding detainees and tempered the anomalies through the generous use of legal process, with military tribunals providing the initial process.

Because of the legal climate and the possibility that its war effort would become unpopular and thus more liable to legal attack, it should also have sought Congress's endorsement of these legal structures through framework legislation that would have supplemented the military process with review by Article III courts under a deferential standard.

Unfortunately, however, the Bush administration took a grudging approach to the granting of process and resorted to unilateral strategies that were easily portrayed as lawyers' tricks. For instance, at first the administration argued that it could rely on ex parte assessments by the executive branch to determine whether those caught on the battlefield were in fact enemy combatants, even if they were United States citizens. This was a mistake even as matter of theory, not to mention prudence. The key question determining whether the war or law enforcement paradigm should apply is whether the individual's action should be judged inside or outside our social compact. A citizen is within our social compact and should be treated within the war paradigm only if he has chosen to be an enemy combatant. He thus certainly deserves a more impartial and deliberate process to challenge his status before being treated as outside the pale.

Thus, there was a substantial risk that the Court would hold, as it did in *Hamdi v. Rumsfeld*, that an American citizen had a right to a more impartial process to challenge his designation as an enemy combatant.[4] Indeed, in *Hamdi* only a single justice, Justice Clarence Thomas, would have automatically deferred to the executive's determination on Hamdi's combatant status.

While the Court directly resolved only the question of a United States citizen's due process rights, the Bush administration should have extended this right at the outset to noncitizens as well. By showing it was scrupulous in taking care not to have incorrectly detained noncombatants, the administration could have forestalled criticism and showed that its regime was not lawless, but carefully considered. Even more important, the more internal process it gave on such key issues, the less likely the Supreme Court would hold that individuals had full rights to habeas corpus. Some swing Justices, like Stephen Breyer, care about preventing errors and are not much concerned about the rubric under which that error correction occurred. In *Hamdi* itself, the Court indicated that the military tribunals, at least in the first instance, might provide sufficient process for a challenge to enemy combatant status.

For similar reasons, the administration from the outset should have publicly provided a process for determining when individuals were no longer substantial threats or could provide substantial information. Because members of al Qaeda are irregular enemy combatants, not common criminals, the United States cannot be put to the choice of trying these detainees and releasing them to the battlefield to fight again. But their irregular nature makes it less clear that they will fight again: No territorial power can compel them. A process for reviewing their dangerousness and information value might even have given detainees incentives to rethink their commitment to jihad and consider how they could make concrete commitments to show that they would not go back to the fight.

Whatever the administration did, however, lawyers in the United States were going to file lawsuits on behalf of the prisoners seeking more and better process and rights indistinguishable from Americans accused of crimes. The basic response of the administration to this prospect was to keep detainees at Guantánamo. Because Guantánamo is not part of the United States and yet is controlled by it, these legal strategists believed it was the perfect place to hold the prisoners more easily than they could in foreign territory and yet be immune from the reach of United States courts. To split metaphysical sovereignty from control was extremely clever, but it was clearly vulnerable to attack as a legal fiction. Although the Supreme Court a half-century ago refused jurisdiction over habeas claims in a case that arose in allied-occupied Germany, such precedent cannot be relied on to hold up when translated to a new context in a high-profile case like this one. Thus, the Supreme Court's decision in *Bush v. Rasul*,[5] in which it insisted on taking jurisdiction of habeas cases at Guantánamo, should have been seen as a substantial risk.[6]

It is the Bush administration's legal strategy that in large measure has made Guantánamo a symbol of lawlessness in the administration's war on terror. Its creation at least in part for strategic litigation advantage suggests to the outside world that the United States was playing legal games rather than following principles of law. And because the administration was making these decisions without legislative input, it could be portrayed as eccentric and malevolent rather than a faithful agent of the American people.

Instead of resorting to a legal sleight of hand, the administration should have gone to Congress to bolster its case. If Congress had from the beginning endorsed the framework for holding detainees outlined above, the Court would have been unlikely to disturb this settlement. The reasons for such deference are both doctrinal and practical. As a doctrinal matter the Court gives substantial deference to Congress's weighing of the costs and benefits of various procedures. In a recent book, Professor Eric Posner and Adrian Vermeule suggest that the Court should give this kind of deference to the executive in cases concerning terrorism because the Court's institutional competence in devising responses to terrorism is much less than that of the executive.[7] But the executive may not have the appropriate incentives to make the trade-off between liberty and security. It is more likely to discount all liberty interests because of its recognition that the greatest risks to its political standing come from a lapse in security, however improbable the cause, rather than from complaints about liberties foregone.

More important from a strategic perspective, whatever degree of deference the Court should give to the executive as a matter of normative principle, as a matter of realpolitik the Court is much more reluctant to disturb the judgment endorsed by Congress as well as the president. Such action would fly much more clearly in the face of the popular will.

Moreover, such a framework statute would also have permitted the United States to hold these prisoners, as they did German prisoners and other previous captives, in the United States, thus dispensing with the negative symbolism of a place that can easily be portrayed as a legal netherworld. It may be argued that the administration still needed a jurisdiction outside the territorial United States to make prisoners' habeas petitions less likely to succeed. The construal of rights protected by habeas, however, has been historically flexible and context dependent. If the courts were satisfied that the prisoners were getting the amount of process that Congress judged reasonable for enemy prisoners, it would be unlikely to require substantive changes.

The ready availability of a congressional solution raises the question of why it was not sought. One explanation is that the administration thought that using Congress would detract from its project of using the crisis to bolster executive authority. In particular, Vice President Cheney, who had seen the decline of executive authority occasioned by Watergate and Vietnam, has spoken out frequently of the need to restore executive power. This strategy, however, was imprudent.

First, it was not likely to succeed. The Supreme Court had only two consistent supporters of executive power—Justices Scalia and Thomas. Even Chief Justice Rehnquist, who had worked in the Office of Legal Counsel, an office dedicated to preserving executive power, had ruled against the executive in such important cases as that concerning the Independent Counsel Act[8] and had celebrated the Court's curbing of executive overreaching in Youngstown.[9]

Second, it is a mistake to risk substantial harm to an important policy in order to build up precedents for an undefined future eventuality. The interpretation of executive power has waxed and waned over the course of American history, dependent largely on justices' reaction to the felt necessities of the time and the constellation of political power in Congress and in the nation. Even had the Bush administration won a victory for the executive branch in the context of detention, it would be distinguished away if future justices believe that circumstances warrant.

INTERROGATION METHODS

Once again the administration had serious issues to address in determining the interrogation methods to be used on those detained. On the one hand, any administration should have wanted to be able to use interrogation methods that would elicit information to stop attacks on the order of 9/11. On the other hand, any administration should have been eager to show that the United States acted humanely with respect to even egregious wrongdoers and in particular followed the strictures of the Torture Convention. Restraint and adherence to our own laws underscores the attractiveness of our civilization in the global battle of ideas against radical Islam. This American tradition goes back to the Revolutionary War when George Washington insisted that the American army take prisoners even after Hessians slaughtered his soldiers without quarter at Fort Washington.

That balance might have been best struck, again, by going to Congress and seeking framework legislation. Congress should and would have authorized the administration to use harsh interrogation methods short of torture in the circumstances where such methods were necessary to get information to forestall attacks. A system requiring personal and recorded authorization by a Cabinet official in specific cases would provide substantial safeguards that these methods would be used only selectively and where necessary. To be sure, such congressional deliberation would have been a messy process and would have publicized the administration's methods when secrecy could itself have value by making it harder for the enemy to prepare for questioning. But nothing on a matter so controversial is kept secret long in Washington, and when Congress set limits to the administration's interrogation process as it did in 2006, it was also a messy process. The debate that Congress could have provided at the outset would have helped educate the world to the reasons that such interrogations were needed in the interest of the safety not only of the United States but of other nations that were threatened by the mass slaughter of modern terrorism.

But whether or not the administration chose to go to Congress to reinforce the legality of its interrogations methods, it could hardly have chosen a worse strategy than it pursued. In a memo written to Alberto Gonzales on August 1, 2002, the Office of Legal Counsel provided a general interpretation of the Torture Convention by limiting the concept of torture to the infliction of physical pain "equivalent in intensity to the pain accompanying serious physical injury such as organ failure or impairment of bodily function."[10] According to the memo, the only psychological harm that amounted to torture would be that "leading to significant duration, e.g. lasting months or even years." Finally, the memo concludes that the president has the constitutional authority to set even those strictures aside if they impair his ability to order interrogations pursuant to his authority as commander in chief.

It is not my purpose here to dispute these conclusions as legal matters, but to show that whatever its correctness, the memo was utterly counterproductive and should have been seen as such at the time. Indeed, my strongest reaction as a former official at the Office of Legal Counsel was not that of other observers who attacked the legal analysis or even the morality of the memorandum. Instead I saw it as a bureaucratic blunder committed not so much by the attorneys at OLC but by the White House counsel and others in the administration who asked for this kind of analysis.

First, to anyone who has worked in the collaborative process of the executive branch, it was clear that this memo would be leaked, and leaked at the most inconvenient time to the administration. One rule I had at the Office of Legal Counsel was to consider how the phrasing and framing of a memo I wrote would look on the first page of the *Washington Post*. From this persective, it should have been clear that the abstract analysis and sweeping language in both its statutory and its constitutional analysis would allow opponents of the administration to paint the memo as radical and unbounded, undermining support for harsh interrogation tactics as well as the administration's general legal credibility.

Assuming that the administration chose not to obtain a framework authorization statute from Congress, a far better way to achieve the administration's objectives would have been to catalogue the kind of interrogation methods the administration actually wanted to use and explain in some detail why those methods would not amount to torture. This memo would have been a far more limited and less controversial opinion, although some would still have disagreed with its analysis. It should also have omitted the unnecessary claim that the president could in some circumstances disregard the convention.[11] This sweeping claim seems to have been motivated by an interest in restoring general executive branch authority. But it is fanciful to believe that unilateral declarations by the executive branch can accomplish this goal. And by putting that expansion of executive power in the context of what seemed to be an almost limitless power to torture detainees, the memo set back the cause it was trying to promote.

WAR CRIMES TRIALS

The administration once again had legitimate objectives in establishing military tribunals to prosecute some of the detainees for war crimes. It wanted to bring those who violated the laws of war to justice and deter subsequent violations. But it did not want to use the Article III court system and all its protection. To do so would in some cases have exposed national security information. More fundamentally, our trial system would have taken a very long time and provided a panoply of rights which, however important to protect individual liberties within civil society, should not be extended to irregular combatants outside the social compact. Swift military justice is part of the necessary shock and awe against war criminals.

So far, however, the administration has succeeded in conducting only one war crimes trial. One reason for the delay was that the administration's first set of rules for conducting the trials faced such vigorous criticism that they were sent for revisions. Even after revision, many military lawyers within the administration objected to some of the provisions, creating a kind of bureaucratic inertia that delayed indictments. But the most important reason for delay was the war criminal defendants' successes in the lengthy constitutional litigation over the procedures. In *Hamdan v. Rumsfeld* the Court held that some of the administration's procedures violated the Uniform Code of Military Justice as well as Article III of the Geneva Convention which, according to the Court, Congress had made applicable to military tribunals.

This signal defeat was quite possibly related to previous mistakes in legal strategy. Strikingly, the Court gave no deference to the administration's interpretation of either the Uniform Code of Military Justice or Article III of the Geneva Convention, despite precedent for deferring to the executive's interpretations of treaties and statutes governing the military. Whatever the doctrinal categories of deference, the general credibility of executive branch positions will hugely influence the actual degree of deference the Court applies. This credibility was damaged by previous administration legal analysis, like that contained in the memo on interrogations, which the administration itself later repudiated.

In *Hamdan* itself, Justice Breyer noted that the president could "return to Congress to seek the authorization he believes necessary." Of course, the president would not have had to return to Congress and would not have faced substantial bureaucratic foot-dragging had he sought congressional authorization for the military tribunals in the first place. The administration almost certainly would have been successful, because even after the Supreme Court defeat in *Hamdan*, it got most of the procedures previously proclaimed unilaterally with some exceptions, including restrictions on use of hearsay and classified information. But the president was in a stronger political position in 2003 and probably even in 2001 than at the end of 2006.

It could be argued that the administration's ability to get most of what it wanted by Congress vindicated its strategy to try first to avoid congressional action. But the administration would probably have gotten a better deal if it had gone to Congress before its Supreme Court defeat. It could have sought authority for trials of war criminals while holding out the prospect of going it alone if Congress refused. And it would have avoided the delay in trials caused by the Supreme Court defeat. The legal strategy with respect to war crimes was not the worst aspect of the administration's performance, but it still cannot be counted a success.

SURVEILLANCE

The Bush administration also had a choice about whether to obtain express authorization to undertake surveillance of individuals in the United States who were in contact with those in or near the battlefields of terrorism. It decided to rely instead on the president's authority as commander in chief and the general authority of the statute that authorized the administration to undertake military actions against the terrorist organizations.

It was a mistake not to obtain express congressional authorization for surveillance when it could easily have been obtained. Indeed, it may have run more substantial risks to rely on executive authority in this regard than in the area of detentions and interrogations. First, Congress here had already passed framework legislation in the Foreign Intelligence Surveillance Act (FISA), which regulated the authority of the executive to wiretap individuals resident in the United States. That legislation by its terms appears inconsistent with the authority exercised by the administration because it requires warrants, which the administration has not sought. It appears to contemplate its applicability in time of war, because it provided additional time to obtain such warrants in wartime. Second, because the surveillance being undertaken was of residents in the United States, there was an even greater risk that courts would not extend precedent to protect executive discretion in this new kind of war.

WASTING ASSETS

The Bush administration's legal strategy in the war on terror has been deeply flawed. Because of its interest in establishing powerful precedent in favor of executive powers, it took bold positions that carried substantial risks of judicial repudiation and failed to obtain legislative endorsement at times of political opportunity. As a result, the Supreme Court said on two occasions that the president was acting illegally, confirming an impression that he was a rogue operator outside established law and popular opinion. The lesson for future administrations seems clear. First, recognize that we live in a time of much more activist courts even in the era of foreign affairs. That fact may be bemoaned, but it cannot be ignored, and the reality of their possible interventions must be factored into strategy from the outset. Second, rely more on Congress than on courts, particularly when the president enjoys support in the initial states of conflict or his party controls Congress.

It is the executive power to persuade from a position of strength rather than formal legal powers that is the president's greatest asset. But it is generally a wasting asset, and the president should therefore translate it into more lasting legislative tools before its dissipation. The president has suffered reverses in the war in Iraq because he did not call in enough troops after the fall of Baghdad. He has had substantial losses in his legal wars because he did not call on citizens through their representatives to rally around a new, but carefully circumscribed, system of wartime detention and surveillance.

FOOTNOTES

1 This point is ably made in Jack Goldsmith and Cass Sunstein, "Military Tribunals and Legal Culture: What a Difference Sixty Years Makes," *Constitutional Commentary* 19:261 (2003).

2 David McGowan of the University of San Diego has superbly discussed these issues in depth in his recent article, "Decency, Due Care, and Lawyering in the War on Terror," San Diego Legal Studies Paper No. 07-96. Available at SSRN: http://papers.ssrn.com/sol3/papers.cfm?abstract_id=975124.

3 Ilya Somin and I have just described in far more detail the huge democratic deficit that besets international law. See John O. McGinnis and Ilya Somin, "Should International Law be Part of Our Law?" *Stanford Law Review* 59:1175 (2007).

4 *Hamdi v. Rumsfeld*, 542. U.S. 507 (2004).

5 542 U.S. 466 (2004).

6 In fact, two mid-level lawyers warned that the litigation risk was at least not insubstantial. See Memorandum for William B. Haynes, General Counsel, Department of Defense, from Patrick C. Philbin and John C. Yoo, Deputy Attorneys General, Office of Legal Counsel, Re: Possible Habeas Jurisdiction over Aliens Held in Guantánamo Bay, Cuba (December 28, 2001).

7 Eric Posner and Adrian Vermeule, *Terror in the Balance* (Oxford University Press, 2006).

8 *Morrison v. Olson*, 487 U.S. 654 (1988).

9 William Rehnquist, *The Supreme Court: How It Is, How It Was* (1988)

10 See Memorandum for Alberto Gonzales, Counsel to the President, from Jay Bybee, Acting Assistant Attorney General, Office of Legal Counsel, Re: Standards for Interrogation under 18 U.S.C. 2340-2340A (August 1, 2002).

11 In fact, a subsequent memo from the Office of Legal Counsel revoking the 2002 memo expressly stated that is was unnecessary to reach the issue of the president's constitutional authority. See Memorandum for the Deputy Attorney General from Daniel Levin, Acting Assistant Attorney General, Office of Legal Counsel, Re: Legal Standards Applicable under 18 U.S.C. 2340-2340A (December 30, 2004).

5

Too Early to Tell?
The Legacy of George W. Bush

Editor's Introduction

Whatever his legacy, nothing about George W. Bush's tenure as president has been ordinary. He came to office under unusual circumstances, having lost the popular vote by a whisker to Vice President Al Gore. He claimed the victory only after a deeply divided Supreme Court ruled in his favor, upholding his razor-thin and disputed plurality of votes in Florida, which decisively tipped the Electoral College math his way. Understandably, the extended campaign season generated intense passions on both sides, and the Supreme Court ruling did little to heal the divisions that had developed. In the end many of Gore's backers felt their candidate had been cheated of his rightful due, while numerous Bush supporters believed an attempt to steal the presidency had been narrowly averted. The strength of these emotions foreshadowed the powerful and divergent feelings the president would evoke throughout his presidency.

Undaunted by his controversial election, Bush forged ahead with an ambitious agenda, sponsoring large tax cuts, crafting a federal policy on stem-cell research, instituting his No Child Left Behind education initiative, and responding to a diplomatic crisis with China over detained American service members.

Then, on September 11, 2001, his presidency, the nation, and the world were transformed as the brutal terrorist attacks ushered in a new era in global and domestic affairs. Issues that had previously divided the country dissipated into insignificance as the nation, and much of the world, rallied behind the president. In pursuit of Al Qaeda, Bush ordered the invasion of Afghanistan, and the Taliban regime, which had provided sanctuary to Osama bin Laden and his terrorist organization, soon fell.

With the Taliban removed, the Bush administration shifted its attention to Saddam Hussein and Iraq. Citing Hussein's past aggression against his neighbors, his pursuit and use of weapons of mass destruction, and a belief that overthrowing the dictator would usher in a new, democratic era in the Middle East, among other reasons, Bush ordered the troops into combat. While Hussein was quickly toppled and eventually executed, the aftermath of the invasion proved more complicated than anticipated and remains so, over five years later. Public opinion, which had in large measure supported the initial invasion, has shifted in the face of over 4,000 American dead, hundreds of billions of dollars in costs, the failure to find weapons of mass destruction, the Abu Ghraib prisoner-abuse scandal, and a host of other setbacks. Nevertheless, the security situation has improved significantly of late, following the president's "surge" initiative, which increased troop strength and adjusted tactics on the ground. Though the divisions brought about by the war show few signs of abating, both sides agree that whatever the outcome, Bush's legacy will largely be determined by developments in Iraq.

Domestically, the president's record remains open to interpretation, depending on one's partisan vantage point and to what degree one attributes the performance of the national economy to an administration's policies. Currently, with the economy sputtering, gas prices soaring to new heights, health-care costs skyrocketing, the mortgage crisis leading to unprecedented foreclosure rates, and a ballooning national debt, Bush's economic record might seem wanting to some. However, his supporters argue that without his tax cuts, the state of the economy could be much worse, and point to both the No Child Left Behind Act and his Medicare prescription drug benefit plan as important domestic achievements, though these programs too have been characterized as boondoggles in certain quarters.

The aftermath of Hurricane Katrina is also likely to shape how the president is viewed by future generations. When New Orleans, a major American city and cultural mecca, was nearly destroyed by massive flooding, many found the administration's response lacking. Still others laid the blame for the debacle on the city's Democratic mayor and the state's Democratic governor.

As the George W. Bush administration draws to a close, the articles in this chapter consider the president's place in history. Whatever the final judgment, one aspect of the president's legacy—perhaps the only aspect on which everyone can agree—is the intense and divisive emotions he evokes. The pieces that follow reflect the profound feelings he has elicited among supporters and detractors alike.

In the first piece, "Reckoning: The Economic Consequences of Mr. Bush, Joseph E. Stiglitz details what he sees as the president's brazen fiscal irresponsibility. Upon taking office, President Bush was bequeathed a budget surplus. But now, under his watch, according to Stiglitz, "we have become dependent on other nations for the financing of our own debt." Stiglitz also takes aim at the president's Iraq policy, the financial cost of which he believes could run into the trillions. "Some portion of the damage done by the Bush administration could be rectified quickly," Stiglitz concludes, "A large portion will take decades to fix."

David Gelernter offers a rousing defense of the president in "Bush's Greatness: There's a Good Reason He Infuriates the Reactionary Left." Denouncing the president's critics, Gelernter describes their enmity towards him as a form of "racist" hatred and compares their opposition to the president's Iraq policy to standing by and doing nothing while someone is murdered.

In "HNN Poll: 61% of Historians Rate Bush Presidency Worst," Robert S. McElvaine reports on an informal and unscientific poll of historians sponsored by the *History News Network* in which Bush was ranked dead last among all U.S. presidents. Joan Swirsky counters with her piece, "The Stellar Legacy of President George W. Bush," in which she lauds the president as a courageous and visionary leader.

Reckoning[*]

The Economic Consequences of Mr. Bush

By Joseph E. Stiglitz
Vanity Fair, December 2007

When we look back someday at the catastrophe that was the Bush administration, we will think of many things: the tragedy of the Iraq war, the shame of Guantánamo and Abu Ghraib, the erosion of civil liberties. The damage done to the American economy does not make front-page headlines every day, but the repercussions will be felt beyond the lifetime of anyone reading this page.

I can hear an irritated counterthrust already. The president has not driven the United States into a recession during his almost seven years in office. Unemployment stands at a respectable 4.6 percent. Well, fine. But the other side of the ledger groans with distress: a tax code that has become hideously biased in favor of the rich; a national debt that will probably have grown 70 percent by the time this president leaves Washington; a swelling cascade of mortgage defaults; a record near-$850 billion trade deficit; oil prices that are higher than they have ever been; and a dollar so weak that for an American to buy a cup of coffee in London or Paris—or even the Yukon—becomes a venture in high finance.

And it gets worse. After almost seven years of this president, the United States is less prepared than ever to face the future. We have not been educating enough engineers and scientists, people with the skills we will need to compete with China and India. We have not been investing in the kinds of basic research that made us the technological powerhouse of the late 20th century. And although the president now understands—or so he says—that we must begin to wean ourselves from oil and coal, we have on his watch become more deeply dependent on both.

Up to now, the conventional wisdom has been that Herbert Hoover, whose policies aggravated the Great Depression, is the odds-on claimant for the mantle "worst president" when it comes to stewardship of the American economy. Once

Franklin Roosevelt assumed office and reversed Hoover's policies, the country began to recover. The economic effects of Bush's presidency are more insidious than those of Hoover, harder to reverse, and likely to be longer-lasting. There is no threat of America's being displaced from its position as the world's richest economy. But our grandchildren will still be living with, and struggling with, the economic consequences of Mr. Bush.

REMEMBER THE SURPLUS?

The world was a very different place, economically speaking, when George W. Bush took office, in January 2001. During the Roaring 90s, many had believed that the Internet would transform everything. Productivity gains, which had averaged about 1.5 percent a year from the early 1970s through the early 90s, now approached 3 percent. During Bill Clinton's second term, gains in manufacturing productivity sometimes even surpassed 6 percent. The Federal Reserve chairman, Alan Greenspan, spoke of a New Economy marked by continued productivity gains as the Internet buried the old ways of doing business. Others went so far as to predict an end to the business cycle. Greenspan worried aloud about how he'd ever be able to manage monetary policy once the nation's debt was fully paid off.

This tremendous confidence took the Dow Jones index higher and higher. The rich did well, but so did the not-so-rich and even the downright poor. The Clinton years were not an economic Nirvana; as chairman of the president's Council of Economic Advisers during part of this time, I'm all too aware of mistakes and lost opportunities. The global-trade agreements we pushed through were often unfair to developing countries. We should have invested more in infrastructure, tightened regulation of the securities markets, and taken additional steps to promote energy conservation. We fell short because of politics and lack of money—and also, frankly, because special interests sometimes shaped the agenda more than they should have. But these boom years were the first time since Jimmy Carter that the deficit was under control. And they were the first time since the 1970s that incomes at the bottom grew faster than those at the top—a benchmark worth celebrating.

By the time George W. Bush was sworn in, parts of this bright picture had begun to dim. The tech boom was over. The nasdaq fell 15 percent in the single month of April 2000, and no one knew for sure what effect the collapse of the Internet bubble would have on the real economy. It was a moment ripe for Keynesian economics, a time to prime the pump by spending more money on education, technology, and infrastructure—all of which America desperately needed, and still does, but which the Clinton administration had postponed in its relentless drive to eliminate the deficit. Bill Clinton had left President Bush in an ideal position to pursue such policies. Remember the presidential debates in 2000 between Al Gore and George Bush, and how the two men argued over how to spend America's anticipated $2.2 trillion budget surplus? The country could well have afforded to ramp up domestic investment in key areas. In fact, doing so would have staved off recession in the short run while spurring growth in the long run.

But the Bush administration had its own ideas. The first major economic initiative pursued by the president was a massive tax cut for the rich, enacted in June of 2001. Those with incomes over a million got a tax cut of $18,000—more than 30 times larger than the cut received by the average American. The inequities were compounded by a second tax cut, in 2003, this one skewed even more heavily toward the rich. Together these tax cuts, when fully implemented and if made permanent, mean that in 2012 the average reduction for an American in the bottom 20 percent will be a scant $45, while those with incomes of more than $1 million will see their tax bills reduced by an average of $162,000.

The administration crows that the economy grew—by some 16 percent—during its first six years, but the growth helped mainly people who had no need of any help, and failed to help those who need plenty. A rising tide lifted all yachts. Inequality is now widening in America, and at a rate not seen in three-quarters of a century. A young male in his 30s today has an income, adjusted for inflation, that is 12 percent less than what his father was making 30 years ago. Some 5.3 million more Americans are living in poverty now than were living in poverty when Bush became president. America's class structure may not have arrived there yet, but it's heading in the direction of Brazil's and Mexico's.

THE BANKRUPTCY BOOM

In breathtaking disregard for the most basic rules of fiscal propriety, the administration continued to cut taxes even as it undertook expensive new spending programs and embarked on a financially ruinous "war of choice" in Iraq. A budget surplus of 2.4 percent of gross domestic product (G.D.P.), which greeted Bush as he took office, turned into a deficit of 3.6 percent in the space of four years. The United States had not experienced a turnaround of this magnitude since the global crisis of World War II.

Agricultural subsidies were doubled between 2002 and 2005. Tax expenditures—the vast system of subsidies and preferences hidden in the tax code—increased more than a quarter. Tax breaks for the president's friends in the oil-and-gas industry increased by billions and billions of dollars. Yes, in the five years after 9/11, defense expenditures did increase (by some 70 percent), though much of the growth wasn't helping to fight the War on Terror at all, but was being lost or outsourced in failed missions in Iraq. Meanwhile, other funds continued to be spent on the usual high-tech gimcrackery—weapons that don't work, for enemies we don't have. In a nutshell, money was being spent everyplace except where it was needed. During these past seven years the percentage of G.D.P. spent on research and development outside defense and health has fallen. Little has been done about our decaying infrastructure—be it levees in New Orleans or bridges in Minneapolis. Coping with most of the damage will fall to the next occupant of the White House.

Although it railed against entitlement programs for the needy, the administration enacted the largest increase in entitlements in four decades—the poorly designed Medicare prescription-drug benefit, intended as both an election-season bribe and a sop to the pharmaceutical industry. As internal documents later revealed, the true cost of the measure was hidden from Congress. Meanwhile, the pharmaceutical companies received special favors. To access the new benefits, elderly patients couldn't opt to buy cheaper medications from Canada or other countries. The law also prohibited the U.S. government, the largest single buyer of prescription drugs, from negotiating with drug manufacturers to keep costs down. As a result, American consumers pay far more for medications than people elsewhere in the developed world.

You'll still hear some—and, loudly, the president himself—argue that the administration's tax cuts were meant to stimulate the economy, but this was never true. The bang for the buck—the amount of stimulus per dollar of deficit—was astonishingly low. Therefore, the job of economic stimulation fell to the Federal Reserve Board, which stepped on the accelerator in a historically unprecedented way, driving interest rates down to 1 percent. In real terms, taking inflation into account, interest rates actually dropped to negative 2 percent. The predictable result was a consumer spending spree. Looked at another way, Bush's own fiscal irresponsibility fostered irresponsibility in everyone else. Credit was shoveled out the door, and subprime mortgages were made available to anyone this side of life support. Credit-card debt mounted to a whopping $900 billion by the summer of 2007. "Qualified at birth" became the drunken slogan of the Bush era. American households took advantage of the low interest rates, signed up for new mortgages with "teaser" initial rates, and went to town on the proceeds.

All of this spending made the economy look better for a while; the president could (and did) boast about the economic statistics. But the consequences for many families would become apparent within a few years, when interest rates rose and mortgages proved impossible to repay. The president undoubtedly hoped the reckoning would come sometime after 2008. It arrived 18 months early. As many as 1.7 million Americans are expected to lose their homes in the months ahead. For many, this will mean the beginning of a downward spiral into poverty.

Between March 2006 and March 2007 personal-bankruptcy rates soared more than 60 percent. As families went into bankruptcy, more and more of them came to understand who had won and who had lost as a result of the president's 2005 bankruptcy bill, which made it harder for individuals to discharge their debts in a reasonable way. The lenders that had pressed for "reform" had been the clear winners, gaining added leverage and protections for themselves; people facing financial distress got the shaft.

AND THEN THERE'S IRAQ

The war in Iraq (along with, to a lesser extent, the war in Afghanistan) has cost the country dearly in blood and treasure. The loss in lives can never be quantified. As for the treasure, it's worth calling to mind that the administration, in the run-up to the invasion of Iraq, was reluctant to venture an estimate of what the war would cost (and publicly humiliated a White House aide who suggested that it might run as much as $200 billion). When pressed to give a number, the administration suggested $50 billion—what the United States is actually spending every few months. Today, government figures officially acknowledge that more than half a trillion dollars total has been spent by the U.S. "in theater." But in fact the overall cost of the conflict could be quadruple that amount—as a study I did with Linda Bilmes of Harvard has pointed out—even as the Congressional Budget Office now concedes that total expenditures are likely to be more than double the spending on operations. The official numbers do not include, for instance, other relevant expenditures hidden in the defense budget, such as the soaring costs of recruitment, with re-enlistment bonuses of as much as $100,000. They do not include the lifetime of disability and health-care benefits that will be required by tens of thousands of wounded veterans, as many as 20 percent of whom have suffered devastating brain and spinal injuries. Astonishingly, they do not include much of the cost of the equipment that has been used in the war, and that will have to be replaced. If you also take into account the costs to the economy from higher oil prices and the knock-on effects of the war—for instance, the depressing domino effect that war-fueled uncertainty has on investment, and the difficulties U.S. firms face overseas because America is the most disliked country in the world—the total costs of the Iraq war mount, even by a conservative estimate, to at least $2 trillion. To which one needs to add these words: so far.

It is natural to wonder, What would this money have bought if we had spent it on other things? U.S. aid to all of Africa has been hovering around $5 billion a year, the equivalent of less than two weeks of direct Iraq-war expenditures. The president made a big deal out of the financial problems facing Social Security, but the system could have been repaired for a century with what we have bled into the sands of Iraq. Had even a fraction of that $2 trillion been spent on investments in education and technology, or improving our infrastructure, the country would be in a far better position economically to meet the challenges it faces in the future, including threats from abroad. For a sliver of that $2 trillion we could have provided guaranteed access to higher education for all qualified Americans.

The soaring price of oil is clearly related to the Iraq war. The issue is not *whether* to blame the war for this but simply how much to blame it. It seems unbelievable now to recall that Bush-administration officials before the invasion suggested not only that Iraq's oil revenues would pay for the war in its entirety—hadn't we actually turned a tidy profit from the 1991 Gulf War?—but also that war was the best way to ensure low oil prices. In retrospect, the only big winners from the war have been the oil companies, the defense contractors, and al-Qaeda. Before the war, the oil markets anticipated that the then price range of $20 to $25 a barrel would continue for the next three years or so. Market players expected to see more demand from China and India, sure, but they also anticipated that this greater demand would be met mostly by increased production in the Middle East. The war upset that calculation, not so much by curtailing oil production in Iraq, which it did, but rather by heightening the sense of insecurity everywhere in the region, suppressing future investment.

The continuing reliance on oil, regardless of price, points to one more administration legacy: the failure to diversify America's energy resources. Leave aside the environmental reasons for weaning the world from hydrocarbons—the president has never convincingly embraced them, anyway. The economic and national-security arguments ought to have been powerful enough. Instead, the administration has pursued a policy of "drain America first"—that is, take as much oil out of America as possible, and as quickly as possible, with as little regard for the environment as one can get away with, leaving the country even more dependent on foreign oil in the future, and hope against hope that nuclear fusion or some other miracle will come to the rescue. So many gifts to the oil industry were included in the president's 2003 energy bill that John McCain referred to it as the "No Lobbyist Left Behind" bill.

CONTEMPT FOR THE WORLD

America's budget and trade deficits have grown to record highs under President Bush. To be sure, deficits don't have to be crippling in and of themselves. If a business borrows to buy a machine, it's a good thing, not a bad thing. During the past six years, America—its government, its families, the country as a whole—has been borrowing to sustain its consumption. Meanwhile, investment in fixed assets—the plants and equipment that help increase our wealth—has been declining.

What's the impact of all this down the road? The growth rate in America's standard of living will almost certainly slow, and there could even be a decline. The American economy can take a lot of abuse, but no economy is invincible, and our vulnerabilities are plain for all to see. As confidence in the American economy has plummeted, so has the value of the dollar—by 40 percent against the euro since 2001.

The disarray in our economic policies at home has parallels in our economic policies abroad. President Bush blamed the Chinese for our huge trade deficit, but an increase in the value of the yuan, which he has pushed, would simply make us buy more textiles and apparel from Bangladesh and Cambodia instead of China; our deficit would remain unchanged. The president claimed to believe in free trade but instituted measures aimed at protecting the American steel industry. The United States pushed hard for a series of bilateral trade agreements and bullied smaller countries into accepting all sorts of bitter conditions, such as extending patent protection on drugs that were desperately needed to fight AIDS. We pressed for open markets around the world but prevented China from buying Unocal, a small American oil company, most of whose assets lie outside the United States.

Not surprisingly, protests over U.S. trade practices erupted in places such as Thailand and Morocco. But America has refused to compromise—refused, for instance, to take any decisive action to do away with our huge agricultural subsidies, which distort international markets and hurt poor farmers in developing countries. This intransigence led to the collapse of talks designed to open up international markets. As in so many other areas, President Bush worked to undermine multilateralism—the notion that countries around the world need to cooperate—and to replace it with an America-dominated system. In the end, he failed to impose American dominance—but did succeed in weakening cooperation.

The administration's basic contempt for global institutions was underscored in 2005 when it named Paul Wolfowitz, the former deputy secretary of defense and a chief architect of the Iraq war, as president of the World Bank. Widely distrusted from the outset, and soon caught up in personal controversy, Wolfowitz became an international embarrassment and was forced to resign his position after less than two years on the job.

Globalization means that America's economy and the rest of the world have become increasingly interwoven. Consider those bad American mortgages. As families default, the owners of the mortgages find themselves holding worthless pieces of paper. The originators of these problem mortgages had already sold them to others, who packaged them, in a non-transparent way, with other assets, and passed them on once again to unidentified others. When the problems became apparent, global financial markets faced real tremors: it was discovered that billions in bad mortgages were hidden in portfolios in Europe, China, and Australia, and even in star American investment banks such as Goldman Sachs and Bear Stearns. Indonesia and other developing countries—innocent bystanders, really—suffered as global risk premiums soared, and investors pulled money out of these emerging markets, looking for safer havens. It will take years to sort out this mess.

Meanwhile, we have become dependent on other nations for the financing of our own debt. Today, China alone holds more than $1 trillion in public and private American I.O.U.'s. Cumulative borrowing from abroad during the six years of the Bush administration amounts to some $5 trillion. Most likely these creditors will not call in their loans—if they ever did, there would be a global financial crisis. But there is something bizarre and troubling about the richest country in the world not being able to live even remotely within its means. Just as Guantánamo and Abu Ghraib have eroded America's moral authority, so the Bush administration's fiscal housekeeping has eroded our economic authority.

THE WAY FORWARD

Whoever moves into the White House in January 2009 will face an unenviable set of economic circumstances. Extricating the country from Iraq will be the bloodier task, but putting America's economic house in order will be wrenching and take years.

The most immediate challenge will be simply to get the economy's metabolism back into the normal range. That will mean moving from a savings rate of zero (or less) to a more typical savings rate of, say, 4 percent. While such an increase would be good for the long-term health of America's economy, the short-term consequences would be painful. Money saved is money not spent. If people don't spend money, the economic engine stalls. If households curtail their spending quickly—as they may be forced to do as a result of the meltdown in the mortgage market—this could mean a recession; if done in a more measured way, it would still mean a protracted slowdown. The problems of foreclosure and bankruptcy posed by excessive household debt are likely to get worse before they get better. And the federal government is in a bind: any quick restoration of fiscal sanity will only aggravate both problems.

And in any case there's more to be done. What is required is in some ways simple to describe: it amounts to ceasing our current behavior and doing exactly the opposite. It means not spending money that we don't have, increasing taxes on the rich, reducing corporate welfare, strengthening the safety net for the less well off, and making greater investment in education, technology, and infrastructure.

When it comes to taxes, we should be trying to shift the burden away from things we view as good, such as labor and savings, to things we view as bad, such as pollution. With respect to the safety net, we need to remember that the more the government does to help workers improve their skills and get affordable health care the more we free up American businesses to compete in the global economy. Finally, we'll be a lot better off if we work with other countries to create fair and efficient global trade and financial systems. We'll have a better chance of getting others to open up their markets if we ourselves act less hypocritically— that is, if we open our own markets to their goods and stop subsidizing American agriculture.

Some portion of the damage done by the Bush administration could be rectified quickly. A large portion will take decades to fix—and that's assuming the political will to do so exists both in the White House and in Congress. Think of the interest we are paying, year after year, on the almost $4 trillion of increased debt burden—even at 5 percent, that's an annual payment of $200 billion, two Iraq wars a year forever. Think of the taxes that future governments will have to levy to repay even a fraction of the debt we have accumulated. And think of the widening divide between rich and poor in America, a phenomenon that goes beyond economics and speaks to the very future of the American Dream.

In short, there's a momentum here that will require a generation to reverse. Decades hence we should take stock, and revisit the conventional wisdom. Will Herbert Hoover still deserve his dubious mantle? I'm guessing that George W. Bush will have earned one more grim superlative.

Bush's Greatness[*]

There's a Good Reason He Infuriates the Reactionary Left

By David Gelernter
The Weekly Standard, September 13, 2004

It's obvious not only that George W. Bush has already earned his Great President badge (which might even outrank the Silver Star) but that much of the opposition to Bush has a remarkable and very special quality; one might be tempted to call it "lunacy." But that's too easy. The "special quality" of anti-Bush opposition tells a more significant, stranger story than that.

Bush's greatness is often misunderstood. He is great not because he showed America how to react to 9/11 but because he showed us how to deal with a still bigger event—the end of the Cold War. The collapse of the Soviet Union in 1989 left us facing two related problems, one moral and one practical. Neither President Clinton nor the first Bush found solutions—but it's not surprising that the right answers took time to discover, and an event like 9/11 to bring them into focus.

In moral terms: If you are the biggest boy on the playground and there are no adults around, the playground is your responsibility. It is your duty to prevent outrages—because your moral code demands that outrages be prevented, and (for now) you are the only one who can prevent them.

If you are one of the *two* biggest boys, and the other one orders you not to protect the weak lest he bash you and everyone else he can grab—then your position is more complicated. Your duty depends on the nature of the outrage that ought to be stopped, and on other circumstances. This was America's position during the Cold War: Our moral obligation to overthrow tyrants was limited by the Soviet threat of hot war, maybe nuclear war.

But things are different today. We are the one and only biggest boy. We can run from our moral duty but we can't hide. If there is to be justice in the world, we must create it. No one else will act if the biggest boy won't. Some of us turn to the United Nations the way we wish we could turn to our parents. It's not easy to say, "The responsibility is mine and I must wield it." But that's what the United States has to say. No U.N. agency or fairy godmother will bail us out.

Of course our moral duty remains complicated. We must pursue justice, help the suffering, and overthrow tyrants. But there are limits to our power. We must pick our tyrants carefully, keeping in mind not only justice but our practical interests and the worldwide consequences of what we intend. Our duty in this area is like our obligation to show charity. We have no power to help everyone and no *right* to help no one. In the event, we chose to act in Afghanistan and Iraq to begin with—good choices from many viewpoints.

The end of the Cold War means that our practical duties have changed too, in a limited way. Since the close of World War I in 1918, our main enemy has been the terrorist-totalitarian axis—still true today. Different nations and organizations have occupied this axis of evil, but the role itself has been remarkably stable. Until the end of the Cold War, the Soviet Union was the main terrorist-totalitarian power (except when it was eclipsed by Nazi Germany and Warlord Japan). The Berlin Wall fell in 1989; in 1990, Saddam marched into Kuwait. Radical Arab terrorism and totalitarianism go way back; the Nazis and then the Soviets supported them. When the Soviets fell, Arab tyrants and terrorists were ready for the limelight. *Our* job was to find new ways to do what we had always done—fight and (ultimately) beat our terrorist and totalitarian enemies.

President Bush had to respond to these post-Cold War realities; 9/11 meant that our pondering period was over. He announced, with deeds and not just words, that we *would* meet our moral obligations, police the playground, and overthrow tyrants; we *would* meet our practical obligations and continue to lead the fight against this new version of the terrorist-totalitarian axis.

We have often been told that we face, today, a whole new kind of war. Only partly true. For more than half a century we have battled totalitarian regimes (the Soviets, North Vietnam, Cuba . . .) *and* the terrorists they sponsored. Today we are battling totalitarian regimes (Baathist Iraq and the Taliban's Afghanistan, Iran, North Korea) *and* the terrorists they sponsor. What's changed? Since we became modern history's first monopower, our obligations and maneuvering room are both greater. But the basic nature of the struggle is the same.

Lincoln said, "Let us, to the end, dare to do our duty as we understand it." Bush answered: "Okay; let's roll." *We accept our obligation to be the world's policeman.* If not us, who? If not now, when?

The war in Iraq is dual-purpose, like most American wars. Take the Civil War. At the beginning, the North fought mainly for pragmatic reasons. No nation can tolerate treason, or allow itself to be ripped to bits or auctioned off piece-wise by malcontents. Midwesterners couldn't allow the Mississippi to fall into foreign hands; they needed their outlet to the sea. And so on. Slavery was overshadowed. But as the war continued, slavery emerged as *the* issue, and the war's character changed.

The Iraq war started as a fight to knock out a regime that invaded its neighbors, murdered its domestic enemies with poison gas, subsidized terrorism, and flouted the international community. Obviously such a regime was dangerous to American interests. But as the war continued and we confronted Saddam's gruesome tyranny face to face, the moral issue grew more important, as emancipation did in the Civil War. For years the Iraqi people had been screaming, in effect: "Oh, my God. Please help me! Please help me! I'm dying!" How could America have answered, "We don't want to get involved"? We are the biggest kid on the playground. If we won't help, who will?

I have just quoted the death-cries of Kitty Genovese, who died on the streets of New York 40 years ago. And I have quoted the response of an onlooker who didn't feel like helping. Her case still resonates in America's conscience, and tells us more than we want to know about the president's enemies.

The *New York Times* ran the story in March 1964.

For more than half an hour 38 respectable, law-abiding citizens in Queens watched a killer stalk and stab a woman in three separate attacks in Kew Gardens.

Twice the sound of their voices and the sudden glow of their bedroom lights interrupted him and frightened him off. Each time he returned, sought her out and stabbed her again. Not one person telephoned the police during the assault; one witness called after the woman was dead.

The left wanted America to watch Saddam stab Iraq to death and do nothing. That is the left's concept of moral responsibility in the post-Cold War world.

Miss Genovese screamed: "Oh, my God, he stabbed me! Please help me! Please help me!"

The Iraqi people were dying. The left had no pity. The Bush-haters were opposed to American "arrogance." The *New York Times* shrugged.

It was 3:50 by the time the police received their first call, from a man who was a neighbor of Miss Genovese. In two minutes they were at the scene. . . .

The man explained that he had called the police after much deliberation. He had phoned a friend in Nassau County for advice. . . .

"I didn't want to get involved," he sheepishly told the police.

Let's not get involved, said the Bush-haters. It's none of our business. Let the U.N. do it.

One couple, now willing to talk about that night, said they heard the first screams. The husband looked thoughtfully at the bookstore where the killer first grabbed Miss Genovese.

"We went to the window to see what was happening," he said, "but the light from our bedroom made it difficult to see the street." The wife, still apprehensive, added: "I put out the light and we were able to see better."

Asked why they hadn't called the police, she shrugged and replied, "I don't know."

We have paid a steep price in Iraq, a thousand dead; but if you choose duty, you must choose to pay. Speaking for America, the president has said: *We choose duty.* What do we get in return? Nothing. Except the privilege of looking at ourselves in the mirror, and facing history and our children.

Opposition to Bush's policy in Iraq goes even further than the Kitty Genovese defense. Its real nature finally came clear when I heard about an anti-Bush harangue by a survivor of Hitler's Germany. He was a young boy when he and his family got out, just in time. "I hate Bush," this man said—or words to that effect—"because America today reminds me of Germany then. Bush is on his way to creating a fascist America." Other Bush-haters have said similar things.

Notice (it is a thing we will have to explain) that this man hates Bush not because of but despite the facts. Has the Republican Congress decreed a U.S. version of the Nuremberg race laws? Has the administration transformed every American news source into a propaganda machine? Demanded that Jews (or anyone) be fired? That Jewish (or any other kind of) shops, businesses, professionals be boycotted? Propaganda posters everywhere? Students thrown out of schools? Secret police grabbing people off the streets? Children urged to inform on parents? All opposition parties banned? Churches harassed? A "Bush Youth" that every "Aryan" boy must join? Storm-troopers holding torchlight parades, singing hate-mongering war songs? Gigantic communal fines levied against Jews (or anyone else)? State-sponsored pogroms? Massive regimentation and rearmament? A führer cult and special schools to train disciples? Brutal suppression of all regime opponents? *No?* Actually America under Bush resembles Nazi Germany *in no way whatsoever*, isn't that so? Then why did you lie and say it did?

One hears many similar accusations nowadays. The Bush administration is spending blood for oil, hopes to expand its imperialist reach, intends to dominate and oppress the Iraqi people, is the world's leading threat to peace. Hates Muslims, despises our allies, plans to suppress the Bill of Rights. There is a name for this kind of hatred—the kind that shrugs off reality, loves to mock its targets and treat them as barely human, capable of any outrage, unspeakably stupid and evil. There is a name for the kind of hatred that applies automatically to any member of a designated group—in this case to *American conservatives* and especially *white, religious American conservatives*. The name of this hatred is *racism*.

We can't understand hatred like the German survivor's or Michael Moore's or a million self-righteous left-wingers' unless we understand that their Bush-hatred is *racist* hatred.

"Race" has traditionally meant any group that *seems* like a group, with a recognizable group identity—Americans, British, Jews, Japanese were all called "races." The Oxford English Dictionary says that a "race" is (among other things) "a group or class of persons . . . having some common feature or features." Thus "the race of good men" (1580), "a race of idle people" (1611), "a new race of poets" (1875). The newspaper humorist Don Marquis once wrote about "the royal race of hicks." Racist hatred has clearly recognizable characteristics:

- *The hater knows all about his target automatically; no research required.* Recall how many leftists were shocked when Bob Woodward informed them, in his Bush book, that the president was an alert, hands-on manager. They had known this to be false *a priori*.
- *The hater harbors a stupendous conceit.* Not long ago an Ivy League philosophy professor explained the political homogeneity of so many philosophy

departments. Pure merit, he said; you have to be *smart* to be a philosophy professor, and conservatives are *dumb*, so what can you expect?

- *The hater is moved by a terrible, frantic eagerness to set himself apart from "them."* In the spring of 2003, an American pop-singer announced to her London audience, "Just so you know, we're ashamed the president of the United States is from Texas."

- *The hater just knows that his opponent acts not on principle but out of greed or stupidity.* At an anti-Iraq war demonstration in March 2004, the actor Woody Harrelson read a poem. "I recognize your face, I recognize your name. / Your daddy killed for oil, and you did the same." We often hear this "blood for oil" accusation. After the first Gulf War we had Iraqi and Kuwaiti oilfields in our grasp. If our goal was to steal oil, why did we give them back? Are we *that* stupid?

- *The hater has no shame—because he knows (not by reason but automatically) that he is right.* Thus a decent and likable retired businessman, rich and with every reason to be grateful to America—the survivor of Nazi Germany I've mentioned—accuses the president of closet fascism.

That's racist hatred.

I don't say that all Bush-haters are racist. By no means. We have a long tradition of super-heated politics in this country. Everyone is entitled to hate the president and do his best to get rid of him.

The racist attacks I have in mind come from the reactionary left—not from the average registered Democrat, in other words, but from the liberal elite.

Reactionaries recoil from new ideas and try to suppress and defeat them. They want things to stay the same. Hence their racist hatred of uppity white conservatives, who have developed the cheek to threaten the left's cultural power. Such institutions as Fox News and the conservative Washington think tanks are hugely disturbing to reactionary liberals. The president faces the same thinking as he tries to set policy for post-Cold War America. Reactionary liberals want everything to stay *just the same*. All trends must continue *just as they have been*. (Judges must continue to subvert democracy; Congress must continue to create new entitlements.) We must treat the new totalitarians *just the same* as we once were *forced* to treat the Soviets—gingerly. Our goal must be not to liberate their victims, not to defeat and disarm their military machines, but to arrange détente with their dictators—just as we once did. (Détente with Saddam was French and Russian policy until we screwed things up.) Our antiquated pre-cell phone, pre-microchip laws and regulations must stay *just the same* (kill the Patriot Act!), and we must sit still and wait politely for the next terrorist outrage, just as we always have.

Bush has a simple message for the reactionary left: The times change and we change with them. He is a progressive conservative—and a progressive president in the best sense. And he has established his greatness in record time.

HNN Poll*

61% of Historians Rate the Bush Presidency Worst

By Robert S. McElvaine
History News Network, April 1, 2008

> "As far as history goes and all of these quotes about people trying to guess what the history of the Bush administration is going to be, you know, I take great comfort knowing that they don't know what they are talking about, because history takes a long time for us to reach"—George W. Bush, Fox News Sunday, Feb. 10, 2008.

A Pew Research Center poll released last week found that the share of the American public that approves of President George W. Bush has dropped to a new low of 28 percent.

An unscientific poll of professional historians completed the same week produced results far worse for a president clinging to the hope that history will someday take a kinder view of his presidency than does contemporary public opinion.

In an informal survey of 109 professional historians conducted over a three-week period through the History News Network, 98.2 percent assessed the presidency of Mr. Bush to be a failure while 1.8 percent classified it as a success.

Asked to rank the presidency of George W. Bush in comparison to those of the other 41 American presidents, more than 61 percent of the historians concluded that the current presidency is the worst in the nation's history. Another 35 percent of the historians surveyed rated the Bush presidency in the 31st to 41st category, while only four of the 109 respondents ranked the current presidency as even among the top two-thirds of American administrations.

At least two of those who ranked the current president in the 31–41 ranking made it clear that they placed him next-to-last, with only James Buchanan, in their view, being worse. "He is easily one of the 10-worst of all time and—if the magnitude of the challenges and opportunities matter—then probably in the bottom five, alongside Buchanan, Johnson, Fillmore, and Pierce," wrote another historian.

The reason for the hesitancy some historians had in categorizing the Bush presidency as the worst ever, which led them to place it instead in the "nearly the worst" group, was well expressed by another historian who said, "It is a bit too early to judge whether Bush's presidency is the worst ever, though it certainly has a shot to take the title. Without a doubt, it is among the worst."

In a similar survey of historians I conducted for HNN four years ago, Mr. Bush had fared somewhat better, with 19 percent rating his presidency a success and 81 percent classifying it as a failure. More striking is the dramatic increase in the percentage of historians who rate the Bush presidency the worst ever. In 2004, only 11.6 percent of the respondents rated Bush's presidency last. That conclusion is now reached by nearly six times as large a fraction of historians.

There are at least two obvious criticisms of such a survey. It is in no sense a scientific sample of historians. The participants are self-selected, although participation was open to all historians. Among those who responded are several of the nation's most respected historians, including Pulitzer and Bancroft Prize winners.

The second criticism that is often raised of historians making such assessments of a current president is that it is far too early. We do not yet know how the things that Mr. Bush has done will work out in the future. As the only respondent who classified the current presidency among the ten best noted, "Any judgment of his 'success' or lack thereof is premature in that the ultimate effects of his policies are not yet known." True enough. But this historian went on to make his current evaluation, giving Bush "high marks for courage in his willingness to attack intractable problems in the Near East and to touch the Social Security 'Third Rail.' "

Historians are in a better position than others to make judgments about how a current president's policies and actions compare with those of his predecessors. Those judgments are always subject to change in light of future developments. But that is no reason not to make them now.

The comments that many of the respondents included with their evaluations provide a clear sense of the reasons behind the overwhelming consensus that George W. Bush's presidency is among the worst in American history.

"No individual president can compare to the second Bush," wrote one. "Glib, contemptuous, ignorant, incurious, a dupe of anyone who humors his deluded belief in his heroic self, he has bankrupted the country with his disastrous war and his tax breaks for the rich, trampled on the Bill of Rights, appointed foxes in every henhouse, compounded the terrorist threat, turned a blind eye to torture and corruption and a looming ecological disaster, and squandered the rest of the world's goodwill. In short, no other president's faults have had so deleterious an effect on not only the country but the world at large."

"With his unprovoked and disastrous war of aggression in Iraq and his monstrous deficits, Bush has set this country on a course that will take decades to correct," said another historian. "When future historians look back to identify the moment at which the United States began to lose its position of world leadership, they will point—rightly—to the Bush presidency. Thanks to his policies, it is now easy to see America losing out to its competitors in any number of areas: China is rapidly becoming the manufacturing powerhouse of the next century, India the high tech and services leader, and Europe the region with the best quality of life."

One historian indicated that his reason for rating Bush as worst is that the current president combines traits of some of his failed predecessors: "the paranoia of Nixon, the ethics of Harding and the good sense of Herbert Hoover. . . . God willing, this will go down as the nadir of American politics." Another classified Bush as "an ideologue who got the nation into a totally unnecessary war, and has broken the Constitution more often than even Nixon. He is not a conservative, nor a Christian, just an immoral man. . . ." Still another remarked that Bush's "denial of any personal responsibility can only be described as silly."

"It would be difficult to identify a President who, facing major international and domestic crises, has failed in both as clearly as President Bush," concluded one respondent. "His domestic policies," another noted, "have had the cumulative effect of shoring up a semi-permanent aristocracy of capital that dwarfs the aristocracy of land against which the founding fathers rebelled; of encouraging a mindless retreat from science and rationalism; and of crippling the nation's economic base."

"George Bush has combined mediocrity with malevolent policies and has thus seriously damaged the welfare and standing of the United States," wrote one of the historians, echoing the assessments of many of his professional colleagues. "Bush does only two things well," said one of the most distinguished historians. "He knows how to make the very rich very much richer, and he has an amazing talent for [messing] up everything else he even approaches. His administration has been the most reckless, dangerous, irresponsible, mendacious, arrogant, self-righteous, incompetent, and deeply corrupt one in all of American history."

Four years ago I rated George W. Bush's presidency as the second worst, a bit above that of James Buchanan. Now, however, like so many other professional historians, I see the administration of the second Bush as clearly the worst in our history. My reasons are similar to those cited by other historians: In the wake of the terrorist attacks on September 11, 2001, the United States enjoyed enormous support around the world. President Bush squandered that goodwill by taking the country into an unnecessary war of choice and misleading the American people to gain support for that war. And he failed utterly to have a plan to deal with Iraq after the invasion. He further undermined the international reputation of the United States by justifying torture.

Mr. Bush inherited a sizable budget surplus and a thriving economy. By pushing through huge tax cuts for the rich while increasing federal spending at a rapid rate, Bush transformed the surplus into a massive deficit. The tax cuts and other policies accelerated the concentration of wealth and income among the very richest Americans. These policies combined with unwavering opposition to necessary government regulations have produced the worst economic crisis since the Great Depression. Then there is the incredible shrinking dollar, the appointment of incompetent cronies, the totally inexcusable failure to react properly to the disaster of Hurricane Katrina, the blatant disregard for the Constitution—and on and on.

Like a majority of other historians who participated in this poll, my conclusion is that the preponderance of the evidence now indicates that, while this nation has had at least its share of failed presidencies, no previous presidency was as large a failure in so many areas as the current one.

The Stellar Legacy of President George W. Bush[*]

By Joan Swirsky
New Media Journal, September 18, 2007

The accomplishments of President George W. Bush, I believe, will endow him with one of the most sterling legacies of all American presidents—right up there with those of other great wartime presidents, including George Washington, Abraham Lincoln, FDR, and Harry Truman.

THE VISION THING

After the September 11th attacks on our country, the president responded with both righteous indignation and military action—and also the appreciation that *all* administrations for the past over-60 years failed miserably in bringing peace to the Middle East. The president envisioned a breathtakingly original idea: introducing democracy to the largely feudal regimes of that region.

He rejected the terminal pacifism of his immediate predecessor—and that predecessor's waffling pro-war/anti-war wife—and first went after Al Qaeda in Afghanistan, and then, logically, Iraq, whose mass-murdering dictator had flouted dozens of U.N. resolutions, annihilated thousands of his citizens with poisoned gas, rewarded the families of Palestinian homicide bombers with hefty cash rewards, and was, according to virtually every intelligence agency on earth, accumulating weapons of mass destruction.

The president's vision struck all the right chords and was embraced by democracy-loving countries throughout the world, voted upon by the usually terrorist-supporting United Nations, and endorsed unanimously by the U.S. Senate and a vast majority of the Congress.

What has happened since then has been quite predictable. Conservatives and most Republicans are still with the president, but the liberals—who only went along to avoid being labeled the weaklings and traitors that come with their

---

DNA—quickly reverted to their base's basest politically-correct and multicultural-ism-is-good philosophy, i.e., that "making nice" is a preferred wartime "strategy," war is bad, all "cultures" are equal, and terrorists are really "victims" of U.S. "imperial" oppression.

And that is not to omit their irrational hatred of President Bush, who dealt a deadly—indeed unrecoverable—blow to their fragile narcissism by winning two presidential elections, and to the irrational conceit that they were and are both morally and intellectually superior not only to the president but to everyone on earth who doesn't agree with them.

Now that the 2008 presidential campaign is prematurely upon us, and the Democrats are in control of the Congress, the liberals have once again proven that, more than anything, they want America to lose—lose the war in Iraq, lose the momentum to help others share in the great promise of democracy, and lose the reputation of our heroic military as the finest on the face of the earth. That is not to omit the ignominious actions of a few weak-kneed Republicans, who because they are up for reelection, have "doubts" about the war in Iraq and have chosen to imitate Bill Clinton and his wife's finger-in-the-wind, poll-driven style of decision-making.

It's not as if the liberals haven't offered alternative suggestions to our current policy in Iraq. First they said we should dismantle Guantánamo, end the Patriot Act, and stop our government from listening in on terrorist phone calls. And both before and after the recent report to Congress of General David Petraeus—which affirmed that his "surge" is working, Iraq is being pacified, and the future for that country promises our own country *victory*—they've suggested that the United States should:

- Cut
- Run
- Appease
- Capitulate
- Apologize
- Give up
- Declare failure

In fairness, they have no choice. Without coming out and admitting it, they have tacitly acknowledged that there is not a wartime leader among them. The liberals now running for president have dodged this admission by stating, as John Edwards did, that the War in Iraq is not a war at all but rather a "bumper sticker"; as Barack Obama did by suggesting what *Investor's Business Daily* calls a "surrender" strategy; and as Hillary Clinton did, ala John Kerry, by saying that she was for the war before she was against it.

Commenting on the "the Democrats' moral bankruptcy" vis-à-vis their cynical and shameful reaction to General David Petraeus's recent report to Congress, *IBD* cited "overwhelming margins" in polls conducted by both *IBD*/TIPP and CBS/*New York Times* that "have found that the public overwhelmingly wants the commanders in the field—not the politicians in Washington—to call the shots" about the war.

"It's hard to see how Bush can be denied a lion's share of the credit for Iraq's success when, as recently as last December, all bets were that official Washington would shove the diplomatic approach endorsed by the Baker-Hamilton Iraq Study Group down the president's throat," IBD said. "The White House bet against that conventional wisdom, and now it's clear who won. Democrats, on the other hand, bet the farm on America losing the Iraq war. Now their moral chips are gone."

THE MONEY THING

A graduate of both Yale University and the Harvard business school, President Bush came to appreciate during his eight-year tenure as governor of Texas that Americans—and the millions of people who flock to our shores each year, both legally and illegally—not only flourish under our capitalist system but also like the idea of "keeping their own money." To that end, he proposed the largest tax cuts in American history, which, since 2003, has resulted in the creation of 8.3 million new jobs, American exports that rose 27 percent between 2004 and 2006, and an economy that has grown 13 percent.

In spite of the wars in Afghanistan and Iraq, rising gas prices, Iran's aggressive nuclear program, the subprime real-estate mortgage problem, recent "corrections" in the stock market, and the relentless doomsday predictions of leftist "experts" like Paul Krugman of the *NY Times* and countless others, our economy went through the roof and is still the envy of every country on earth!

As Donald Lambro, chief political correspondent for *The Washington Times*, has documented, "Stocks are booming, interest rates, inflation and unemployment are low, and companies are making money." But Lambro disagrees with the Office of Management and Budget's prediction that the annual deficit, estimated at $400 billion just a few years ago, will be $205 billion by the end of this fiscal year.

"The OMB is much too conservative," he says. "If the economy continues to perform well . . . we will likely reach a surplus well before 2012."

Economist and TV personality Lawrence Kudlow calls the astounding Bush economy "the greatest story never told." In fact, when the Dow Jones exploded by exceeding 14,000, only *The Wall St. Journal* carried this good news on its front page.

In stark contrast to President Bush's vision for an "ownership" society, Democrats have offered the following suggestions:

- Raise taxes
- Institute socialized medicine, which has failed in virtually every country that has tried it and would bankrupt our county
- Punish the wealthy CEOs who fuel our economy, boost employment, and give disproportionate charitable contributions to the world's welfare
- Enact an "open borders" policy for illegal immigrants, which will also bankrupt our country

- Do away with the Electoral College so that presidents in the future will be elected by only urban populations in NY, NJ, LA, etc. —an electorate that would insure government control and de facto socialism for decades to come

THE EDUCATION THING

President Bush looked at decades of academic failure of the poor and disenfranchised children in our country and accurately, I believe, concluded this resulted from a complete absence of accountability. So he instituted No Child Left Behind, which has made teachers, parents, and children themselves accountable for math and English literacy, and therefore for the ability of the current school-age generation to compete in our ever-competitive world.

In stark contrast to President Bush's vision for a truly educated populace, Democrats have offered the following suggestions:

- Do away with accountability
- Support the dinosaur unions that hate this concept
- Complain that the pampered children of today are being "pressured"
- Count on the leftwing media *not* to inform you that private schools, charter schools, parochial schools, and home-schooling—all of which demand accountability—consistently generate significantly better test results and more educated children than do public schools

THE SOCIAL SECURITY THING

President Bush looked at the same numbers as the liberals did and concluded that our Social Security system—which allows seniors to retire and receive enough money to live on, or at least get by on—is going broke in the not-too-distant future. Visionary that he is, he offered a sweeping SS reform that would insure that the system would not implode and leave multimillions of tax-paying people who have contributed to the system without the safety nets they deserve.

In stark contrast to his vision, Democrats—and their leftist AARP echo chamber—have offered the following suggestion:

- Keep this devolving system exactly as it is

THE MEDICARE THING

President Bush enacted a Medicare Drug reform bill in which 39 million seniors now get "bargains" for their medications and also bypass many of the bureaucratic boondoggles that have proven so daunting and disastrous in the past.

In predictable opposition to the president's vision for this sweeping reform,

Democrat liberals have offered the following:
- Don't change the horrific status quo!

THE SUPREME COURT THING

Today, thanks to the wisdom and prescience of President Bush, the United States has two extraordinary justices on the Supreme Court: Chief Justice John Roberts, and Samuel Alito. Liberals fought these nominations ferociously, just as they've fought the president's nominations of other stellar jurists to the appellate courts of our nation. To the liberal mind, those who interpret the Constitution as it was written are not acceptable. They prefer justices who reinterpret and invent out of whole cloth statutes that fit their socialist agenda.

THE KATRINA DISASTER

A day after the horrific Hurricane Katrina hit several southern states President Bush visited the areas and promptly enacted the most far-reaching financial and support-system help in the history of our country, but not soon enough or good enough for his rabid liberal antagonists.

While the heroic people of Mississippi, led by their *Republican* Governor Haley Barbour, fought back and recovered with nary the "victim" whine that is the Democrats' mantra, the powers-that-be in Louisiana and their liberal whiners-in-chief in the Congress purposefully ignored the president's multiple visits and great largesse to the region and kept up their drumbeat of criticism in order to avoid the cold hard truths of this cataclysmic event.

And what were those truths? That Ray Nagin, the *Democrat* Mayor of New Orleans; Mary Landrieu, the *Democrat* senator from New Orleans; and Kathleen Blanco, the *Democrat* Governor of Louisiana, were all to blame—and still are, as were their predecessors—for literally decades of neglecting Louisiana's deteriorating and crumbling levies, as well as for their mind-boggling ineffectualness in dealing with the disaster as it unfolded and has continued to unfold.

Lawrence Kudlow has documented the Democrats' failures in hard terms. He says that according to a government report entitled "The Federal Government Is Fulfilling Its Commitment to Help the People of the Gulf Coast Rebuild," the U.S. has spent "a monstrous $127 billion, including tax relief to Louisiana—which has amounted to $425,000 per person."

Now what would the average person do with $425,000? For one thing, they would thank God for this largesse and also use it to build not a semblance of their former homes but virtual castles. But that is not what happened, thanks to the graft-addicted thieves of the New Orleans political hierarchy.

"Where did the rest of that money go?" Kudlow asks—a question the so-called mainstream media avoids like the plague, just as they avoid asking why New Orleans, since Katrina, has become "the murder capital of the world . . . with a murder rate that is 40 percent higher than before Katrina, and twice as high as other dangerous cities like Detroit, Newark, and Washington, D.C."

Kudlow reminds us that Hillary Clinton and her socialist ilk think that giving money to wastrels like this is a "government investment"— "and that's just what's in store for America if she wins the White House next year."

Even the higher-ups in New Orleans admitted that they "lost" a billion dollars, which leads even the most un-cynical person to wonder into which Democrat pockets those greenbacks found their way!

GRAND IDEAS V. GUTTER POLITICS

While Republicans and conservatives were devastated by the midterm elections in which Democrats gained control of the Congress, nothing, in my opinion, could have been better!

Now that the Democrats have had nine months to "lead" our country, they have demonstrated for the entire country—and the entire world—that they have a spectacular lack of ideas, initiatives, and legislation.

In their first hundred days in power, all they did was launch over 300 investigations, troll for more than that number of documents, and had over 600 oversight hearings. And nearly half of the 39 bills they signed into law were to name a federal property or to build a road! Hence their lower-than-basement polling, with a mere 14 percent of Americans approving their performance—the lowest rating in the entire history of the Gallup polls.

As Kimberley A. Strassel writes in the *Wall St. Journal*, when the new majority's "first 100 hours [were] done and gone, by mid-January, the Democratic Party proceeded to fall apart . . . "

This is because hate is initially energizing but ultimately impotent. Liberals—after the mental depression they experienced when President Bush won both the 2000 and 2004 elections—were so enraged that all they could do was act like the children they are by calling names, insulting, lashing out at, vilifying, lying about, attempting to obstruct, and manufacturing all manner of phony issues to undermine the president.

But now that they're in power, they are still stuck on Bush and have proven themselves endemically incapable of leading our country. And that includes the Hollywood crowd that has worked overtime and poured literally billions of dollars to turn out anti-American and anti-Bush movies and documentaries that have earned them "awards" from their left-leaning cronies but close-to-zilch at the box office.

During all of the president's successes, the Democrats—all of them essentially anti-establishment holdovers from the leftist anti-war days of the 1960s—have relentlessly supported the opinions of those who paved the path for the September 11th attack: former President Clinton, former Secretary of State Madeleine

Albright, former National Security Advisor Sandy Berger, current Senator Hillary Clinton, and dozens of other members of the so-called "loyal" opposition, and that is not to omit the current crop of leftists who are still singing the same song—as always out of tune—about our nation's greatness.

THE RAGE OF CONSERVATIVES

Yes, conservatives are also angry at President Bush for, among other things, suggesting the ill-qualified Harriet Miers to the Supreme Court, supporting illegal immigration, engaging in "out of control" federal spending, and also for insisting—against all empirical evidence—that Islam is "the religion of peace."

They are also especially irate that the president failed to go on the offensive about the minute-by-minute, hourly, daily, monthly, non-stop distortions and lies that emanate from the liberal media, and that his public-relations team—if it existed at all—was so incredibly ineffective. Just as they are angry that he capitulated to the bogus fetish of man-made global warming.

And that is not to omit his failure to direct his Attorney General, Alberto Gonzales, to aggressively prosecute:

- *The New York Times* and other leftwing newspapers for their treasonous leaks about our national security secrets
- Patrick Fitzgerald for prosecutorial misconduct in his obsessive pursuit of I. Lewis "Scooter" Libby in the Plamegate fiasco, which ultimately revealed that Valerie Plame was not a covert agent, her leftwing husband Joe Wilson was a fraud, and that Libby had committed *no* crime!
- U.S. Attorney Johnny Sutton for his malicious prosecution of Border Guards Jose Compean and Ignacio Ramos for doing their jobs in guarding America so admirably when they fired at a Mexican drug smuggler

THE FOREST AND THE TREES

It is not only that George W. Bush, unlike all of those who preceded him over the past nearly-60 years—except for Ronald Reagan—have lacked the vision of our current Commander-in-Chief, it is also that he has distinguished himself by his moral clarity, his advocacy for traditional values and the value of life, his inveterate and consistent decency, his humility, his unflagging optimism about the greatness of our country's future, and his unfailing respect toward even those who sputter with impotent rage in his presence and hurl invective toward him behind his back and to the media.

As William Kristol, publisher of *The Weekly Standard*, has noted, "the unnecessary mistakes and the self-inflicted wounds that have characterized the Bush administration should not stop people from looking at the broad forest rather than the often unlovely trees."

Kristol reminds his readers that we have not had a "second terrorist attack on U.S. soil—not something we could have taken for granted. Second, a strong economy—also something that wasn't inevitable. And third, and most important, a war in Iraq that has been very difficult, but where—despite some confusion . . . we now seem to be on course to a successful outcome."

In a riveting article in *The New York Sun,* entitled "The Long View," the president's recently retired counselor, Karl Rove, who acknowledged that he could "hardly be considered an objective observer," explained that: "History's concern is with final outcomes, not the missteps or advances of the moment. History will render a favorable verdict if the outcome in the Middle East is similar to what America saw after World War II."

Rove reminded his readers that: "The *Washington Post* scorned President Truman as a 'spoilsman' who 'underestimated the people's intelligence.' *New York Times* columnist James Reston wrote off President Eisenhower as 'a tired man in a period of turbulence.' At the end of President Reagan's second term, the *New York Times* dismissed him as 'simplistic' and a 'lazy and inattentive man.'"

These "harsh judgments," Rove said, "have not weathered well over time. Fortunately, while contemporary observers have a habit of getting presidents wrong, history tends to be more accurate."

"I have come to understand," Rove continued, [that] "true leadership leans into the wind. It tackles big challenges with uncertain outcomes rather than taking on simple, sure tasks. It does what is right, regardless of what the latest poll or focus group says."

Indeed. And there is one more thing by which history will judge President Bush and for which future generations will thank him—his magnificent obsession with America's safety and security.

6

Who Will It Be?
The 2008 Campaign, the Candidates, the Issues

Editor's Introduction

The 2008 presidential campaign is shaping up to be one of the most exciting and important contests in American history. Each of the major-party candidates persevered against considerable odd to earns the nomination. On the Republican side, Senator John McCain's second run for the Oval Office got off to a shaky start, leading many political analysts to predict an early exit for the Arizona Senator. Refusing to give in, McCain dusted off his "Straight-Talk Express" tour bus, which had served him so well during his 2000 campaign, scaled down his operation, and pressed on. As the bids of former New York City Mayor Rudolph Guiliani and former Tennessee Senator Fred Thompson failed to gather steam, McCain regained his leading-candidate status and soon defeated spirited challenges from former governors Mitt Romney of Massachusetts and Mike Huckabee of Arkansas.

Meanwhile, first-term Illinois Senator Barack Obama, who electrified the 2004 Democratic Convention with his soaring oratory, squared off against Senator Hillary Clinton, a dominant figure in Democratic politics for over 15 years. Following his surprise victory in the Iowa Caucuses, Obama effectively became the front-runner, the first truly viable African-American presidential candidate in American history. As the months past, Senator Obama built up a small but insurmountable lead in delegates to capture the nomination, albeit after a bruising battle with Senator Clinton.

The articles contained in this chapter explore the candidates themselves as well as the themes and issues that are likely to impact the outcome of the race. In the first piece, "The World According to John McCain," Michael Hirsh delves into the Republican nominee's distinguished career. Hailing from a renowned military family, Senator McCain graduated from the U.S. Naval Academy and served as a pilot during the Vietnam conflict. His plane was shot down over Hanoi in 1967, and he was held prisoner for over five years. During his captivity, he was tortured and spent two years in solitary confinement. For propaganda purposes, the Vietnamese offered to free him, but he refused, insisting he would only leave if all the prisoners captured before him were allowed out as well. Upon his release in 1973, he returned to the United States where he continued to serve in the Navy, most notably as liaison to the U.S. Senate in Washington, D.C. In 1981 he retired from the Navy and embarked on his political career. He was elected to the U.S. House of Representatives from Arizona's First District in 1982. In 1986 he successfully ran for the Senate seat of the departing conservative icon Barry Goldwater. As a senator McCain has earned a reputation as a "maverick," willing to buck the wishes of his party leaders on a number of issues.

Senator Barack Obama is the subject of the next piece, "Destiny's Child," by Ben Wallace-Wells, who details the candidate's unique upbringing as well as his career as an author, academic, community organizer, and state senator. The first African-American editor of the *Harvard Law Review*, Senator Obama is the son of a Kenyan father and a white American mother. Fusing sparkling eloquence with a natural charisma, he has developed a passionate following, especially among African-Americans and the young, earning comparisons to both John and Robert Kennedy.

One of the chief areas of disagreement between Obama and McCain is the Iraq War. Senator Obama has opposed the conflict since its outset, declaring it a strategic mistake. While pledging to start bringing the troops home soon after assuming the presidency, Senator Obama has stressed that he will do so with caution and with the advice and consent of military leaders. Senator McCain, on the other hand, was one of the chief proponents of the war and remains committed to its successful conclusion. He also was a firm backer of President Bush's "surge," which deployed additional troops to the theater and instituted a new tactical approach to the conflict. In "On Iraq War Anniversary, Candidates Stake Out Their Claims," Adam Nagourney reports on Obama, McCain, and Clinton's statements on the war and the strategies they say they'd employ were they to be elected president.

As violence has stabilized in Iraq, the state of the U.S. economy has come into greater focus. With few exceptions, most analysts consider the situation rather grim, and many believe we are currently experiencing a recession. Food and gas prices, mortgage foreclosures, health-care costs, the national debt, the strength of the dollar, and a variety of other factors suggest that the economy is faring poorly. Addressing the sources of this unease will be among the chief tasks of the next president. Jane Sasseen, in "The Candidates' Plans to Fix the Economy," details the candidates' proposed economic initiatives.

Along with the war in Iraq and the economy, health care is a major issue in the coming election. Insurance premiums keep rising, serving as a hidden tax on workers and employers alike. Meanwhile nearly 50 million Americans are without health care. But having insurance is no safeguard against the financial toll of a medical emergency. Indeed, a considerable percentage of bankruptcies result from health-care bills; most of these so-called medical bankruptcies are declared by people who had insurance at the time of their emergency. Julie Appleby, in "Candidates Diverge on Health Care Plans," the last entry in this chapter, examines each candidate's health-care proposals.

The World According to John McCain[*]

By Michael Hirsh
Newsweek, March 29, 2008

"We need to listen," John McCain was saying, "to the views . . . of our demo-cratic allies." Then, though the words weren't in the script, the Arizona sena-tor repeated himself, as if in self-admonishment: "We need to listen." A lot of meaning was packed into that twice-said line, which was a key theme of McCain's first major foreign-policy speech since becoming the GOP's nominee-apparent. McCain was telling America, and the whole world: if I'm elected there will be, at long last, a return to what Jefferson called "a decent respect to the opinions of mankind." There will be no more ill-justified lurches into war, no more unilateral-ism, no more George W. Bush. Above all, McCain seemed to be saying that while Hillary Clinton and Barack Obama tear each other to pieces, I'm going to be the wise and welcoming statesman patching up America's global relations even before I get to the Oval Office. Not surprisingly, after the speech last week at the Los Angeles World Affairs Council, McCain's campaign could not talk enough about international cooperation—what McCain had called a "new compact." "He has such a deep relationship with so many Europeans and those in other regions, in-cluding Asia and the Middle East," said one adviser, Rich Williamson, who added that McCain has kept up his global profile by "going each year to the Munich Security Conference."

It was all very reassuring. There's just one problem: John McCain doesn't always behave according to his own statesmanlike script. In fact, while attending that same Munich conference in 2006, the Arizona senator had another one of what have come to be known as McCain Moments. In a small meeting at the Hotel Bay-erischer Hof, McCain was conferring with Frank-Walter Steinmeier, the foreign minister of Germany—one of America's most important allies—when the others heard McCain erupt. He thought the German was being insufficiently tough on the brutal regime in Belarus. Raising his voice at Steinmeier—who's known for speaking in unclear diplomatese—McCain "started shaking and rising out of his chair," said one participant, a former senior diplomatic official who related the anecdote on condition of anonymity. "He said something like: 'I haven't come to Munich to hear this kind of crap'." McCain's old pal Joe Lieberman jumped in. "Lieberman, who reads him very well, put his hand on McCain's arm and said gently, 'John, I think there's been a problem in the translation.' Of course Lieberman doesn't speak German and there hadn't been any problem in the translation . . . It was just John's explosive temper."

Certainly this was no great crisis, and the Germans later said all was forgiven. (On Sunday Sen. McCain's campaign strongly denied this account of the incident; Sen. Lieberman earlier recalled it as a misunderstanding over the translation.) But McCain's Munich outburst could not be called an isolated incident. Fearless and righteous, McCain has long been known to unleash a lacerating anger on those who cross him—Senate colleagues, foreign interlocutors, even the interrogators who once held his life in their hands at the Hanoi Hilton. (Lieberman, his fellow centrist, recently seems to have assigned himself the role of McCain's monitor. Just two weeks ago, when McCain mistakenly said Iran was training Al Qaeda in Iraq fighters, it was the Connecticut senator who again pulled him aside, gently reminding him that the Iranian regime has been accused of training fellow Shiite extremists, not Sunni Al Qaeda.) For someone who is just an election away from the White House—and who is running on his image as a tested statesman—there remain serious questions about how exactly McCain might behave as president.

Partly this is because McCain himself is not easy to pin down. There is McCain the pragmatist: worldly-wise and witty, determined to follow the facts to the exclusion of ideology—a man willing to defy his own party and forge compromise, even with liberals like Ted Kennedy (on granting illegal immigrants some amnesty) and John Kerry (on normalizing relations with Vietnam). And then there is the zealous advocate, single-minded about pressing his cause, sometimes erupting in outrage at detractors and willing to stand alone—without any allies at all, if need be.

There is much to like in both McCains. He's pragmatic in the service of the national interest; he rises to passion when he believes that America's best values are at stake. Even some of those who fret about his zeal and temper say they plan to vote for him (just as many ultraconservatives who worry about his centrism say they'll reluctantly pull the lever as well). Lieberman says McCain's anger "is part of his strength. And his guts. There are some things we should get righteously angry about."

Sometimes these two McCains—the crusader and the pragmatist—have combined to make him a powerful and leaderly force for change, which seems to be what Americans want now. It was McCain the savvy military analyst who looked hard at the emerging Iraqi insurgency in the fall of 2003, decided a lot more U.S. troops were needed, and then went head-to-head with the mulish Donald Rumsfeld over the issue. (McCain was, in effect, the first person in Washington to call for a "surge.") Ultimately, four years later, he brought the Congress—and the president—with him. "I went against the will of my own party when it wasn't politically expedient," McCain has said.

What's also true, however, is that he had long supported calls to topple Saddam Hussein, and was an enthusiastic promoter of the war in Iraq. Despite his best efforts to project himself as a healing president, the antic Arizonan has already worried many voters. His Beach Boys wisecrack about whether to "bomb, bomb, bomb" Iran is perhaps too easily mocked.

But McCain has said over and over that as president he will rise to what he calls the "transcendent challenge of the 21st century"—the fight against radical Islamic terrorism. And he's gone beyond that: he's indicated that anyone who disagrees with that premise—read Barack Obama and Hillary Clinton—is simply incompetent. As he declared in Los Angeles: "Any president who does not regard this threat as transcending all others does not deserve to sit in the White House, for he or she does not take seriously enough the first and most basic duty a president has—to protect the lives of the American people."

This is what troubles some about McCain's zeal for certain causes: he can be pragmatic in the pursuit of them, but seems to see them in largely black and white terms, not unlike George Bush, and rejects too much of the gray. Terror cells may be spreading, but their crazed ideology—all that talk of establishing a medieval caliphate—keeps dying every time it is exposed to the open air. And what about other major threats, like global warming? McCain, in an interview with *Newsweek*, said those were important, "but I do not believe that anyone who fails to understand the dimensions and enormity of this [extremist] challenge is qualified to serve as president of the United States." In Iraq, where last week the Iraqi government failed to quell renewed hostilities from cleric Moqtada al-Sadr's Mahdi Army—forcing U.S. troops to step in once again—McCain declared recently: "We're succeeding. I don't care what anybody says." The diatribe against Belarus was another case in point: no one doubts that Alexander Lukashenko is an evil if fairly insignificant dictator, but sometimes one has to talk to evil people.

On similar grounds, McCain has refused to consider meeting with the current Iranian government. Some critics worry that despite McCain's stated commitment to diplomatic coercion against Tehran, such an uncompromising approach could lead to hostilities. "The typical thing you'd expect from a war veteran, especially someone with his searing experience, is more caution than he shows," says Winslow Wheeler, a defense-budget expert who observed McCain for years as an aide to different senators.

This tendency to pursue causes so relentlessly—like his almost visceral dislike of Russia's quasi-dictatorial Vladimir Putin, whom he wants to cast out of the G8 (contrary to European wishes)—even concerns some GOP stalwarts. "I tried to talk to him about Russia, but he just stiffened," a former senior GOP foreign-policy official, who would speak only on condition of anonymity, said. "To me that's one of the most troublesome things about him. Advisers need to be able to walk into the Oval Office and say, 'Look, Mr. President, I think you're wrong.' That's not easy to do anyway. But if you think your head's going to be taken off and he will never forgive you, then you've got a real problem." As Wheeler puts it: "Joe Lieberman's not going to be there at 3 o'clock in the morning, in bed with him, when the phone call comes."

McCain himself has long been aware of what he called, in his 2002 book "Worth the Fighting For," his "legendary" temper. "I am combative, there is little use in pretending otherwise," he wrote. While he insisted then that people tend to exaggerate his anger (most people with tempers say the same), he admitted that it "has caused me to make most of the more serious mistakes of my career." But it is not just McCain's anger that worries his detractors; it's the fierce righteousness that is joined to it. During his first Senate run, in 1986, McCain grew so tired of hearing complaints about his anger that he thundered to his staffers ("as they struggled to keep straight faces," recorded author Robert Timberg): "I don't have a temper! I just care passionately." The participant who witnessed McCain's 2006 spat with Steinmeier agrees with this distinction. "He is, plain and simple, the most openly emotional politician in the United States," he says. "Other people have had tempers. Eisenhower had a famous temper. Clinton has a temper. Reagan had a temper. But it's that McCain is so emotional. He does jump to conclusions." In the Senate, McCain is known for getting up and walking out if he doesn't like what he's hearing. "You really don't have the luxury of walking out when you're president; you have a broader obligation," says a longtime Democratic Senate staffer who would describe private meetings only if he were not named. McCain denies he ever walked out of a meeting for that reason, saying that his Senate record shows "calm, sober hours of negotiations, good faith and respect for those who hold opposing notions." But he adds: "I feel passionately about issues, and the day that passion goes away is the day I will go down to the old soldiers' home and find my rocking chair."

Not even his harshest critics suggest that McCain—whose character and sanity were tested by some of the most savage torture a human being could endure—is unstable. And even many Democratic admirers, such as former senators Bob Kerrey and Gary Hart, think he'd be an outstanding president. Lieberman, perhaps his most avid supporter in the Senate, says it's "fair" to ask whether the displays of temper that so characterized McCain's Senate career are suitable for the Oval Office. But he adds: "I've never seen him get angry to the point of a loss of control."

Which fights is he likely to pick as president? As a Vietnam veteran, tempered in the failure of that war, McCain has made many thoughtful and careful judgments about the use of force during his more than 20 years in the Senate. In 1983, as a congressman, he called for the withdrawal of the Marines from Beirut—defying a president he professed to admire, Ronald Reagan. He voted against intervention in Haiti and in favor of a cutoff of funds for the "Black Hawk Down" mission in Somalia. He was leery of a ground war against Iraq in 1991, though he ultimately voted for it. But since then, McCain has also shown a willingness to use force that suggests he has escaped from his Vietnam-bred caution.

McCain himself denies there's been much change in his views, and aides say he's been fairly consistent in embracing the concept so many Vietnam vets have:

the "Powell doctrine." Named after former Joint Chiefs chairman and Secretary of State Colin Powell, the doctrine says the U.S. military should not be used unless the mission and exit strategy are clear and overwhelming force is applied. In Beirut and Somalia, McCain saw that the missions were muddled, says Mark Salter, his longtime speechwriter and alter ego. "He thought, 'What in the world are these few hundred Marines doing but making themselves targets?' " (Soon afterward, on Oct. 23, 1983, 241 Marines died in a terrorist bombing.)

McCain began to grow somewhat more sanguine after the stunning successes in the gulf war—the start of the "smart bomb" era—and the fall of the Soviet Union. He came to expand his view of America's calling, especially after Serbs slaughtered 8,000 Muslims at Srebrenica in 1995. In the late 1990s he forcefully backed the air war in Kosovo, and signed the Project for a New American Century letter along with neocons like Paul Wolfowitz and Richard Perle that called for Saddam Hussein to be ousted.

A decade later, after 9/11, McCain proved more eager than Bush was to take on Saddam in the middle of the war against Al Qaeda, declaring in early 2002 that Iraq was "the next front." He has since pledged to keep U.S. troops there indefinitely, saying he's in accord with none other than Osama bin Laden that Iraq is the central battleground in the War on Terror. "General Petraeus and I and Osama bin Laden are in agreement," McCain said recently. "It is hard to understand why Senator Clinton and Senator Obama do not understand that."

McCain knows that his candidacy will rise or fall on how the public sees Iraq and the larger War on Terror. "How people judge Iraq will have a direct relation to how they judge me," he recently told reporters on his campaign plane. "In some ways, it's out of my control." Last week, as violence scorched Baghdad and Basra, there were renewed questions about whether McCain even now "gets" Iraq and the delicate counterinsurgency campaign being run by Gen. David Petraeus. When he traveled there last year, appearing in a flak jacket in an open Baghdad market to demonstrate the success of the surge, "many of us were very uncomfortable," says a former member of the U.S. command in Baghdad who would reveal internal discussions only on condition of anonymity. "We felt he was pushing things too hard and too fast."

Despite McCain's nuanced record on the use of force, his team understands that he's got something of an image problem. Hence it was no surprise that the first lines of his remarks last week were designed to remove any lingering doubts that McCain is a warmonger, according to Salter. "I detest war," McCain declared. "When nations seek to resolve their differences by force of arms, a million tragedies ensue . . . Whatever gains are secured, it is loss the veteran remembers most keenly."

Still, McCain's Vietnam experience, not surprisingly, shapes him yet. "His position on Iraq is heavily influenced by his Vietnam experience," says Gary Hart, who was an usher at McCain's 1980 wedding. "I think that he has an emotional stake in not losing. He, like other veterans, believes that we could have 'won the Vietnam War,' but the politicians panicked and caved in to public sentiment and withdrew prematurely."

If there is one issue that haunts the reinvigorated McCain candidacy even more, it is whether he will start a new war with Iran. McCain told *Newsweek* that he "will continue to exhaust every other option before committing young Americans to harm's way," but that "we cannot afford to have Iran acquire nuclear weapons." Lieberman says McCain is precisely the man to keep America out of a war. "He's going to do everything he can to avoid military confrontation with Iran," he says. "There's an old expression: the best way to achieve peace is to prepare for war." McCain has called for expanding the U.S. Army and Marines by about 100,000 service members, but he also understands that the global struggle against terrorists and their state sponsors is counterinsurgency writ large, requiring aid and the winning of "hearts and minds" as much as military ops. "In this struggle, scholarships will be far more important than smart bombs," he said in Los Angeles. If John McCain becomes president, which will be used more?

Editor's Note: In this story, Newsweek *describes a meeting at the 2006 Munich security conference in which Sen. John McCain allegedly erupted at the German foreign minister, whom McCain thought was being insufficiently tough on the brutal regime in Belarus. There are, however, conflicting versions of the episode, and we should have made that clear. Other people who were in the room at the time dispute the account, and several of those who were there, including those who recall a brief flareup of anger from the senator (which the senator denies), believed the incident was minor, based on a misunderstanding caused by a translation problem, and was quickly cleared up. Sen. McCain should have been given an opportunity to give his version of events in the print version, and we regret that the piece did not note the different recollections of the moment, including the denials that there was any display of anger.*

Destiny's Child[*]

By Ben Wallace-Wells
Rolling Stone, February 22, 2007

Shortly after Barack Obama was elected to the United States Senate in 2004, he began residing, Monday through Thursday, in a one-bedroom apartment a few blocks from the Capitol. For a forty-three-year-old man who had been married for thirteen years and who had two young daughters, it was an isolating experience. The building has a yoga studio and a running track and a decidedly own-and-urban view of some ratty rooftops in the city's tiny Chinatown district; its decor, glass and brick, is less U.S. senator than junior management consultant. In his return to bachelor life, Obama found himself "soft and helpless. My first morning in Washington, I realized I'd forgotten to buy a shower curtain and had to scrunch up against the shower wall in order to avoid flooding the bathroom floor." The other new Democrat elected to the Senate that year, Ken Salazar of Colorado, took an apartment in the same building with his brother John, who is himself a congressman; they spent their time watching documentaries about leathery old cowboys on the Western Channel. Obama spent most of his time reading briefing books.

When Obama first got to Washington, he wanted to be a wonk, to keep his head down and concentrate on small issues. "The plan was: Put Illinois first," one of his aides tells me. Obama himself admits that his initial agenda had a "self-conscious" modesty. His early legislative accomplishments have been useful and bipartisan—he has even sponsored bills with ultraconservative Sen. Tom Coburn, who believes that high school bathrooms breed lesbianism—but they have been small-scale and off the headlines: a plan to make it easier for citizens to find out about government spending, increased research into ethanol, more job training and tax credits for "responsible fathers." This is the kind of head-down diligence that plays well in the Senate. "I am amazed by his sheer stamina," says Sen. Dick Lugar, a Republican from Indiana who has become something of a mentor to Obama.

But Washington has plenty of wonks, and Obama wasn't going to distinguish himself through diligence alone. He came to the Capitol equipped with his own, swelling celebrity; the Senate was not a perfect fit. Beyond his considerable charm, Obama can be righteous and cocky. He came to Washington pushing the hope that politics could be better—but now he can give the impression that he'd rather be just about anywhere other than in Washington. "It can be incredibly frustrating," he tells me. "The maneuverings, the chicanery, the smallness of politics here." Listening to a bloviating colleague at his first meeting of the Senate Foreign Relations Committee, Obama slipped a three-word note to a member of his staff: "Shoot. Me. Now." On a recent day, as Obama made his way through the Capitol's corridors, his fellow senators seemed like good-natured sportscasters, jolly and easy with their power, bantering about the fortunes of baseball teams in their home states . . . Obama is aloof and quiet. He prefers to listen, attentive as a rector, not quite of this world, silently measuring it. "The typical politician pushes himself on people to get them to pay attention," says Frank Luntz, the Republican campaign strategist. "Obama is quieter. He doesn't push—he has a laid-back feel that pulls you in. That is so rare."

Obama's ascent from rookie senator to presidential contender is one of the more startling and sudden acts in recent political history. Those around him aren't quite sure what has happened, and neither, for that matter, is the senator himself. Obama says he experienced the change as a call from the crowds that always stalk him, a summoning to a new role. First there was Hurricane Katrina, when the talk shows called him, assuming he had something to say. Then there were the throngs that lined the roads on his trip to Africa last summer, and the same excitement from domestic audiences on his book tour last fall. "I realized I didn't feel comfortable standing on the sidelines when so much was at stake," he tells me. "It was hard to maintain the notion that I was a backbencher." The early, wonkish humility was gone, replaced by a man who began to speak of himself in sprawling, historic terms. "Just being the president is not a good way of thinking about it," Obama says now. "You want to be a great president."

It is early January, a few weeks before Obama is set to announce his campaign for the presidency. He is sitting in his Senate office, dangling one leg over the other knee and speaking very, very slowly. It's not just that Obama searches for the right word; it's that the search seems to take him to distant worlds. When I first interviewed him last summer, his office was quiet and offbeat, a warren of tiny corridors and desks, the atmosphere of a faculty lounge. Now the place is intense, the faces drawn, the harried feel of a war room.

Most politicians come to national prominence at the head of a movement: Bill Clinton had neoliberalism, George W. Bush had compassionate conservatism, Reagan had supply-side economics. Even Obama's rivals have political calling cards: John Edwards has devoted himself to a poverty-fighting populism, Hillary Clinton is defined by a hawkish centrism. These identities give them infrastructures, ideologies, natural bases of support. Obama is trying to pull a less-conventional trick: to turn his own person into a movement. "I'm not surprised you're having trouble categorizing him," one of his aides says. "I don't think he's wedded to any ideological frame." With Obama, there is only the man himself—his youth, his ease, his race, his claim on the new century. His candidacy is essentially a plea for voters to put their trust in his innate capacity for clarity and judgment. There is no Obama-ism, only Obama.

"People don't come to Obama for what he's done in the Senate," says Bruce Reed, president of the centrist Democratic Leadership Council. "They come because of what they hope he could be." What Obama stands for, if anything, is not yet clear. Everywhere he goes he is greeted by thrilled crowds, trailed constantly by a reporter from *The Chicago Tribune* who is writing a book about the senator with a preliminary title so immodest that it embarrassed even Obama's staff: *The Savior*. The danger here is that the public has committed the cardinal sin of political love, forcing Obama onto the national stage before knowing him well enough to gauge whether he's ready for it. The candidate they see before them is their own creation—or, rather, it is the scrambling of a skinny, serious, self-reflective man trying to mold his public's conflicted yearnings into something greater. "Barack has become a kind of human Rorschach test," says Cassandra Butts, a friend of the senator's from law school and now a leader at the Center for American Progress. "People see in him what they want to see."

The Trinity United Church of Christ, the church that Barack Obama attends in Chicago, is at once vast and unprepossessing, a big structure a couple of blocks from the projects, in the long open sore of a ghetto on the city's far South Side. The church is a leftover vision from the Sixties of what a black nationalist future might look like. There's the testifying fervor of the black church, the Afrocentric Bible readings, even the odd dashiki. And there is the Rev. Jeremiah Wright, a sprawling, profane bear of a preacher, a kind of black ministerial institution, with his own radio shows and guest preaching gigs across the country. Wright takes the pulpit here one Sunday and solemnly, sonorously declares that he will recite ten essential facts about the United States. "Fact number one: We've got more black men in prison than there are in college," he intones. "Fact number two: Racism is how this country was founded and how this country is still run!" There is thumping applause; Wright has a cadence and power that make Obama sound like John Kerry. Now the reverend begins to *preach*. "We are deeply involved in the importing of drugs, the exporting of guns and the training of professional KILLERS. . . . We believe in white supremacy and black inferiority and believe it more than we believe in God. . . . We conducted radiation experiments on our own people. . . . We care nothing about human life if the ends justify the means!" The crowd whoops and amens as Wright builds to his climax: "And. And. *And!* GAWD! Has GOT! To be SICK! OF THIS [. . .]"

This is as openly radical a background as any significant American political figure has ever emerged from, as much Malcolm X as Martin Luther King Jr. Wright is not an incidental figure in Obama's life, or his politics. The senator "affirmed" his Christian faith in this church; he uses Wright as a "sounding board" to "make sure I'm not losing myself in the hype and hoopla." Both the title of Obama's second book, *The Audacity of Hope*, and the theme for his keynote address at the Democratic National Convention in 2004 come from Wright's sermons. "If you want to understand where Barack gets his feeling and rhetoric from," says the Rev. Jim Wallis, a leader of the religious left, "just look at Jeremiah Wright."

Obama wasn't born into Wright's world. His parents were atheists, an African bureaucrat and a white grad student, Jerry Falwell's nightmare vision of secular liberals come to life. Obama could have picked any church—the spare, spiritual places in Hyde Park, the awesome pomp and procession of the cathedrals downtown. He could have picked a mosque, for that matter, or even a synagogue. Obama chose Trinity United. He *picked* Jeremiah Wright. Obama writes in his autobiography that on the day he chose this church, he felt the spirit of black memory and history moving through Wright, and "felt for the first time how that spirit carried within it, nascent, incomplete, the possibility of moving beyond our narrow dreams."

Obama has now spent two years in the Senate and written two books about himself, both remarkably frank: There is a desire to own his story, to be both his own Boswell and his own investigative reporter. When you read his autobiography, the surprising thing—for such a measured politician—is the depth of radical feeling that seeps through, the amount of Jeremiah Wright that's packed in there. Perhaps this shouldn't be surprising. Obama's life story is a splicing of two different roles, and two different ways of thinking about America's. One is that of the consummate insider, someone who has been raised believing that he will help to lead America, who believes in this country's capacity for acts of outstanding virtue. The other is that of a black man who feels very deeply that this country's exercise of its great inherited wealth and power has been grossly unjust. This tension runs through his life; Obama is at once an insider and an outsider, a bomb thrower and the class president. "I'm somebody who believes in this country and its institutions," he tells me. "But I often think they're broken."

Obama was born in Honolulu in 1961, back when the Hawaiian islands were still a wary and weird part of America, half military base, half pan-Pacific outpost. His own background was even more singular and chancy: Obama's father was a Muslim from Kenya, the son of a farmer, who grew up tending his father's goats and who, through an almost impossible succession of luck, won a scholarship to the University of Hawaii. At the time, Barack's mother, Ann Dunham, was eighteen, a student at the university, the daughter of a blue-collar couple from Kansas. When Barack was two, his father left the family and returned to Kenya. Barack's mother remarried, moving with her son to her new husband's home in Indonesia.

To Barack, the country seemed exotic (he briefly owned a pet monkey named Tata) but also "unpredictable and often cruel." He recalls watching floods swamp the countryside and seeing the "desperation" of poor farm families who "scrambled to rescue their goats and their hens even as chunks of their huts washed away." (In January, the conservative online magazine *Insight* alleged that Obama had attended a hyper-religious Islamic madrassah as a child in Indonesia—a charge that the senator has denied.)

Obama spent four years in Jakarta before moving back to Honolulu, where he lived with his grandparents and won a scholarship to the private Punahou Academy, the place in Hawaii where all the Ivy League-bound kids go. (In his autobiography, he notes that when he hung out with a black friend, they together comprised "almost half" of the African-American population of Punahou.) He cops to "experimentation" as a teen, saying he smoked weed and even did "a little blow." He played basketball—"with a consuming passion that would always exceed my limited talent." Even today, his friends say, Obama talks a mean game. "He's a bit of a trash-talker," says Butts. "You see that competitive side of him come out when he's playing Scrabble or basketball."

After graduating from Columbia University, Obama spent four years as a street-level organizer in Chicago, where he met and worked with Wright, before attending Harvard Law School, where he was made the first black president of the law review. Winning the position required political savvy: "He was able to work with conservatives as well as liberals," recalls his friend Michael Froman, now an executive at Citigroup. Laurence Tribe, the renowned constitutional scholar, considers Obama one of his two best students ever: "He had a very powerful ability to synthesize diverse sources of information."

When Obama returned to Chicago, he turned down big-money firms to take a job with a small civil rights practice, filing housing discrimination suits on behalf of low-income residents and teaching constitutional law on the side. He had thought he might enter politics since before he left for law school, and eventually he did, winning a seat in the state Senate at the age of thirty-seven.

"He was a little off-putting at first—that whole Harvard thing," says Rich Miller, a veteran observer of Illinois politics. "But the bottom line is pretty much everybody I know had a high opinion of him, Republican or Democrat. In this state it's hard for anyone to get along, and even though he was very liberal, he was able to pass a hell of a lot of bills."

Many of the stands Obama took were pretty radical for a candidate who would end up aiming for national office. He led an ambitious but failed effort to provide health care for every citizen of Illinois, fought against predatory lending practices and wrote a bill making Illinois the first state to require police to tape their interrogations of murder suspects. But in 2003, when Obama began to run for the U.S. Senate, his legislative track record wasn't enough to get him elected. He was one of seven Democrats in the field, third or fourth on name recognition and even farther behind in funds. He barely stood a chance.

Then, running preliminary polls, his advisers noticed something remarkable: Women responded more intensely and warmly to Obama than did men. In a seven-candidate field, you don't need to win every vote. His advisers, assuming they would pick up a healthy chunk of black votes, honed in on a different target: Every focus group they ran was composed exclusively of women, nearly all of them white.

There is an amazingly candid moment in Obama's autobiography when he writes of his childhood discomfort at the way his mother would sexualize African-American men. "More than once," he recalls, "my mother would point out: 'Harry Belafonte is the best-looking man on the planet.'" What the focus groups his advisers conducted revealed was that Obama's political career now depends, in some measure, upon a tamer version of this same feeling, on the complicated dynamics of how white women respond to a charismatic black man. "I remember when we realized something magical was happening," says Obama's pollster on the campaign, an earnest Iowan named Paul Harstad. "We were doing a focus group in suburban Chicago, and this woman, seventy years old, looks seventy-five, hears Obama's life story, and she clasps her hand to her chest and says, 'Be still, my heart.' *Be still, my heart* —I've been doing this for a quarter century and I've never seen that." The most remarkable thing, for Harstad, was that the woman hadn't even seen the videos he had brought along of Obama speaking, had no idea what the young politician looked like. "All we'd done," he says, "is tell them the Story."

From that moment on, the Story became Obama's calling card, his political rationale and his basic sale. Every American politician has this wrangle he has to pull off, reshaping his life story to fit into Abe Lincoln's log cabin. Some pols (John Edwards, Bill Clinton) have an easier time of it than others (George Bush, Al Gore). Obama's material is simply the best of all. What he has to offer, at the most fundamental level, is not ideology or even inspiration—it is the Story, the feeling that he embodies, in his own, uniquely American history, a longed-for break from the past. "With Obama, it's all about his difference," says Joe Trippi, the Democratic consultant who masterminded Howard Dean's candidacy. "We see in him this hope that the country might be different, too."

It has become fashionable, given Obama's charisma and compassion, to compare him to Robert F. Kennedy, whose 1968 campaign for the presidency achieved near-rock-star status. But Obama is not Kennedy. Bobby Kennedy grew up studying how to use America's power, and in his forties he began to venture out and notice its imperfections. Barack Obama came up in a study of those flaws, and now, thrust into a position of power in his forties, is trying to figure out what to do with it.

It is in his ambitious, halting attempts to put together a coherent foreign policy that you can most clearly see Obama trying to figure out the algorithm of American power. When he took his seat in the Senate, aides say, he was coming to foreign-policy questions "relatively cold." The imbalance between his near-zero experience and the expectations that accompanied his arrival was absurd: Obama says he "laughed out loud" when he was asked, at his very first press conference in Washington, "Senator, what's your place in history?"

But Obama had something that most first-time senators lack: the clout of celebrity. You could almost see the wheels turning in the minds of Washington's best and brightest: Go to work for Obama, they were thinking, and you might end up running the world. "You spend your life preparing for Bobby Kennedy to walk in the door," says one D.C. pollster, "and then one day he walks in your door."

One of the biggest names to work with Obama is Samantha Power, the scholar and journalist who was awarded the Pulitzer Prize for *A Problem From Hell: America and the Age of Genocide*. "In 2004, I came out of election night just completely depressed," Power says. "We thought Kerry would win and we'd all get a chance to change the world. But then it was like, 'Nah, same old thing.'" Obama gave her a place to channel her energy. She advised him on the genocide in Darfur, an issue that most politicians at the time were studiously avoiding. "He's a sponge," Power says. "He pushes so hard on policy ideas that fifteen minutes after you've started talking, he's sent you back to the drawing board. He doesn't get weighted down by the limits of American power, but he sees you have to grasp those limits in order to transcend them."

Power is part of a generation of thinkers who, like Obama, came of age after the Cold War. They worry about the problems created by globalization and believe that the most important issues America will confront in the future (terrorism, avian flu, global warming, bioweapons, the disease and nihilism that grow from concentrated poverty) will emanate from neglected and failed states (Afghanistan, the Congo, Sierra Leone). According to Susan Rice, a Brookings Institution scholar who serves as an informal adviser to Obama, their ideas come from the "profound conviction that we are interconnected, that poverty and conflict and health problems and autocracy and environmental degradation in faraway places have the potential to come back and bite us in the behind, and that we ignore such places and such people at our peril."

Over the past two years, Obama has come to adopt this worldview as his own. He came back fascinated from a quick trip to a U.S. project in Ethiopia, where American soldiers had parachuted in to help the victims of a flood: "By investing now," he said, "we avoid an Iraq or Afghanistan later." The foreign-policy initiatives he has fought for and passed have followed this model: He has secured money to fight avian flu, improve security in the Congo and safeguard Russian nuclear weapons. "My comment is not meant to be unkind to mainstream Democrats," says Lugar, "but it seems to me that Barack is studying issues that are very important for the country and for the world."

When I meet with Obama in his office, it becomes clear that his study of foreign policy has only deepened his belief in the potential of American power. "In Africa, you often see that the difference between a village where everybody eats and a village where people starve is government," he tells me. "One has a functioning government, and the other does not. Which is why it bothers me when I hear Grover Norquist or someone say that government is the enemy. They don't understand the fundamental role that government plays."

There are limitations to this view of the world, of course, and there are those who believe that for all his study, Obama has been too cautious on the big issues. When he was running for the Senate, Obama was an early and vocal opponent of the war in Iraq. "I think our foreign policy has been all bluster and saber-rattling and continued mistakes over the last several years," he says. But since he arrived in the Senate, many of those who hoped Obama would become a great liberal champion have been disappointed. He has voted with conservatives on tort reform and industry-friendly provisions in the bankruptcy bill, and the troop-pullout bill he introduced in January was a late and unremarkable entry in the debate over Iraq. "Those of us in the Chicago progressive community still believe in Barack Obama," says Joel Bleifuss, editor of the left-wing magazine *In These Times.* "But at the moment we're pretty much taking it on faith."

"Obama has set himself a very high bar," says Michael Franc, a conservative scholar at the Heritage Foundation. "People like him for being a fresh face, an out-of-the-box thinker. But on the matrix of issues that will decide this election—Iraq, Iran, the war on terrorism—I haven't seen anything from him that strays very far from conventional liberal thinking. To the extent that he sounds like just another Democrat, he's needlessly ceding an advantage he might otherwise create for himself."

Obama seems to recognize that he is caught between the public's eagerness for a fresh approach and its desire for a John Wayne figure who will stand tall against the terrorists. "What we've seen from the Bush administration is a lot of tough talk and poor decisions," he says, as if acknowledging a painful political truth. "But people do want tough."

Over the past six months, as Obama has drawn closer to declaring his candidacy, there have been the beginnings of the first real backlash against him. In early November, the Chicago papers ran a series of stories detailing his relationship with a crooked developer, Tony Rezko. In a complicated but legal deal with Rezko, who bought a vacant lot next door to Obama's in Chicago, the senator was able to secure his own house at $300,000 below the asking price. *The Chicago Sun-Times* gleefully headlined its account from media darling to media-hounded. The report uncovered no evidence of wrongdoing, but its emergence serves as a reminder that Obama cannot remain above the fray forever. The more successful he is at positioning himself as a political outsider, the more he will inevitably be subjected to the same forces that hobble political insiders. This is the unavoidable truth about falling in love with politicians: The time comes when you have to give them up.

With Obama, there are crowds—always the crowds. In December, in what marked the true beginning of his presidential campaign, he traveled to Manchester, New Hampshire, to test the political waters. The crowd begins with the retirees: Three hours before Obama is due to arrive, hobbling eighty-year-olds show up and badger the staff like teeny-boppers, trying to figure out which entrance the senator will use so they can catch a glimpse of him up close. The creaky old political operatives on hand debate whether this crowd was larger than the one they had seen when John F. Kennedy came to town. One woman compares Obama to Jesus.

In other politicians, charisma often seems like compensation for some deeper, irreducible need: Bill Clinton comes so close, and listens so closely, because he wants to be hugged; George Bush slaps backs and gives his best friends nicknames because he, the draft-dodging son of a fighter pilot, needs to be the manliest creature in the room. With Obama, the charisma seems to stem from a remarkable ease with himself. When Frank Luntz, the conservative political consultant, walked into the young senator's office for the first time, Obama sat on the couch and gestured for Luntz to take the big, formal chair behind the desk. "I've been in many, many senators' offices, and never once have I been offered the senator's chair," Luntz says. "I asked him what he was doing, and he said, 'If I knew you any better, I'd be lying down.' What he was saying was that he was so comfortable with who he was, there was no need for any pretense or power trips."

Now, as Obama takes the stage, his charisma is almost palpable. He speaks about a young soldier he met, returned from Iraq: "An explosion had shattered his face. He had been blinded in both eyes. . . . His arm was no longer functioning. He had two young daughters, just like I do." Meeting the soldier, Obama recalls, "I looked not at him but at his wife, who loved him so much. You thought about their lives going forward." The lesson the senator took from the meeting, he says, was this: "Politics is not a sport. The debates we have in Washington are not about tactical advantages. They are about who we are as people, what we believe in and what we are willing to do to make sure we have a country that our children deserve." Afterward, he signs autographs in the crowd for what seems like hours: He can't, he won't, get away.

This kind of thing has its own effect, a ratcheting-up of the natural tendency of politicians to love themselves as much as the crowds do. In every politician, himself included, Obama says, there is "that ego-driven ambition that I want to *be* somebody. *I* want to be in front of the microphone, *I* want to be in front of the TV, *I* want to be the most important guy on the committee, *I* want it to be my bill." You can see this cockiness seeping through. Asked at fund-raisers whether the new role he's assumed is taking a toll on him, Obama waves it off: "Nah, I'm a thoroughbred."

"Look, there's no real preparation for a presidential race," says David Axelrod, Obama's chief political adviser. "Hillary Clinton, there's no question, she's played the course, she knows the sand traps and the lie of the greens. McCain's been through it once before, too. My feeling about this is, we don't know exactly how Barack will respond. I'll be really frank with you: Barack doesn't know exactly how he'll respond."

Throughout the fall, as Obama explored the idea of running for president, he often seemed to hesitate, almost fearful in the face of the exultation that greeted him wherever he went. In late August, for the third time in his life, he traveled to Kogelo, the tiny, grassless village in western Kenya where his father had grown up the son of a Muslim goat herder and where the senator's grandmother still lives. There is something absurd about the collision of Obama's worlds, right now, dozens of microphones thrust in the face of this eighty-five-year-old woman who has spent her life in this amazingly obscure place and barely knows her grandson. But this is part of the Obama legend, the globalized Abe Lincoln: This is his log cabin, a generation removed. When his caravan pulls into the village, thousands of people are waiting for him, a vast and disciplined crowd standing in long, silent lines, like those old photos of British colonials reviewing the Zulus. They are rooting for him to say something big, something feeling, about Africa, about the relation between America and Kenya, about the way history is beginning to shift. Obama, instead, backs away. "I don't come here as a grandson but as a U.S. senator," he tells them. "My time is not my own. Don't expect me to come back here very often." And then again: "I'm not going to be here all the time." He goes on in this vein: He wants to help Kenyans, but he also wants them to help themselves. He begins to sound like any other politician, a deputy to the trade commissioner. The crowd, full of hope, almost visibly deflates.

But on the same trip, it also began to become clear what it might mean if Barack Obama were somehow, despite it all, to become president of the United States— the resonance it might have not just within the United States but beyond. On a bright morning, the senator's convoy pulled into the Kibera district of Nairobi, which is called, perhaps unscientifically, the largest slum in all of Africa. It is undoubtedly the most compact: There are up to 750,000 people living in less than two square miles of malign-looking shacks, with no electricity and no running water. The whole place stinks of human waste. Kibera has become a common stopping point for American notables touring Africa's stricken zones—congressmen, Chris Rock, Madeleine Albright—and the place has assumed a kind of indifference to visiting celebrity. This is not the case with Obama. The senator has no speech planned today—he is here for a meeting on microfinance—but thousands of people have choked the dirt paths through the ghettos. *Obama biro, yawne yo!* they shout—"Obama's coming, clear the way!" His name, in its local rhythms, sounds almost like a religious chant. Kenyan police on horses, thin and jumpy animals, try to beat back the surging crowd.

When Obama is finished with his meeting, he comes out of a hut: a skinny American dude, looking more like thirty-five than forty-five, his face treadmilled-thin, all teeth and cheekbones, holding a megaphone at his side. The roar is deafening. For a second, Obama looks stunned. He lifts the megaphone to his lips, but he can't make himself heard. When he lowers it, he's grinning. For the first time, it seems as if some resistance has broken in Obama: His reluctance has been replaced by something deeper and more spontaneous. He raises the megaphone again. "Hello!" he calls out in the local dialect. The wave of sound that greets him is awesome. He half-loses it, just starts yelling into the megaphone: "Everyone here is my brother! Everyone here is my sister! I love Kibera!" The crowd is so loud that he can't be heard more than twenty feet from where he is standing, and so he begins to wade into the crowd, shouting into the megaphone again and again: "You are all my brothers and sisters!" The look on his face is one of pure joy. Months later, his eyes still glitter when he recalls the sheer spectacle of it all. "It was a remarkable experience," he says.

The residents in Kibera know little about Obama besides his race, the fact that his father is from this country and what the Kenyan papers have told them: that he represents a younger and more empathetic vision of America. It's enough. Here, at last, is what it would mean to have a black president of the United States, one with a feel for what it means to suffer the rough edge of American power. In

Kibera, something raw and basic about global politics began to stir, to make itself heard. These people, among the poorest in the world, are hoping for something more. And in the shouting crowds and the ecstasy of the moment, it has begun to seem, for the first time, as if Obama wants it all, too.

Correction: The original, published version of this article incorrectly stated that the "Washington Times" alleged that Obama had attended a madrassah in Indonesia. The allegation was actually published by Insight, a conservative online magazine owned by the same parent company as the "Times." "Rolling Stone" regrets the error.

On Iraq War Anniversary, Candidates Stake Out Their Differences[*]

By Adam Nagourney

International Herald Tribune, March 18, 2008

This week's fifth anniversary of the invasion of Iraq provoked an intense exchange over the war among the three presidential candidates, illustrating the deep divisions over how to proceed there even as the violence has ebbed. The exchange left little doubt that the issue would be a major area of difference between the two parties this fall.

Though the milestone could have easily been overshadowed by the crisis on Wall Street, Senators John McCain, Hillary Rodham Clinton and Barack Obama aggressively seized on Iraq in their campaigning Monday. That they did so, in the face of risks for each of them in the handling of the issue, was evidence of the large role all sides believe the war will continue to play in months ahead, even as the weakening economy takes center stage.

Of the three, Clinton, Democrat of New York, moved the most aggressively, and perhaps most unexpectedly, given the extent to which her vote in 2002 to authorize the war has caused her problems with Democratic primary voters.

She delivered a speech in Washington in which she renewed her pledge to begin withdrawing troops within 60 days of becoming president. But she also used her platform to attack both Obama, who she again said had been inconsistent on the war, and McCain.

McCain, the Arizona Republican who has championed the war and was long an advocate of the eventual policy of increasing the American troop presence in Iraq, was in Baghdad to mark the anniversary and said in an interview there that Clinton's approach was a prescription for defeat at the hands of Al Qaeda.

Obama, Democrat of Illinois, engaged Clinton for challenging the depth of his opposition to the war. He talked again of having spoken out against it from the outset, a distinction that has served him well in the primaries. Obama has been parrying criticism from Clinton and McCain, who have similarly questioned his credentials to be commander in chief.

While Iraq may have faded from public consciousness a bit, in reflection of a drop in the number of casualties and rising concern about the economy, it remains a politically defining issue for both parties, one sure to shape the arguments about national security this fall. The day's back-and-forth amounted to a preview of that debate.

"Despite the evidence, President Bush is determined to continue his failed policy in Iraq until he leaves office," Clinton said at a lightly attended speech at George Washington University. "And Senator McCain will gladly accept the torch and stay the course, keeping troops in Iraq for 100 more years if necessary.

"They both want to keep us tied to another country's civil war, a war we cannot win. And that, in a nutshell, is the Bush-McCain Iraq policy: Don't learn from your mistakes—repeat them."

Clinton argued that the troop "surge" advocated by McCain had failed to produce the kind of change the White House promised, as evinced by the fact that the troop level in Iraq at the end of the surge will be the same as at the beginning.

Talking to CNN in Baghdad, McCain, who has long said that his candidacy could rise or fall on what happens in Iraq, maintained that Clinton "obviously does not understand or appreciate the progress that has been made on the ground." But more tellingly, he returned to what has been the main Republican argument against Democrats since the attacks of Sept. 11, 2001, suggesting that they would not protect the nation from terrorism.

"If Mrs. Clinton's plan to begin withdrawal in 60 days is enacted," he said, "I just think what that means is Al Qaeda wins."

Clinton sought to make a case that Obama could not be counted on to withdraw American forces as rapidly as possible. She said he had not taken action in the Senate to stop the war and pointed to remarks by Samantha Power, who stepped down this month as an Obama foreign policy adviser after calling Clinton a "monster" and suggesting that as president, Obama would not necessarily abide by the troop withdrawal schedule he has laid out as a presidential candidate.

In an interview with the BBC, Power had said that Obama's pledge to withdraw one or two combat brigades per month was "a best-case scenario," not necessarily what could be achieved should he take office.

"One choice in this election is Senator McCain, who is willing to keep this war going for 100 years," Clinton said. "You can count on him to do that. Another choice is Senator Obama, who has promised to bring combat troops out in 16 months. But according to his foreign policy adviser, you can't count on him to do that."

Obama responded at a town hall meeting in Monaca, Pennsylvania.

"Let me be absolutely clear: I opposed this war in 2002, in 2003, 2004, 2005, 2006 and 2007," he said, speaking over the crowd's applause. "I have been consistent in saying we have to be as careful getting out as we were careless getting in. I've been clear that this was a strategic error, unlike Senator Clinton, who has voted for this war and has never taken responsibility for it."

The Candidates' Plans to Fix the Economy[*]

Presidential Contenders Aim to Convince Voters Each Can Revive Growth

By Jane Sasseen
BusinessWeek, March. 28, 2008

If there was ever any doubt the economy has moved to center stage in the Presidential campaign, this was the week that dispelled it. Coming on the heels of the Bear Stearns (BSC) rescue and deepening worries about the state of the housing and financial markets, all three contenders in the race, Senators Hillary Clinton (D-N.Y.), John McCain (R-Ariz.), and Barack Obama (D-Ill.) hit the hustings to give major speeches outlining their views on what needs to be done to revive the economy.

It's getting to the point where I can't keep up anymore," says Daniel Clifton, head of Washington research for investment firm Strategas Research.

Indeed, in the rhetorical equivalent of one-upsmanship, Clinton gave not one but two major addresses. After a speech she gave on Mar. 24 in Philadelphia on the housing crisis, Obama was in lower New York on Mar. 27, at the Cooper Union, to offer his views on how to improve the broad regulatory structure governing the financial markets and stem the problems in the housing markets. And just a few hours later, Clinton was back again, this time outlining her plan to bolster training and education programs for workers who lose their jobs.

In between, McCain also laid out his views on the crisis hitting housing and the financial markets.

"THE NO. 1 ISSUE"

"They are all trying to have an 'I feel your pain' moment with voters, although they're going about it in somewhat different ways," says Ann Mathias, the head of Washington research for the Stanford Group, an investment adviser.

The shift into high gear on the economy should come as little surprise: With each passing day, pollsters say, voters are becoming increasingly worried. "First and foremost, the economy is the No. 1 issue now," says Democratic pollster Peter Hart. And he argues it's no longer just a long-term or vague worry. Not only does the majority of the country believe the U.S. will go into a recession, if it is not there already, about 55% of those surveyed in March say the slowing economy has already affected them in a major way. Sixty-five percent say they have been greatly affected by rising gasoline and home heating oil prices, for instance, and 33% say the economy is having an impact on their retirement savings. "The problems are impacting real people's lives in real ways," says Hart.

CLINTON'S PLAN TO HELP THE UNEMPLOYED

Those issues clearly play to Clinton's strengths with struggling working- and middle-class voters—a key reason she has upped the ante with a handful of proposals aimed at showing her leadership and command of policy detail. Analysts say such an emphasis could help increase her lead in the critical Apr. 22 Pennsylvania primary. If successful, that message could provide some momentum going into Indiana, North Carolina, and the other remaining states. While that alone wouldn't be enough to win her the delegates needed to beat Obama, Clinton is clearly counting on it to help in her fight to win superdelegates to back her campaign.

"For Hillary the economic issue is obviously a godsend," says Hart. "It gives her a way of relating to the voters she's done best with, a way of talking about their concrete problems."

That aim was on full display in her Mar. 27 speech. Having devoted her earlier talk to the housing crisis, this time Clinton used a broad speech on the economy to introduce new proposals to spend $10 billion over five years on improving education and training programs, particularly for displaced workers. Clinton pledged to expand current government retraining programs, which are now targeted only to those who lose their jobs due to trade, to be available to all workers, regardless of how they ended up unemployed.

Every dislocated worker would be eligible for basic training, job search benefits, and other assistance. Clinton also promised to expand the existing Pell Grant program, which provides federal financial aid to students, to workers who enroll in education or training programs to bolster their skills after losing their jobs.

"We may be competing in a new global economy, but our policies to equip American workers for the 21st century are stuck back in the 20th century," Clinton told an audience in Raleigh, N.C.

OBAMA FAVORS A STRICTER REGULATORY ENVIRONMENT

For Obama, the challenge was clear: Step up and offer voters a more detailed view of how he'd handle the current problems. "Hillary trumped him on the economy in recent days," says Clifton. "He has to regain the upper hand and say, 'Here's my solution.'"

Much of Obama's emphasis was on the measures needed to shore up the regulatory structure surrounding financial markets. In his New York speech, Obama called for new standards for transparency and improved oversight of the financial sector to prevent the sort of crisis now roiling the markets. He argued that the deregulatory emphasis of the last decade has left the economy vulnerable to bubbles and special interests that have shaped the economy for their own benefit.

"Under Republican and Democratic Administrations, we failed to guard against practices that all too often rewarded financial manipulation instead of productivity and sound business practices," Obama said. "We let the special interests put their thumbs on the economic scales. The result has been a distorted market that creates bubbles instead of steady, sustainable growth."

To reduce the risks that have been created as a result, Obama argued a new regulatory structure is needed that would include strengthening the liquidity and capital requirements for financial institutions, streamlining the overlapping regulatory agencies that oversee them, and increasing government oversight of the risks many institutions are taking.

To deal with the housing crisis, Obama renewed his support for legislation currently before Congress that would provide government backing for new mortgages if lenders agree to reduce the principal value to what the homes are currently worth. Nearly 9% of today's homes carry mortgages that are worth more than the house's market value, which raises fears that many homeowners will walk away from their mortgages. Obama also proposed a $10 billion Foreclosure Prevention Fund that would help homeowners who are victims of fraud refinance their homes. He called for a modification of bankruptcy laws to help victims of predatory lending remain in their homes and for a significant extension of unemployment insurance.

McCAIN DISMISSES EXPANDED ROLE FOR GOVERNMENT

For all their efforts to differentiate themselves as the heated Democratic race continues, however, the two Democrats have strikingly similar approaches to the financial crisis. Moreover, pollster Hart says Clinton's recent heavy emphasis on lunch-bucket economics does not show signs of bolstering her polling numbers.

The real difference that is becoming increasingly obvious, says Mathias, is between the two Democratic candidates on one side, and McCain, the Bush Administration, and Treasury Secretary Henry Paulson on the other. In his Mar. 25 speech, McCain argued against an expansive role for the government in responding to the crisis. And in a statement on Mar. 27, he added he believed "the role of the government is to help the truly needy, prevent systemic economic risk, and enact reforms that prevent the kind of crisis we are currently experiencing from ever happening again."

McCain derided the Democrats' proposals as little more than multibillion-dollar bailouts for big banks and speculators. "There is a tendency for liberals to seek big government programs that sock it to American taxpayers while failing to solve the very real problems we face," he said.

Candidates Diverge on Health Care Plans[*]

By Julie Appleby
USA Today, March 25, 2008

Republican presidential candidate John McCain says the United States is approaching a "perfect storm" of problems that "will cause our health care system to implode" if the next president doesn't act.

Democratic rivals Barack Obama and Hillary Rodham Clinton would agree. But that's about where agreement over health care ends.

While McCain sees soaring medical costs as the initial problem to address, Obama and Clinton have competing plans that focus first on expanding coverage. They say too many Americans don't have adequate health insurance, and 47 million aren't covered at all.

These sharply different philosophies are at the core of the three candidates' potential solutions for how Americans should get and pay for their health care in the coming decade.

Each is reacting to a host of problems that are driving up costs for businesses and consumers: a 78% jump in insurance premiums since 2002, as tracked by the Kaiser Family Foundation; a Medicare system heading for red ink as baby boomers age; and a shrinking percentage of employers offering coverage.

Those factors, combined with the growing number of uninsured, have created the broadest public appetite for change since Clinton led a failed effort to overhaul health care during her husband's presidency. Health care ranks near the top of Americans' worries in a *USA Today*/Gallup Poll last month.

Concerns about health costs and the uninsured will help make this "the first presidential election that will have a good share of the campaign fought around health care," says Tommy Thompson, former secretary of Health and Human Services under President Bush.

It's unclear how that political fight will take shape—and whether any plan from the next president will survive through Congress. Health policy analysts say the battle lines already in place over the future of the health care system will offer

Americans a stark choice in the November election.

Health care consultant Robert Laszewski and Drew Altman, president of the non-partisan Kaiser foundation, and others describe three major areas in which the candidates and their two parties split:

- The Democratic candidates want to cover all or nearly all people, often by expanding government programs. McCain says worry about costs first and expand coverage later.
- McCain and many congressional Republicans would not require anyone to buy insurance or make insurers sell to those with existing medical problems. Democrats would require most, if not all, people to have insurance and insist that insurers sell to everyone who applies.
- Republicans would lean more on tax incentives to get people to buy their own insurance and less on coverage through their jobs. Democrats would bolster the current system of employer coverage.

These alternatives have both potential as well as pitfalls, Altman and Laszewski say.

McCain's ideas could continue to leave millions of people without insurance, they say, and could increase the number of employers dropping or limiting health plans. Covering more people, as Clinton's and Obama's plans attempt, could cost more than expected, they say.

Meanwhile, a bold initiative in Massachusetts aims to cover most of the uninsured by requiring everyone to have coverage and subsidizing care for lower-income residents. The plans offered by Clinton and Obama have similar elements.

The year-old Massachusetts effort helped increase enrollment in health insurance by more than 300,000. That success also means more people qualify for subsidies to help buy coverage, so the program may cost about $150 million more than expected this year.

The Massachusetts plan and other state efforts to cover the uninsured have helped make health care a campaign issue. A bigger reason for the current interest is a public perception that Washington has failed to act, says Robert Blendon, a health policy professor at Harvard.

"The sense is that very little has happened about the uninsured or making insurance more affordable for people," he says.

The different proposals among the candidates—and in Washington—boil down to three issues: Who gets health insurance, how should they get it and who pays.

COVER EVERYONE?

Clinton's and Obama's plans are similar in many ways, but they disagree on at least one key point: Clinton would require all people to have insurance. Obama would only require parents to have coverage for their children.

McCain would emphasize tax credits to help purchase health coverage and not require anyone to have insurance.

Blendon says that to cover a large share of the uninsured, the Democrats are "willing to consider laws that require most businesses to offer insurance to employees and at least require all parents to have insurance coverage for their kids."

The Republicans, he says, "are more focused on getting people who have insurance lower-cost options . . . including helping people who buy their own insurance to have more choices."

Laszewski, president of Health Policy and Strategy Associates, a Washington, D.C.-based consulting firm that works with insurers, hospitals and drug companies, says, "Either one could work," but both options face hurdles.

For example, Massachusetts—where some people still can't afford coverage— shows that "you can get a lot (of people) covered, but you can't get everyone covered," he says. Laszewski also sees flaws in McCain's push for tax credits to help buy coverage. "How will they make health insurance affordable for the oldest and sickest with one standard tax credit?" he asks. A tax credit could help younger, healthier people buy coverage, but it might not be enough for older people or those with health problems.

FORCE INSURERS TO SELL?

Clinton and Obama want insurers to sell coverage to all who apply. That would change many state laws, which allow insurers who sell policies to individuals to reject those with medical conditions ranging from hay fever to cancer.

More than 18 million people buy their own insurance because they are self-employed or their jobs don't offer it, according to America's Health Insurance Plans, the industry's lobbying group.

Len Nichols, an economist at the New America Foundation, a centrist think tank in Washington, says without a mandate for everyone to get insurance, some people would wait until they are sick to buy coverage. That would deprive insurance companies of premiums paid by healthy clients that offset costs of treating the sick.

McCain says too many rules already govern insurance and are driving up costs. To reduce insurance regulations, McCain's proposal would allow consumers to shop for lower-cost insurance in any state, not just where they live—a change from most state laws.

JOB COVERAGE OR TAX CREDITS?

Offering tax credits to buy health insurance, as McCain supports, would change how most Americans pay for coverage.

Currently, workers in the 60% of companies that offer health insurance get those benefits tax-free. Many Republicans, including McCain, say tax-free benefits are unfair to those who don't get coverage through their jobs and can't deduct insurance costs unless they are self-employed.

Under McCain's plan, job-based insurance would be taxable income. For a worker whose employer-offered family plan now costs an average $12,000 a year, that would mean a tax increase of $3,360, if in the 28% bracket.

McCain wants all individuals to get a tax credit—$2,500 or $5,000 for families—to either buy their own health policies or offset the taxes on coverage through their jobs.

Laszewski warns that for older or sicker workers, especially those buying coverage on their own, a policy could cost far more than the tax credit.

Len Burman, director of the centrist Urban-Brookings Tax Policy Center, says McCain's plan would improve the current system because it offers low-income residents a refundable tax credit to buy insurance. He also says that tax credits could likely lead some employers to drop health coverage.

Clinton and Obama want most Americans to keep getting coverage through their jobs. Large employers that don't offer health plans would have to contribute to the cost of covering their employees under Clinton's plan. Obama wants big companies to pay into a public fund for health care.

Both Democrats also want to open new ways to buy coverage, possibly through a system similar to one that covers federal workers and includes a variety of benefits.

WHAT ARE THE CHANCES?

Numerous efforts to revamp health care have failed since Democrat Harry Truman's administration in the 1940s. The last major push was during President Bill Clinton's first term in 1993-94. Hillary Clinton led a task force that called for universal health coverage to overhaul the nation's health care system, but the complexity of the plan and industry opposition doomed it in Congress.

"Two huge things are different now," New America's Nichols says. First, premiums have shot up, he says. Second, U.S. companies are increasingly competing with firms in other countries where health insurance is rarely offered, such as China or India, he says. That means U.S. employers pay for benefits, while their competitors don't.

Controlling rising costs could prove to be the hardest, although all three presidential hopefuls say their plans would do that.

Thompson, the former health secretary, says both parties agree on two ways to hold down costs. One is to promote technology, such as electronic medical records, to increase efficiency. The other is to streamline care for millions of Americans who have chronic illnesses, such as diabetes and asthma. Early care for those patients could reduce expensive hospital stays or other avoidable complications.

Many economists, including Paul Ginsburg of the Center for Studying Health System Change, say tougher measures may be needed to put a dent in health care spending, which topped $2.1 trillion in 2006—16% of the economy.

Harder-hitting measures, such as limits on new medical treatments until proved effective, wouldn't be well received.

"No one has a frontal assault on health care costs because that is somewhere between politically unpopular and political suicide," says Altman of the Kaiser foundation, which studies health policy.

WILL ANY CHANGES SUCCEED?

None of the candidates is proposing a government-run health system like in Canada or Great Britain. "A one-size-fits-all, big government takeover" isn't the answer, McCain says.

Clinton says her proposal is "not a government takeover of health care." She would, as one option, allow people to enroll in a plan similar to Medicare.

Obama says the government should control "skyrocketing profits of the drug and insurance industries," but should not change coverage for millions of Americans who get insurance through work.

Analysts disagree on whether any changes will succeed. Thompson says that "2009 will be the biggest successful year in the transformation of health care that we have seen since the passage of Medicare and Medicaid in the 1960s." Harvard's Blendon, however, foresees "a huge stalemate" except around the issue of covering more children, unless there is a sweep of Congress by one party.

Blendon says the two parties are so far apart on solutions—and have become so polarized—there is little common ground.

"There used to be a sense of a moderate middle that shared some of the values and concerns of each party," he says. "Now there are not a lot of people in the middle."

Bibliography

Books

Aitken, Jonathan. *Nixon: A Life*. Washington, D.C.: Regnery Pub., 1993.

Ambrose, Stephen E. and Douglas G. Brinkley. *Rise to Globalism: American Foreign Policy Since 1938*, 8th rev. ed. New York: Penguin Books, 1997.

Bernstein, Carl and Bob Woodward. *All the President's Men*. New York: Simon & Schuster, 1974.

Beschloss, Michael. *Presidential Courage: Brave Leaders and How They Changed America 1789–1989*. New York: Simon & Schuster, 2007.

Boller, Paul. *Presidential Campaigns: From George Washington to George W. Bush*. New York: Oxford University Press, 2004.

Brinkley, Alan and Davis Dyer, eds. *The American Presidency*. Boston: Houghton Mifflin, 2004.

Crenson, Matthew, and Ginsberg, . *Presidential Power: Unchecked and Unbalanced*. New York: Norton, 2007.

Cronin, Thomas E. and Michael A. Genovese. *The Paradoxes of the American Presidency*. New York: Oxford University Press, 2003.

Donald, David Herbert. *Lincoln*. New York: Simon & Schuster, 1995.

Ellis, Joseph J. *Founding Brothers: The Revolutionary Generation*. New York: Alfred A. Knopf, 2000.

——— . *His Excellency: George Washington*. New York: Alfred A. Knopf, 2004.

Goodwin, Doris Kearns. *No Ordinary Time: Franklin and Eleanor Roosevelt: The Home Front in World War II*. New York: Simon & Schuster, 1994.

————. *Team of Rivals: The Political Genius of Abraham Lincoln*. New York: Simon & Schuster, 2005.

Gould, Lewis L. *The Modern American Presidency*. Lawrence, Kans.: University Press of Kansas, 2004.

Healy, Gene. *The Cult of the Presidency: America's Dangerous Devotion to Executive Power*. Washington, D.C.: Cato Institute, 2008.

Hess, Stephen. *Organizing the Presidency*. Washington, D.C.: Brookings Institution, 1976.

Leibiger, Stuart. *Founding Friendship: George Washington, James Madison, and the Creation of the American Republic*. Charlottesville, Va.: University Press of Virginia, 1999.

McCullough, David G. *Truman*. New York: Simon & Schuster, 1992.

————. *John Adams*. New York: Simon & Schuster, 2001.

Milkis, Sidney M. and Michael Nelson. *The American Presidency: Origins and Development, 1776-2007*, 5th ed. Washington, D.C.: CQ Press, 2008.

Morris, Edmund. *The Rise of Theodore Roosevelt*. New York: Coward, McCann & Geoghegan, 1979.

————. *Theodore Rex*. New York: Random House, 2001.

Neustadt, Richard E. *Presidential Power and the Modern Presidents: The Politics of Leadership from Roosevelt to Reagan*. New York: Free Press, 1990.

Rudalevige, Andrew. *The New Imperial Presidency: Renewing Presidential Power After Watergate*. Ann Arbor, Mich.: University of Michigan Press, 2005.

Schlesinger, Arthur M. *A Thousand Days: John F. Kennedy in the White House*. Boston, Houghton Mifflin, 1965.

————. *The Imperial Presidency*. Boston: Houghton Mifflin, 1973.

————. *The Cycles of American History*. Boston: Houghton Mifflin, 1986.

Web sites

Readers seeking additional information about the American presidency may wish to refer to the following Web sites, all of which were operational as of this writing.

The American Presidency: A Glorious Burden

americanhistory.si.edu/PRESIDENCY/home.html

Maintained by the Behring Center of the Smithsonian National Museum of American History, this site features images of presidential artifacts as well as essays, timelines, and other historical analyses.

The American Presidency Project

www.presidency.ucsb.edu/index.php

An endeavor sponsored by the University of California at Santa Barbara, the American Presidency Project provides access to over 75,000 presidential documents as well as audio and visual resources. The data archive is divided into sections on Relations with Congress, Popularity, Public Appearances, Growth of the Executive Branch, Presidential Selection, State of the Union and Inaugural Address charts, and Presidential Disability.

American President: An Online Reference Resource

millercenter.org/academic/americanpresident

Part of the Miller Center of Public Affairs at the University of Virginia, this multimedia project offers essays on the presidents before, during, and after their tenure in office. Material on the vice presidents, first ladies, and cabinet members and a series of articles that "[delve] into the function, responsibilities, and organization of the modern presidency and traces the history and evolution of presidential duties," can also be accessed.

American Presidents: Life Portraits

Created for the C-SPAN television program of the same name, this site provides a host of material for researchers, including biographical facts, information on presidential places, and key events in presidential lives. Visitors can also take on-line tours of presidential grave sites.

Grolier: The American Presidency

ap.grolier.com/

This on-line collection offers material on the American presidency from various Grolier publications as well as audio and visual clips. The major areas of focus include Profiles, which features biographies of the presidents, vice presidents, first ladies, and defeated candidates, and The Presidency and Electoral Politics, which includes material on the constitution, presidential scandals, and monuments, among other topics.

The White House

www.whitehouse.gov

The official White House Web site informs the public on the president's agenda and activities and also includes on-line tours of the premises. Material examining the history of the building can likewise be accessed.

Additional Periodical Articles with Abstracts

More information about the American presidency and related subjects can be found in the following articles. Readers who require a more comprehensive selection are advised to consult *Readers Guide Abstracts* and other H.W. Wilson Publications.

My Years with Ronald Reagan. Richard Reeves. *American Heritage*. v. 57 pp50–52+ February/March 2006.

The writer, author of *President Reagan: The Triumph of Imagination*, reminisces about his experiences with Ronald Reagan. According to Reeves, Reagan was the candidate of optimism and national destiny, maintaining throughout that Americans were God's chosen and the last best hope. Through good times and bad for eight years, reveal Gallup polls, he was the most admired man in the United States. He had a 63 percent approval rating when he left the presidency, higher than any popular president in the latter half of the century. There were statistical debates about whether he had reformed America's political structure in the manner of Franklin D. Roosevelt, but there was no question that he had established the Republicans as the United States' governing party. There is also no doubt that numerous Americans paid a high price for his policy. Nobody can be sure of the so-called opportunity costs of Reaganism; the money funneled to tax breaks and defense may have cost decades of lost opportunities for improved education and health care.

Eight Great History-Making Presidential Primaries. *American History* v. 43 p14 June 2008.

The writer briefly discusses eight momentous presidential primaries: the 1960, 1968, 1972, 1976, and 1980 Democratic primaries, and the 1912, 1976, and 1980 Republican primaries.

Redeeming Dubya: Legacy of G. W. Bush. Ross Douthat. *Atlantic Monthly* v. 301 pp15–16 June 2008.

The notion that history might rehabilitate George W. Bush appears too ludicrous to be seriously considered, but almost every presidential reputation, however tarnished, eventually finds somebody willing to defend it, Douthat argues. To garner the type of vindication he appears to blithely expect, George W. Bush will have to convince not just centrists but at least some liberals. It might be said that a too-sharp awareness of the U.S. tendency to associate great leadership with world-historical ambition has ruined Bush's presidency, but the enthusiasm for Barack Obama and John McCain suggests that the longing, on the left and right alike, for presidents who will chase greatness has merely been magnified by the debacle in Iraq. This is good news for Bush, who has to hope that the identical propensity that wrecked his government will redeem his reputation, but it is perilous news for the United States.

Untruth and Consequences: Lies Told by Presidents. Carl M. Cannon. *Atlantic Monthly* v. 299 pp56–60+ January/February 2007.

George W. Bush stands accused of equivocating about the decision to take the United States to war, Cannon reports. For the past year and a half, a majority of people in the United States have expressed doubts that the President's reasons for ordering the military to invade Iraq were those he articulated publicly. Even allowing for a heavy dose of anti-Bush feeling on the part of the media, much of the American public has altered its opinion regarding the veracity of the man in the Oval Office. Nonetheless, Bush's place in history will depend not on whether he lied to the U.S. people, but rather how he lied, what consequences his lying had, and how he ultimately responded to them.

The Electoral College: An Idea Whose Time Has Come and Gone. Dewey M. Clinton. *The Black Scholar* v. 37 pp28–41 Fall 2007.

In this article, part of a special issue on the black social agenda in the United States, the writer examines the advantages and disadvantages of the Electoral College. He discusses three principal factions in the debate surrounding the Electoral College: those who favor the status quo; those who want to maintain the institution but reform it; and those who support extreme reform, or the abolition of the college altogether. Among the initiatives favored by those who advocate minor changes is splitting districts in all states, while those in favor of major reforms propose district voting, proportional representation, a national bonus plan, instant-runoff voting, and/or direct election. For his part, Clinton asserts that the Electoral College is an anachronism that should be abolished in favor of a direct popular vote.

Strong, Silent Men Make Good Presidents. Paul Johnson, *Forbes* v. 173 p33 March 1, 2004.

The writer reflects on his increasing admiration for George W. Bush. With voters paying more attention to economic issues, Bush has rightly remained determined to prioritize security. There is nothing flashy about the president; he has some clear ideas, shared by the majority of Americans, and the willpower to support them. Even in Old Europe, the likelihood of his winning a second term is increasingly perceived as a guarantee of stability and continuity.

How Presidents Persuade. Gardiner Morse, *Harvard Business Review* v. 81 pp20–21, January 2003.

In this piece, part of a special issue on motivating employees, Gardiner remarks that few people have seen life in the Oval Office more intimately than David Gergen. As an adviser to presidents Nixon, Ford, Reagan, and Clinton, he played a pivotal role in how these leaders streamlined and presented their messages. In his best-selling *Eyewitness to Power*, Gergen wrote about the leadership qualities and deficiencies that each brought to the White House, and reflected on how the best leaders inspire their followers. In an interview, Gergen discusses the roles of honesty, transparency, and stagecraft in the leader's craft.

From Kennedy's Cold War to the War on Terror. Gareth Jenkins. *History Today* v. 56 pp39–41 June 2006.

There are parallels between John F. Kennedy's foreign policy during the 1960s and that of President Bush, Jenkins contends. The U.S. invasion of Iraq in 2003 is seen by many as a historical watershed, ushering in a new era in which the world's sole superpower feels unconstrained in using preemptive military action to achieve its strategic goals. Nonetheless, there have been continual attacks on the sovereignty of Third World nations throughout the period since the Cold War began. In 1961, Kennedy came to the U.S. presidency with a reputation as a Cold Warrior intent on maintaining the United States' global advantages, and he greatly exaggerated the military capacity of the Soviet Union to scare Americans into supporting the greatest arms buildup in peacetime ever. Kennedy was able to project an image of himself as basically a man of peace, while overseeing an apparatus of covert counterinsurgency worldwide, whereas Bush's mask began to slip even before the invasion of Iraq.

Presidents & the Constitution. *Insights on Law & Society* v. 6 pp4–31 Fall 2005.

A special issue on U.S. presidents and the Constitution is presented. Articles discuss the significant growth in the size, stature, and visibility of the presidency during the 20th century; the rise of the rhetorical presidency; presidents and war powers; the purpose, uses, and repercussions of executive orders issued by U.S. presidents; the expropriation of the war power by the president from Congress; the need for an empowered president to solve the complex problems confronting the United States today; the work of Presidential Classroom, a nonprofit, nonpartisan civic education organization; the reluctance of recent U.S. presidents to apologize or accept responsibility for mistakes; President George W. Bush's recent nominations to the U.S. Supreme Court; and some of the resources currently available on the Web site for *Insights on Law & Society*. A lesson on executive orders and presidential power is also provided.

When Presidents Lie. Eric Alterman. *The Nation* v. 279 pp20, 22+ October 25, 2004.

Although it might sometimes be damaging, presidents should always tell the truth, Alterman argues. From the perspective of personal political consequences, the act of purposeful deception by an American president depends almost completely on the context in which it takes place. Bill Clinton was impeached for his decision to "lie" under oath about adultery, the most costly mistake that he ever made and a betrayal of both his closest supporters and many of his own deeply held personal and political aspirations. In telling the truth to the nation, presidents may often have to deal with complex, tough, and frequently dangerous problems that they would undoubtedly prefer to avoid. Nonetheless, when a president lies about important issues, he sets up an independent dynamic that would otherwise not have existed and that injures everyone.

Enfeebling the Presidency. David B. Rivkin, Jr. and Lee A. Casey, *National Review* v. 58 pp36–38, June 19, 2006.

According to the authors, the current denigration of the presidency is sufficiently robust and comprehensive that it will probably survive George W. Bush's tenure and become a long-term fixture of America's legal and political discourse. The engine driving the hostility to presidential power is a basic suspicion of, and opposition to, the use of U.S. power as a way of defending and advancing American interests at home and abroad. This reaction is rooted in a tendency to see the United States as a negative force in global affairs. Because, in the aftermath of September 11, America has found itself at war against a ruthless and determined foe, necessitating the robust use of various presidential powers, critics have found numerous opportunities to advance their effort to hobble the president, who is both the symbol of strong American government and the actual locus of the initiative in the formulation and implementation of U.S. foreign policy.

The Long Road to a Clinton Exit. *New York Times* pp1+ June 8, 2008.

Hillary Clinton's presidential campaign was brimming with overconfidence, riven by acrimony, and weighed down by the emotional baggage of a marriage between a former and would-be president, the writers contend. Bill Clinton helped neither her campaign, nor his legacy, with unfortunate statements about Barack Obama and emotional outbursts. Mrs. Clinton's staff included advisers who were rivals and who nursed grudges. The candidate made the mistake of dismissing Mr. Obama as a glamorous personality, when, in reality, he has the charisma that many voters find appealing.

Should We Elect the President By Popular Vote? John R. Koza and Robert Hardaway. *New York Times Upfront* v. 140 p22 February 25, 2008.

John R. Koza, Chairman of National Popular Vote, and Robert Hardaway, author of *The Electoral College and the Constitution*, debate the merits and demerits of the Electoral College system of electing the president. Koza argues that the Electoral College effectively disenfranchises voters who do not reside in closely divided battleground states and allows candidates to win the presidency without obtaining the majority of votes nationwide. Hardaway argues in favor of the system, noting that it was intended by the Founding Fathers to ensure that the president had widespread support and could not, having obtained 90 percent of the votes in one area, be elected against the will of the remainder of the country.

Lessons From the Front Line: Impact of Military Service on Presidents. Sarah Kliff, *Newsweek* v. 151 pp30–31, February 11, 2008.

Over half of the nation's presidents have served under a military commander before assuming office, Kliff reports. Six presidents on whom military service had a particular effect according to historian Michael Beschloss, namely George Washington, Andrew Jackson, Theodore Roosevelt, Dwight D. Eisenhower, John F. Kennedy, and George H. W. Bush, are briefly discussed.

What FDR Teaches Us. Jonathan Alter. *Newsweek* v. 147 pp28–30 May 1, 2006.

In this article, adapted from *The Defining Moment: FDR's Hundred Days and the Triumph of Hope*, Alter juxtaposes George W. Bush with Franklin Delano Roosevelt in order to offer insights into both Roosevelt's extraordinary gifts and Bush's current difficulties. Before reaching office, aristocrats Roosevelt and Bush had much in common, but the personal crises they each experienced before becoming head of state had completely different effects on the political style and character of their presidencies. Roosevelt's extraordinary leadership in February 1933 marked the "defining moment" of modern American politics, when Roosevelt rescued both capitalism and democracy within a few weeks and redefined "the Deal" between the nation and its people. He imagined a new United States, marked by commitment to one another, and a new set of governing principles that are still being debated today.

The Cult of the Presidency. Gene Healy. *Reason* v. 40 pp20–28 June 2008.

Healy charts how the roles and responsibilities of the president have changed over the years, to the point where a "cult of the presidency" has developed. "Our system," Healy contends, "with its unhealthy, unconstitutional concentration of power, feeds on the atavistic tendency to see the chief magistrate as our national father or mother, responsible for our economic well-being, our physical safety, and even our sense of belonging."

Learning to Love the Imperial Presidency. Gene Healy. *Reason* v. 39 p23 October 2007.

Since Nixon's resignation, Healy contends, the conservative movement has prioritized the expansion of presidential power, frequently at the expense of the Constitution. This was not always the case; almost unanimously, the conservatives who gathered around William F. Buckley's *National Review* in 1955 associated executive power with liberal activism and saw Congress as the conservative branch, but things started to change with Nixon. Leading conservatives began to view the executive as the conservative branch and went to work developing a conservative case for the imperial presidency. Right-wing resentment over Nixon's downfall helped fuel the change. Conservatives began to consistently vote for major increases in presidential strength, even when these expansions went against traditionally conservative positions, and by the Reagan era, prominent Republicans were urging a repeal of the 22nd Amendment, which restricts presidents to two terms.

Presidential Trivia. Richard Lederer. *The Saturday Evening Post* v. 280 pp16–17 January/February 2008.

In *Presidential Trivia*, Richard Lederer has gathered reams of intriguing information about the presidents, their vice presidents, and their wives. The writer presents several of the fascinating facts revealed in the book.

1932: A New Deal Is Struck. Geoffrey C. Ward. *Smithsonian* v. 35 pp60+ October 2004. This piece, part of a special section examining four elections that changed American history, examines the presidential race of 1932 and its aftermath, focusing on how Franklin Roosevelt revived a glum nation and transformed the relationship of Americans to their government. Before Roosevelt assumed power, ordinary citizens rarely dealt with the federal government, there was no Social Security, unemployment compensation, federal guarantees of bank deposits, or regulation of the stock market, nor was there a commitment to equal opportunity or high employment. All of this changed during the years of the New Deal, with Roosevelt never swaying from his absolute conviction that no problem was so great that it could not be solved by ordinary Americans.

Does Experience Matter in a President? David von Drehle. *Time* v. 171 pp26–30 March 10, 2008.

According to von Drehle, history has demonstrated that when it comes to the presidency, experience does not ensure success. Experience gets its value from the person who has it. In some lives, a little goes a long way. Some people grow and mature through years of government service, others amass credentials elsewhere. At the same time, the value that voters place on an impressive resumé is constantly shifting. When Americans reject the best-credentialed candidates because their heart leads them somewhere else, they are merely reflecting a visceral comprehension that the presidency is not like other jobs. A perfect president is both merciless and compassionate, visionary and pragmatic, crafty and honest, patient and intrepid, blending the eloquence of a psalmist with the timing of a jungle cat—not exactly the type of information that can be gleaned from a resumé.

Do Presidents Matter? Justin Fox. *Time* v. 171 p42 February 18, 2008.

There is little evidence that the White House can change the economy, but economic trouble is bad news for the incumbent party, Fox maintains. Separating cause and effect on presidents and the economy is difficult, and although Democratic administrations over the past 50 years have had faster economic growth and better stock-market performance than Republican ones, the sample size is so small that luck cannot be entirely ruled out. According to Jim Leach, former Republican congressman from Iowa and director of the Institute of Politics at Harvard's Kennedy School of Government, in normal times, presidents only modestly matter to the economy, but in abnormal times such as the present, they matter a great deal. He believes that United States and its financial system face a global crisis of confidence that could end very badly if not handled properly. Leach, who has not endorsed a candidate, says that the crucial characteristic for the incoming president will be the ability to inspire confidence.

Transformation Is Hard: Attempts of U.S. Presidents to Change Foreign Policy. Joseph S. Nye, Jr. *Time* v. 168 p29 July 17, 2006.

President George W. Bush hoped to change the course of U.S. foreign policy, but history shows that the odds are against him, Nye maintains. After 9/11, Bush made three major changes to the grand strategy that the United States had followed for a half-century. Bush reduced reliance on permanent alliances and institutions, extended the traditional right of preemption into a new doctrine of preventive war, and suggested coercive democratization as a solution to the problem of terrorism in the Middle East. The ultimate success or failure of Bush's bid to transform U.S. grand strategy will be judged by history, but successful strategic transformations have been rare over the past century. The writer outlines the history of previous efforts made by U.S. presidents to radically transform U.S. strategy.

Great Campaign Moments. *U.S. News & World Report* v. 144 pp28–54 January 28–February 4, 2008.

In this special section on great moments in past U.S. presidential campaigns, articles chart some of the more dramatic and decisive events in presidential races, among them Nixon's famous "Checkers" speech and the violent protests at the 1968 Democratic convention.

The Real Lincoln. Justin Ewers. *U.S. News & World Report* v. 138 pp66–73 February 21, 2005.

Scholars are increasingly interested in Abraham Lincoln's early years, about which there is little information, Ewers notes. Lincoln left no autobiography and there are fewer than ten pages of personal reminiscences in his *Collected Works*, with the result that his past hardened into hagiography after his death. Now, however, his pre-presidential papers have been consolidated in the new Abraham Lincoln Presidential Library and Museum in Springfield, Illinois, and an exhibition marking the museum's April opening will devote considerable attention to chronicling Lincoln's journey to the presidency. In addition, as the bicentennial of his birth approaches in 2009, scholarship is reexamining his early life, using new sources to examine his personal relationships and rise to power, in the hope of finding the true Lincoln. What researchers have found is a man less decisive, less principled, and much wealthier than history recalls.

Shaping an Office: History of the Presidency. Michael Barone. *U.S. News & World Report* v. 137 p42 December 13, 2004.

Part of a special section on photographs of past U.S. presidents. Americans tend to think of their president as the personification of the country he leads. No one has molded the office of president more than the man who first held it and for whom it was designed—George Washington, a man with a vision of a continental nation that would rise to a leading role in the world. Every subsequent president has also molded the office in his own image, however. Few other democracies meld the position of head of government and head of state, as the United States does, and Americans see their presidents as national leaders who in different ways have helped foster the strengths and virtues of America. Indeed, Americans may now expect more of their presidents than anyone can deliver.

New Hampshire Primaries. Jack W. Germond. *Washingtonian* v. 43 pp35–38+ January 2008.

According to Germond, proponents of the New Hampshire primary are not always correct in their assertion that it is always first and always right. In seven hotly contested primaries, New Hampshire voters have selected the eventual nominees four times, but they exposed the vulnerabilities of front-runners in the other three. New Hampshire voters demonstrated the weakness of Nelson Rockefeller and Barry Goldwater in 1964, Lyndon Johnson in 1968, Edmund Muskie in 1972, Edward Kennedy in 1980, Walter Mondale in 1984, and Robert Dole in 1996, and they also sent a clear warning on George W. Bush in 2000 by presenting him with an 18-point defeat at the hands of John McCain. They have close, repeated contact with the entire field of candidates and their views are more rounded than those formed from television commercials and news coverage.

I Can't Believe He Said That: Gaffes by Presidential Candidates. Jack W. Germond. *Washingtonian* v. 42 pp45–49 September 2007.

A few words can be important and potentially ruinous for a presidential candidate, Germond reports. In the current era, everything a politician says anywhere is pored over by the mainstream press, the cable-television networks, and the bloggers, who have plenty of time and space and no desire to show any restraint. It has even got to the stage where candidates are held accountable for what their supporters say and do. These cases seldom have anything to do with what sort of a president a candidate might be, but one stumble can cost the election. Candidates can spend hundreds of millions of dollars, declaim endlessly on issues, and present 12-point plans for education, the economy, and the environment, but ultimately, the election of the next U.S. president can rest on a gaffe.

Index